WAR DIARIES

WAR DIARIES

Design after the Destruction of Art and Architecture

Edited by
ELISA DAINESE and
ALEKSANDAR STANIČIĆ

UNIVERSITY OF VIRGINIA PRESS
Charlottesville and London

University of Virginia Press
© 2022 by the Rector and Visitors of the University of Virginia
All rights reserved
Printed in the United States of America on acid-free paper

First published 2022

9 8 7 6 5 4 3 2 1

ISBN 978-0-8139-4801-0 (cloth)
ISBN 978-0-8139-4802-7 (paper)
ISBN 978-0-8139-4803-4 (ebook)

Library of Congress Cataloging-in-Publication Data is available for this title.

Cover illustration: Thomas Impiglia, Belgrade: Memory Lab; "Overlooking the Bridge, building as a regenerative force for the rehabilitation of Belgrade" (Bartlett School of Architecture UCL, Dip/MArch Unit 13, 2010).

CONTENTS

Foreword — vii
NASSER RABBAT

Acknowledgments — ix

Introduction: Critical Themes of Design after Destruction — 1
ELISA DAINESE AND ALEKSANDAR STANIČIĆ

1. On Urban Postconflict Development: Toward a Practice-Oriented Research Agenda — 17
   KAI VÖCKLER

2. Ivan Štraus: War Diary and Design Intentions of an Architect in Postwar Sarajevo — 46
   ARMINA PILAV

3. Normalizing War: The Aesthetics of National Resilience — 69
   GABRIEL SCHWAKE

4. Scars of War and Reconstruction in Lebanon — 91
   DEEN SHARP

5. "Simple Plans" and Complex Lives: A Dialogue about Planning and Designing Emergency Settlements — 115
   CHARLIE HAILEY, INTERVIEW WITH PER IWANSSON AND HANS SKOTTE

6. Designing Emergency Architecture — 139
   RAUL PANTALEO AND TAMASSOCIATI, TRANSLATED BY ELISA DAINESE

7. Teaching Culturally Sensitive Design — 154
   ALEKSANDAR STANIČIĆ, INTERVIEW WITH AZRA AKŠAMIJA

Conclusion: Reconceptualizing Design after Destruction 179
ELISA DAINESE AND ALEKSANDAR STANIČIĆ

Bibliography 187
Notes on Contributors 199
Index 203

FOREWORD

"The inhabited cities will be laid waste and the land will be a desolation. So you will know that I am the Lord." (Ezekiel 12:20) This is how the Lord warned the Israelites, his chosen people, when he decreed their first exile to Babylon. And they had better take his threat seriously, for he had already destroyed countless sinful cities that he boasted about in numerous passages in the Tanakh. In fact, having examined more than thirty such passages, I can imagine them stitched together in some sort of primordial Divine War Diaries.

Yahweh, however, was not unique in his use of destruction to vent his anger and wrath. Numerous alpha gods and powerful kings of antiquity brandished the destruction of cities as acts of punishment or retribution, as a projection of absolute power, as divine intervention, or as the fulfillment of oaths or dreams. Their long record of devastation unfolded over time and space from the probably fictional destruction of Sodom and Gomorrah, Troy, and Atlantis to the very real annihilation of Babylon, Carthage, Jerusalem, Tyr, and Rome in antiquity and on to the destruction of premodern Merv, Nishapur, Baghdad, Teotihuacán, and Cusco. Each left behind scattered ruins, slowly fading memories, and competing diaries of conquest and loss.

New factors arose in modern times that altered the possible scenarios of power projection. Industrialization and heavy urbanization, coupled with secular reframing of civil rights and the emergence of capital as the premier metric of personal and global standing, offered the mighty new tools to shape their image. Yet war remained one of their favorites. It was actually magnified by enormous advances in the technologies and strategies of violence. The ravages of the two World Wars culminated in the ruin of Dresden, Hiroshima, and Nagasaki and the atrocities of decolonization from Algeria to Vietnam. The recent civil wars in Africa, the Balkans, and the Middle East painfully show that the old obsession with destruction has never been stronger than it is today.

All along, the destruction of cities has been first and foremost an architectural and urban issue of no less importance than the construction of cities. Even without the intrusion of war, the two acts are per force interlocked in a circular *pas de deux* of sorts. Almost every urban destruction entails a (re)construction, and most urban (re)constructions presuppose a prior demolition. This cycle, which, needless to say, has existed since the first urban turn in ancient Mesopotamia, intensified with the Industrial Revolution in Europe and its tremendous social, economic, urban, and demographic consequences. Massive destruction is no longer the result of wars and revolutions alone, it has also become an act of urban planning. Industrial cities that have expanded dramatically in a short period and acquired complex new facilities, infrastructural systems, and monetization procedures have witnessed the demolition of large parts of their old urban fabric, sometimes without the consent of their inhabitants and even against their will. The most extensive destruction/reconstruction operation was the grand project of Baron Haussmann in Paris (between 1854–69), which tore down hundreds of buildings, laid out modern boulevards, parks, and extensive infrastructures, and drastically changed the face and size of the city. Haussmann's Paris became the blueprint for grand urban projects around the world in the late nineteenth century, from Vienna, Madrid, and Rome to Cairo and Buenos Aires.

This peacetime destruction, masquerading usually as urban renewal or rezoning, later gave us the critical term urbicide. Coined in 1963 by the science fiction author Michael Moorcock, the term was arrogated to the discourse of architecture by Ada Louise Huxtable after the destructive streak of the grand American urban vision in New York City in the mid 1960s. It further spread through the writing of contemporary critics of the wanton destruction caused by the wars fought in the former Yugoslavia, in Africa, and most recently in Syria and Iraq such as Marshall Berman, Bogdan Bogdanović, Robert Bevan, and Stephen Graham. These developments in the conceptualization of destruction have had considerable effects not only on how we think about the fragility of architecture but also on identity and memory, on the mapping and definition of territories and states, on the formulation of ethics, and on the understanding of the city as one of the most intricate artifacts humanity has produced and arranged its collective life around.

But how are architects and planners, the prima facie agents of (re)construction, to incorporate destruction into their design thinking? The debates are ongoing, and the venues of investigation are many. This collection of essays assiduously explores the subject through both case studies and theoretical and historical reflections. But let me not reveal their arguments or summarize them here. (That is what the introduction is for). Instead I will turn to the kind of design reckoning I wish to advocate for any architectural intervention or reconstruction project, be it the result of war, natural disaster, or substantial urban replanning.

Challenged for decades by shifts toward narrowly specialized, visually cutting-edge, and financially driven design, architecture finds itself today excelling in technical, formal, and technological problem solving, but the discipline is ill-equipped to handle the broader moral, social, political, cultural, and environmental conundrums affecting our lives, let alone influence their resolution. We need to reconfigure the definition of our profession to reposition passion, curiosity, reflection, and a solidly civic, socially just, and ethical compass at the center of all design practice. We also need to reclaim an expansive and diverse knowledge base as fundamental to all architectural thinking, a foundation that we have neglected in our rush to digitization. As my late colleague Julian Beinart once exclaimed, in our beleaguered contemporary world there is an excess of ugliness (understood as more than appearance) and an excess of socioeconomic and political inequality. They are related. By addressing the former holistically, design can and should impact the lessening—and ultimately the eradication—of the latter.

These are of course lofty ideas. They may even be idealistic. But this is precisely why I am presenting them as the scaffolding for any engaged and informed architectural intervention. Reconceptualizing idealism as the frame for design can propel the hard work of excellence along a different path than one that is strictly functional, aesthetically exuberant, or opportunely lucrative. Design can be empowered by the imaginative, humane, and moral dimensions of idealism. This promises a different caliber of politically and ethically informed architecture, one that does not shy away from asking the hard questions about its responsibility beyond the actual design and looks into the conditions of its initiation and its broader consequences. Idealism, properly equipped and communicated, can thus be turned into a framework through which architecture can truly participate in building a thriving, just, and nurturing society and, at a more universal level, a kinder and more harmonious humanity.

Nasser Rabbat

ACKNOWLEDGMENTS

The *War Diaries* book project was seeded by generous support from two 2016 fellowships offered by the Italian Academy for Advanced Studies in America, led by David Freedberg (Director) and Barbara Faedda (Executive Director), who immediately recognized the actuality and dangers of the contemporary war waged against art and architecture. The awards took place at Columbia University in New York City, whose settings facilitated our first research on the reconstruction of damaged sites as a cultural practice that mediates political conflicts and offers meaningful criticism of violence and destruction. As the content of the volume took shape, further financial support—via a 2019 Graham Foundation Grant to Individuals—helped to realize the book in its final form.

Several individuals were instrumental at the various phases of the project's conception, refinement, and completion. Most notably, we would like to thank Helen Malko, who helped shape our initial ideas thanks to her work at the International Observatory of Cultural Heritage of the Italian Academy. The anonymous reviewers for the University of Virginia Press brought fresh perspectives to the content of the volume by asking tough questions, uncovering essential connections, and revealing illuminating perspectives. As acquiring editor, Boyd Zenner has contributed immensely to refining the ideas we aimed to capture and convey, applying rigorous attention to details and nuance to the text as well as to the various voices therein. *War Diaries* would not have been possible without their effort, insights, and trust throughout the process.

We wish to thank several colleagues at our respective academic institutions who participate in ongoing dialogues about cross-disciplinary spatial research and postwar design: Tom Avermaete at ETH Zurich, Nasser Rabbat and James Wescoat at Massachusetts Institute of Technology. They supported the research through informal conversations, insight, and guidance, while our respective universities provided invaluable assistance by offering us research-related teaching opportunities.

We also would like to thank all of the students who participated in courses that investigated design methods, approaches, and practices after war destruction: Rik Meijer, Daniella Maamari, Jody Miller, Cameron Kelly, Anita Pop, Matthew Gillingham, and Shyniaya Duffy. Many of these students, and others, joined us in research studios and seminars and shared their willingness to engage with the complex realities of warscapes and reconstruction settings.

To everyone we contacted for the essays and our authors, we are extremely grateful for their gracious sharing of time and knowledge. Through conversations and writings, many scholars and practitioners—in particular András Riedlmayer, Andrew Herscher, Hashim Sarkis, Felicity Scott, Anooradha Siddiqi, Samia Henni, Daniel Barber, David Brownlee, Joan Ockman, Sean Anderson, and Tiffany Chung—provoked critical inquiry into the fraught role of architecture and urbanism in postwar settings. Colleagues and friends—including Ren Thomas, Andrea Jelić, Emily Gunzburger Makaš, and Senada Demirović—generously provided platforms for reflection on our work, and they informed our methodology in new ways.

Finally, we dedicate *War Diaries* to those who inspired it: the people who are surviving war conflicts all over the world and the people who are trying to remediate war's consequences with their creative work.

WAR DIARIES

INTRODUCTION

CRITICAL THEMES OF DESIGN AFTER DESTRUCTION

ELISA DAINESE AND ALEKSANDAR STANIČIĆ

The destruction of buildings and artifacts has shaped not only the physical attributes of the built environment but also societies, cultures, and entire civilizations across the globe—arguably, with zeal equal to their creative production.[1] Whether the result of natural calamities or human-induced erasure of built environments, whether "senseless" annihilation or "creative destruction" under the pretext of progress, the destruction has been theorized and even romanticized throughout history as an intrinsic part of cultural evolution that has paved the way for new realities and innovative ideas. In the past century, however, the information age has redefined the notion of urban warfare, conceiving it as a local phenomenon that produces global effects in our increasingly interconnected world.[2] The technological capacity to share data through mass media—the instant flow of information—has enabled the immediate and broad transfer of political messages underlying destruction. Innovative visual tools are rapidly changing the way we understand, expose, and contest spatial conflicts, blurring even more the line between violence, aesthetics, and creation.[3]

At the same time, the development of high-precision, long-distance weaponry systems has brought a new dimension to this battle, as it has made the selection of targets based on their strategic—or symbolic—value one of the key components of urban warfare.[4] Modern-day annihilations of Aleppo and Homs, in Syria, and more recently Donbas, in Ukraine, illustrate this weaponization of art and architecture and connect these specific destructions with a growing number of physical assaults and aggressions against cultural heritage and spatial landmarks (fig. I.1).[5]

FIGURE I.1. Postcard showing the Serbian government building (background), damaged in the 1999 NATO bombing, taken from the Baumgarten's Generalštab (general staff building) in Belgrade. Editions Francophiles, 1999. (Courtesy of the National Library of Serbia and Aleksandar Kelić)

In these and similar cases, the calculated destruction of the built environment and cultural artifacts has become a new, powerful, and globally recognized weapon for achieving political goals. Ripple effects of this new type of warfare—transmission of fear; destruction of memory and culture; eradication of homes; oppression, occupation, and displacement for the sake of creation of new socio-spatial realities—have constituted devastating outcomes on the politicization of urban and artistic spheres and the livability of reconstructed buildings and cities. The broadcasted demolition of the ancient ruins of Palmyra, Syria, and Nimrud, Iraq, are the most well-known examples of the accelerated politicization of violence against built artifacts; destruction becomes both a display of power and a global spectacle.[6] In other instances the political agenda is manifested in more covert ways, nonetheless producing devastating consequences for the urban and natural environment.[7] The erasure of multicultural urban pasts for the purpose of creating homogenized national ethnicities and territories in former Yugoslavia provides a case in point.[8] Similarly, during the occupation of land through aggressive urban development in Algeria, Iraq, and Palestine/Israel, military techniques often merge with urban design.[9] These and other examples show the severe social consequences that occur when the international community and media have not immediately recognized the extent of the destruction of art and architecture. The ethnic and territorial homogenization achieved through genocide and settlement destruction in areas such as Rwanda and the conflict displacement in the ongoing Somali civil war demonstrates how, by operating below the media radar, military operatives can hijack design as well as the representational tools of architecture.[10]

Meanwhile, those who practice humanitarian planning and emergency architecture struggle to offer resettlement solutions to migrant populations fleeing destruction, while spontaneous and more formal refugee camps in host countries such as Kenya strive to find accommodation for millions of displaced people (fig. I.2).[11] Adding complexity to this issue, the global arms race and the uncontrolled growth of urbanized terrain (as well as the recognition of [urban] territory as a valuable strategic, symbolic, and economic resource) have blurred the line between home front and battlefront.[12] Increasingly after 9/11, we have witnessed the militarization of public space through the production of new spatial elements, the so-called defensive architecture, and the normalization in everyday life of the presence of (the threat of) violence and of the ubiquity of military-style thinking.[13] On the other hand, environmental issues—such as climate change that turns arable land into desert on the Israeli-Palestinian border; water management policies that redefine the six-state territory in the Mekong's delta; and a battle for natural resources that sustains both conflict and cement production in northern Syria—engage in a push-pull relationship with social conflicts, creating vicious circles of contestation and destruction.[14]

FIGURE I.2. Ifo 2, Dadaab Refugee Camp, Kenya, 2011. (© Brendan Bannon)

As a result of the processes of destruction described above, the preservation and reconstruction of architecture, heritage sites, and historic monuments has become central to local and public debates, academic research, and international affairs.[15] As the destruction intensifies, it has brought forth a resurgence of academic and public interest in urban conflicts research—arguably one of the fastest growing subdisciplines in the field of architectural history and theory. However, there is a palpable lack of scientific discourses that focus on the meaning, role, and approaches—creative, aesthetic, and, ultimately, design—in response to these damaging tendencies. Even though past experience has taught us that the decisions made in the early stages of emergency design and reconstruction have long-term and irrevocable consequences, the issue of design often comes secondary in the discussions and practices related to postdisaster urban and social recovery. This gap was pointed out by Lawrence Vale and Thomas Campanella in their discussion of broader narratives of urban resilience and their analysis of how the pragmatic process of urban recovery can be fueled by highly symbolic actions.[16] A broad set of related examinations focuses primarily on the postconflict reconstruction of cultures and societies as discussed, for example, by Miranda Rui Gonçalves and Federica Zullo; while Duyne E. Jennifer

Barenstein and Esther Leemann finally recognized and examined communities' roles and perspectives in postdisaster reconstruction.[17] Another notable reference is the research developed by Dacia Rose Viejo and M. L. S. Sørensen, who have investigated how reconstruction efforts affect communities' long-term coping capacity and preparedness to face future events.[18]

We found the lack of focus on design successes and shortcomings during the first phases of emergency to be alarming, especially since, on the practical side of things, the built environment has expectedly responded to war trends by incorporating the possibility of violence into design, sacrificing its humanitarian agenda for the sake of perceived security.[19] This militarization and objectification of artistic, architectural, and urban production goes against the ethical principles and the very nature of design professionals who have been forced to witness the malicious hijack of the creative disciplines and to serve as mediators between—and even enablers of—various political ideologies both locally and globally. In this context, the challenges put in front of designers wishing to participate in rebuilding strike any thoughtful observer as massive, if not insurmountable.

Among the numerous reasons for the lack of systematic approaches to design are several misconceptions. First, the belief that design practices in a wartime context are no different from processes happening during peacetime and the resulting idea that any practitioner with or without a license can therefore design in a postwar setting. Second, the false notion that design is not a crucial, or even necessary, activity, and that art is not a substantial human need in times of life-threating urgency. Third, the naïve thinking that posits design and violence are not related. Fourth, the misconception that design decisions can be revoked or modified once things settle and peace is reached. And, finally, related to all of the above, the sense that design is a luxurious expense available only to the privileged and its practice is therefore futile during times of war or emergency.

In contrast to these misbeliefs, *War Diaries: Design after the Destruction of Art and Architecture* seeks to build new frameworks for understanding the fundamental role of design in postwar reconstruction and emergency situations by investigating innovative design processes and their outcomes (fig. I.3). It particularly focuses on the theoretical, contextual, and practical frameworks for design responses to urban warfare and violence

FIGURE I.3. Concept submitted in competition for the RTS (Radio-Television of Serbia) memorial on Aberdareva Street, Belgrade, first prize, 2013. Authors *Neoarhitekti* Studio, Belgrade. (Courtesy of Tatjana Stratimirović, Vladimir Milenković, and Snežana Vesnić)

against art and architecture by investigating the perspectives of practitioners who deal with destruction, emergency design, and the long-term consequences of rebuilding from the frontline.

In order to challenge universally existent and persistent dogmas on postwar design, *War Diaries* brings together case studies from global settings. The studies present multiple and multivalent design strategies as they have been applied in some of the areas most affected by armed and internal conflicts in Europe, the Middle East, and East Africa. Centered around contested settlements and cultural production, these examples extend established academic knowledge in architecture, urban studies and planning research.[20] By looking at complex postwar settings and practitioners' various perspectives, these narratives also challenge obvious design misconceptions and question the idea that a purely theoretical research can alone solve the intricacies of postwar design. The focus is on case studies from different local contexts and regions of the world where planners, architects, and artists are involved in concrete initiatives on the ground. Their approaches and practices respond not only to the unique characteristics of local conflicted cultures but also to the nature of conflict and destruction. The framework we propose here provides an instrumental and applied set of discussions that question design tools, experimentations, and methods that challenged, inspired indirectly, or aided directly other cultures and spaces experiencing these various postwar conditions. In this effort, we are seeking a general set of design principles. If design is an essential mediatory tool, as we propose, then it is vital to explore the role that design and designers have played in destroyed settings as they propel processes of recovery (fig. I.4).

War Diaries privileges discussions about design issues and decisions in the cases it explores, and it focuses on the role design plays in (re)building transitional justice, urban resilience, and social tolerance into complex and heterogeneous postconflict societies. Within this overall framework, main threads examine the degree to which damaged sites and architecture are rebuilt as cultural artifacts that mediate political conflicts and offer meaningful criticism of violence and destruction (fig. I.5). Thus, through various artistic, urban, and architectural reports from the field—that is to say, *Diaries*—the book explores how particular design practices facilitate the processes of development and reconstruction. We asked our authors to reflect on compromised and contingent

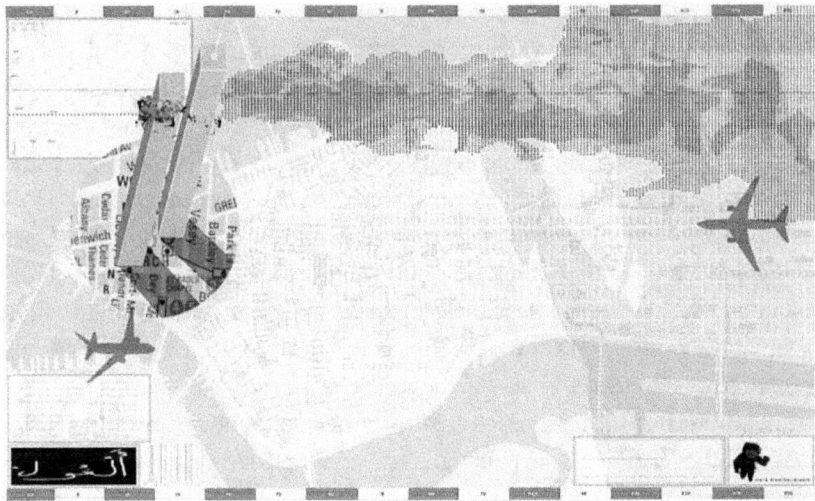

FIGURE I.4. Lieven De Boeck, *Fireworks II, Le Bleu du Ciel*, detail, 2001. Published in Teresa Stoppani, "Architecture of the Disaster," *Space and Culture* 15.2 (2012): 135–50. (Courtesy of Lieven De Boeck)

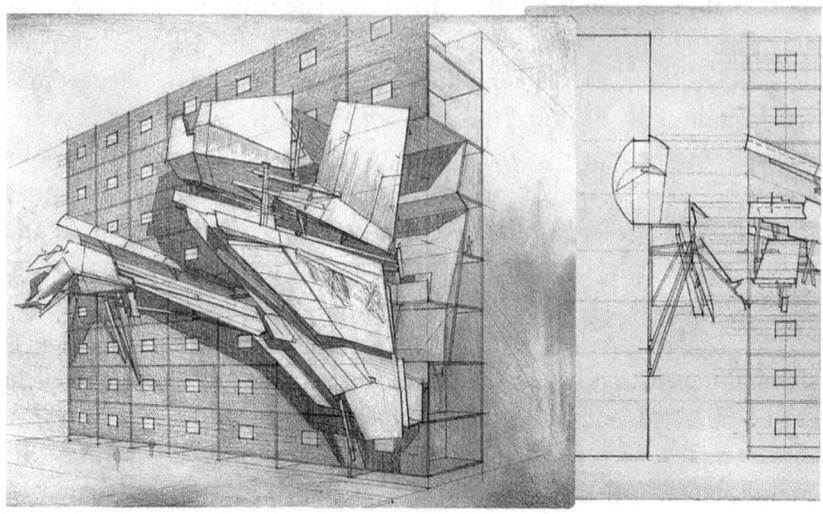

FIGURE I.5. Lebbeus Woods, illustration of a damaged and reconstructed residential block, from *War and Architecture: Three Principles*. (https://lebbeuswoods.wordpress.com/2011/12/15/war-and-architecture-three-principles/)

situations in which the desires of challenged populations or ambiguous design performances have been used to maintain the status quo of disrupted landscapes (often more so than violence itself). The issue at stake is how professionals have questioned the established polity that is conducting and accomplishing investigations, renewal, and redevelopment of attacked sites. Among the main questions we raised with our contributors are, How can art, architecture, and urban planning fight back and regain a humanist and ethical purpose in reconstruction phases? How can new creative practices, pedagogical methods, and planning policies be employed in remediating the political and social consequences of urban destruction in a professionally responsible way? How can the fight against the aestheticization of violence and the promotion of a culturally sensitive design lead the way through the urgency of recovering?

In addition to filling the lacuna of volumes on architectural and artistic design after conflict—surprisingly scarce when we consider the rising weaponization of art and architecture—by tackling these main issues, *War Diaries* also examines some corollary topics. These include, for example, the connection between conflict and media in contested territories, the negotiations between local and international organizations/

interests during reconstruction, and the role various communities can play in the rebuilding and decision-making process.

By examining the role of specialists, the book sheds light not on one specific method but on multiple approaches, methodologies, and attitudes toward destruction that designers have used to question and remediate the effects of violence against cities and cultural heritage sites (fig. I.6). The focus on postconflict design pays special attention to multiple stakeholders and diverse subjects, such as practitioners, educators, direct users, and the broader community. Various formats inform this multiperspective investigation, a method that offers fruitful ways to articulate the complexity of postconflict design and give voice to groups otherwise unheard in current intellectual investigations. Contributors include practitioners involved in emergency and postwar design (Kai Vöckler, Raul Pantaleo and TAMassociati, Per Iwansson and Hans Skotte), artists investigating the politics of identity and memory (Azra Akšamija), and scholars who examine transitional postwar design, emergent built environments, and the aestheticization of violence (Armina Pilav, Charlie Hailey, Gabriel Schwake, and Deen Sharp)—all of whom are involved in or interested in projects on the ground. *War Diaries* also gives significant attention to experimental programs aimed toward educating the

FIGURE I.6. Student design work from the Culturally Sensitive Design course, MIT Department of Architecture, 2017–18. (Courtesy of Stella Zhujing Zhang)

new generation of designers, who are certainly the future of "culturally sensitive design" and the reconstruction of postconflict areas.[21] The approaches, designs, and pedagogical experiences of the different protagonists featured here illuminate the practical and theoretical problems and solutions used in the field to restore historical sites, heal social relationships, and enhance tolerance thresholds addressing a range of scales, from architectural detail to shelter/building to settlement and city.

As such, the book is primarily intended for scholars and practitioners engaged in an emerging field that addresses the destruction of the built environment and seeks to preserve heritage in the midst of modern and contemporary conflicts. Since the volume's emphasis is on actual projects and initiatives on the ground, all chapters deal with the lived experiences or research pedagogies of actors who are actively "waging war" on the destruction of art and architecture. Therefore, we believe the audience for *War Diaries* extends beyond academia to include groups interested in urban resilience, postwar reconstruction, art and activism, geopolitics, and memory studies. We hope this collection makes significant contributions to the curriculums of art and architecture for all levels of students, especially those passionate about studying destruction, preservation, and reconstruction of cultural and built artifacts.

War Diaries offers seven chapters that explore responses in the wake of destruction that range from the transformation of current practices to internal critique to radical reassessment. While each chapter explores the attitudes and positions of an individual, group, or firm on postwar and urgent design, when taken together the essays follow a precise guiding structure that focuses on the processes of rebuilding at the scale of the artifact, the building, the settlement, and the community. Chapter 1, by Kai Vöckler, initiates this discussion by offering a comparative analysis of the social and political issues of postwar reconstruction. From his perspective as an urban designer, Vöckler discusses the spatial implications of violent conflicts in cities and elaborates on the strategies designers can apply to tackle urban divisions. His main interest is on the role played by architects and planners as agents of change; nonetheless, the chapter also introduces the processes and agencies—mainly NGOs—that support architects and planners working in postconflict situations.

Chapters 2, 3, and 4 develop narratives centered around buildings and objects and discuss reconstruction and resettlement at the architectural scale. In chapter 2 Armina Pilav examines the complex role of designers and design during and immediately after the Bosnian War (1992–95) and tackles the ambiguities of architectural engagements within the city of Sarajevo. She compares both the literary works and reconstruction proposals of two architectural visionaries and prolific authors, Ivan Štraus and Lebbeus Woods, who both kept war diaries and theorized about postwar reconstructions. In the years of intimate correspondence that followed their meeting in besieged Sarajevo in 1993, Štraus and Woods exchanged ideas about architecture and war and worked together on a reconstruction proposal for the *Elektropriveda* Building in Sarajevo. Pilav discusses these events and the reconstruction process that ensued, exposing the fragility of a romanticized approach to designing postwar cities and, in particular, the weakened position of architects in the new hierarchy of stakeholders of postwar Sarajevo.

The critique of the role of architects in highly contested environments is expanded further in chapter 3 by Gabriel Schwake, who delves into aestheticization as a political tool weaponized by the state in order to normalize the presence of violence and war in urban society. The chapter examines how Israeli design and aesthetics have been weaponized in the endless struggle for political influence and control in Israel. The study includes an examination of the Israeli "protective spaces" developed by the government as an integral part of everyday housing design. In particular, the writing focuses on the architectural competition for the National Centre of Israeli Resilience initiated by the Israeli Home Front Command and the National Emergency Management Authority. Through these investigations Schwake offers insight on the perspectives and impact of military organizations and practices on architectural design.

The perspective broadens even more in chapters 4 and 5, which explore the role of planners on remediating destruction. Chapter 4, authored by Deen Sharp, investigates in depth the origins of design decisions made during the postwar reconstruction of Beirut. Deen argues that even the processes of reconstruction after violence can result in more violence, displacement, and social discord. To illustrate the link between reconstruction and violent conflict, Deen creates a time line of rebuilding postconflict cities and postconflict societies, which should be understood as developing and interlinked processes. To investigate this connection, Deen provides an account of Lebanon's postwar reconstruction led by, and formed around, the urban development corporation Solidere in downtown Beirut.

Following Deen's interrogation of the connections between war and postwar design and the involvement of foreign investors in Lebanese rebuilding efforts, chapter 5 investigates the role of international foreign planners in the humanitarian design of refugee camps. The chapter offers an examination of the initial design of, and later transformations of, Dadaab's Hagadera Refugee Camp in Kenya, which hosts millions of refugees displaced by the ongoing Somali civil war. The analysis is developed as a dialogue between the author, Charlie Hailey, and Per Iwansson, the architect who oversaw the first design of the camp in the early 1990s, who is a staunch advocate for the "simple plans" approach. Another voice includes Hans Skotte, an architect and planner working on postwar construction.

Continuing the discussion of specific design approaches and how aesthetics can trigger collective healing in postwar societies, architect Raul Pantaleo and TAMassociati take a poetic tone in chapter 6. Centered on the role of the architect-designer, the chapter investigates design and emergency architecture produced by the firm in the war zones and refugee camps in Darfur, Sudan, Afghanistan, and Iraq. The authors invite us to focus on aesthetics in order to trigger collective imagination and provide practical and rapid responses in states of emergency. According to Pantaleo, the examination of aesthetics goes beyond an unavoidable necessity and becomes a moral and ethical prerequisite in postwar situations. The design of social architecture in war-torn and poor regions relies on accurate investigations into details and proportions, thorough energy analyses, considerations of environmental efficiency, and managing limited resources and time constraints to propose solutions.

Complementing Pantaleo's revealing insights into an architect's mind, the concluding chapter of *War Diaries,* chapter 7, offers the perspective of an artist by explicating the artistic productions and teaching experiments centered around a field-shaping course on culturally sensitive design. In an interview with Aleksandar Stančić, Azra Akšamija (of the MIT Department of Architecture) explores the pedagogical and research methods she developed to introduce a cross-disciplinary and inclusive model for education and civic innovation through the lens of art and design, with a focus on creative responses to conflict and crisis. Taking as a field of inquiry the Al Azraq Refugee Camp in Jordan, the students in Akšamija's Culturally Sensitive Design course developed their own design interventions (both artistic and architectural) that aimed at enhancing the intercultural collaborations and quality of life in the camp. Using this experimental pedagogical approach, students not only contemplated the production of future heritage but also touched on some larger ethical issues in the field of postwar art and architectural production.

Collectively, these chapters reveal successful design examples as well as shortcomings and deficiencies in the reconstruction and resettlement process. In addition, they challenge the canonical account of postwar architectural design and propose to understand postdisaster building as a political act with a cultural footprint, which takes place in environments where rebuilding carries even more risks as it tries to recuperate civic values put to the test by destruction. Readers can appreciate the spread of creativity as designers adapt to changing living conditions while understanding the intrinsic connections between their dual roles as activists in the public discourse on postwar urban reconstructions and as translators of sociopolitical forces into architectural form.

Notes

1. On the interconnectedness between violence, architecture, and culture, see Andrew Herscher, "Warchitectural Theory," *Journal of Architectural Education* 61.3 (January 2008): 35–43.
2. On this topic see, for example, Sean Anderson and Stephen Sloan, *Historical Dictionary of Terrorism* (Metuchen, NJ: Scarecrow Press, 1995).
3. Armina Pilav, Marc Schoonderbeek, Heidi Sohn, and Aleksandar Staničić, eds., *Mediating the Spatiality of Conflicts*, International Conference Proceedings, TU Delft Faculty of Architecture and the Built Environment (Delft: BK Books, 2020).
4. Srdjan Jovanović Weiss, "NATO as Architectural Critic," *Cabinet* 1 (2000): 84–89, http://cabinetmagazine.org/issues/1/NATO.php.
5. On monument destruction, conservation, restoration, and international cooperation, see, for example, Lucia Allais, *Designs of Destruction: The Making of Monuments in the Twentieth Century* (Chicago: University of Chicago Press, 2018).
6. Miroslav Melčák and Ondřej Beránek, "ISIS's Destruction of Mosul's Historical Monuments: Between Media Spectacle and Religious Doctrine," *International Journal of Islamic Architecture* 6.2 (2017): 389–415, https://doi.org/10.1386/ijia.6.2.389_1; Douglas Kellner, "9/11, Spectacles of Ter-

ror, and Media Manipulation," *Critical Discourse Studies* 1.1 (2004): 41–64, https://doi.org/10.1080/17405900410001674515.
7. On war destruction, postwar reconstruction, and their relationship to climate change and environmental issues, see, for example, Esther Ruth Charlesworth, *Architects without Frontiers: War, Reconstruction and Design Responsibility* (Amsterdam: Architectural Press, 2006).
8. Robert Bevan, *The Destruction of Memory: Architecture at War* (London: Reaktion Books, 2007); Martin Coward, *Urbicide—The Politics of Urban Destruction* (New York: Routledge, 2009); András Riedlmayer, "The War on People and the War on Culture," *New Combat* 3 (Autumn 1994): 16–19.
9. Rafi Segal, David Tartakover, and Eyal Weizman, eds., *A Civilian Occupation: The Politics of Israeli Architecture* (London: Verso, 2003); Eyal Weizman, *Hollow Land: Israel's Architecture of Occupation* (London: Verso, 2007).
10. On these topics see, for example, Anooradha Siddiqi, "In Favor of Seeing Specific Histories," *Grey Room* 61 (2015): 86–91; and Anooradha Siddiqi, "On Humanitarian Architecture: A Story of a Border," *Humanity: An International Journal of Human Rights, Humanitarianism, and Development* 8.3 (2017): 519–21.
11. The literature on the relationship between destruction, displacement, and refugee camps is vast. On this topic see, for example, Michel Agier, *On the Margins of the World: The Refugee Experience Today* (Cambridge, UK: Polity, 2008); and Andrew Herscher, *Displacements, Architecture and Refugee* (Berlin: Sternberg Press, 2017). On humanitarianism in Africa, see Bronwen Everill and Josiah Kaplan, *The History and Practice of Humanitarian Intervention and Aid in Africa* (Houndsmill, UK: Palgrave Macmillan, 2013).
12. See the seminal work by Stephen Graham, *Cities, War, and Terrorism: Towards an Urban Geopolitics* (Oxford, UK: Blackwell, 2004); and Stephen Graham, *Cities Under Siege: The New Military Urbanism* (London: Verso, 2011).
13. In this volume the militarization of built environments is explained in more detail by Gabriel Schwake in chapter 3.
14. See, for example, E. Gary Machlis, Thor Hanson, Zdravko Špirić, and Jean E. McKendry, eds., *Warfare Ecology: A New Synthesis for Peace and Security* (Dordrecht: Springer Netherlands, 2011); and Esther Ruth Charlesworth, *Humanitarian Architecture: Fifteen Stories of Architects Working after Disaster* (London: Routledge, 2014).
15. For an example, see the exhibition held at MoMA entitled, "Insecurities: Tracing Displacement and Shelter" (October 1, 2016–January 22, 2017), https://www.moma.org.

16. Lawrence Vale and Thomas J. Campanella, eds., *The Resilient City: How Modern Cities Recover from Disaster* (Oxford, UK: Oxford University Press, 2005).
17. Miranda Rui Gonçalves and Federica Zullo, eds., *Post-Conflict Reconstructions: Re-Mappings and Reconciliations* (Nottingham, UK: Critical, Cultural and Communications Press, 2013); Duyne E. Jennifer Barenstein and Esther Leemann, *Post-Disaster Reconstruction and Change: Communities' Perspectives* (Boca Raton, FL: CRC Press, 2012).
18. Dacia Rose Viejo and M. L. S. Sørensen, eds., *War and Cultural Heritage: Biographies of Place* (Cambridge, UK: Cambridge University Press, 2015).
19. On humanitarianism and the relation between it and violence, see, for example, Emily Apter, Thomas Keenan, et al., "Humanism without Borders: A Dossier on the Human, Humanitarianism, and Human Rights," *Alphabet City: Social Insecurity* 7 (2000): 40–67; Eyal Weizman, "Arendt in Ethiopia," in *The Least of All Possible Evils: Humanitarian Violence from Arendt to Gaza* (London: Verso, 2011), 27–62; and Architecture for Humanity, *Design like You Give a Damn: Architectural Responses to Humanitarian Crises* (New York: Metropolis Books, 2006).
20. For instance, see the works developed by Jonathan Rokem and Camillo Boano, eds., *Urban Geopolitics: Rethinking Planning in Contested Cities* (London: Routledge, 2017); Jane Schneider and Ida Susser, eds., *Wounded Cities: Destruction and Reconstruction in a Globalized World* (London: Berg Publishers, 2004); Dilanthi Amaratunga and Richard Haigh, *Post-Disaster Reconstruction of the Built Environment: Rebuilding for Resilience* (Chichester, UK: Wiley-Blackwell, 2011).
21. We discuss this topic further in chapter 7 in the interview with Azra Akšamija.

1

ON URBAN POSTCONFLICT DEVELOPMENT
Toward a Practice-Oriented Research Agenda
KAI VÖCKLER

Cities give rise to a vast range of social and political issues, and since these affect every urban dweller in one way or another and are keenly examined and debated in the public eye, spatial designers—by which I mean architects, planners, and researchers engaged in urban development—have unique opportunities, above and beyond their provision of basic necessities and insights, to also positively influence residents' attitudes and future prospects. The crucial role of the city as an agent of political and social change becomes particularly clear in any postconflict situation, for urban development there is mostly rolled out under unsafe and unstable conditions.[1] A city of this sort is scarred by conflict; it is literally the epitome of the crises in which the metropolis finds itself. As is evident in divided cities all over the world, from Belfast to Nicosia, from Mostar to Beirut, conflicts may negatively embed themselves in the social fabric of a city. Yet simultaneously they turn cities into incubators for new and diverse communities seeking to (re-)establish a peaceful (co-)existence and into testing grounds for innovative strategies, such as how to overcome differences by nonviolent means. As vital centers of communication and, potentially, of reconciliation, cities have a leading role to play in conflict resolution.

Cities obliged to rebuild after a conflict generally face the same major problem: namely, a radically altered demographic. Many residents flee a city during periods of armed conflict, and for a variety of reasons they often never return: for example, they may find the ongoing situation in their homeland politically or economically disadvantageous to their interests and see better prospects for themselves elsewhere. Almost all of the Kosovo-Serbs in Prishtina fled or moved away from the city after 1999, for they saw no future for themselves under the new political regime and were subject moreover to discrimination and violence.[2] Conversely, conflict may drive large segments of the rural population to seek refuge in a city. Thus, by 1999 over one quarter of the population of Prishtina was composed of Kosovo-Albanians recently moved into the city, and many rural dwellers had moved there following wartime destruction of their livelihood.[3] Kabul (Afghanistan) was likewise substantially altered after 2001 by a massive influx of both new rural migrants and those who had initially fled to Pakistan or Iran but had found, upon repatriation, that a return to their native town or village was no longer possible.[4] Existing communities thus change or even disappear while new ones rapidly form and take their place. Neighborhoods become home to communities whose inhabitants were hitherto strangers and whose connections with the city and its history may greatly differ. For rural migrants, the very fact of living in crowded conditions may be alienating, to say nothing of the other challenges posed by postconflict city life.

Living conditions in such contexts are generally hard and precarious. Production is often at a standstill, business links have yet to be forged, and jobs are scarce. State institutions may be only partly operational or in need of reconstruction. Political life is usually still unstable and corruption rife. Moreover, the aforementioned massive influx of displaced persons (rural migrants and returnee refugees) puts a further strain on infrastructure. The population of Kabul, for example, quadrupled within a few years of military interventions in Afghanistan. This combination of factors usually leads to an informal (i.e., unplanned and unregulated) construction boom, since the demand for living and working spaces dramatically increases.[5] Not only urban reconstruction but also new urban development leaves its mark on postconflict situations. Political power vacuums, nationwide, in parallel with the demise of community structures (and hence of mutual monitoring and social control among the civilian population) unleash powerful forces that may seriously damage cities' chances of recovery. For these reasons alone, it is vital to scrutinize the aid and planning strategies deployed in postconflict cities and to intensify the search for possible alternatives.[6] One often underestimated factor is the huge impact that urban development has on the development of social and political structures. It is vital therefore to inquire into how the expertise of architects and planners may be deployed, not only to overcome the consequences of crisis, but also to prevent further conflict in the future. Which brings us to the key question in this volume: What could an "architecture of peace" look like?

To answer this question in full entails hammering out in greater detail the role that spatial designers (meaning architects, planners, and researchers in urban contexts) could or should play in postconflict developments—in other words, determining more precisely which form their specific disciplinary contribution to reconstruction and new development might take. This furthermore implies conscious contextualization: that account be taken of the interplay of social, political, and economic forces in any fragile postconflict situation; and that appropriate strategies be developed to deal with it. This requires not only an interdisciplinary approach, but also adaptation of that approach to the respective local conditions ("localization"). The latter depends in turn on the sound knowledge of local culture that only local partners have, and thus on their significant involvement from the very start of any project development (e.g., research). The first step in any urban postconflict development must accordingly be to identify, categorize, and systematize appropriate strategies in light of their ultimate optimal adaptation to the specific context. This calls for reflection from the outset on the role of the spatial designer—be this the architect/planner directly involved in the work of reconstruction or the researcher investigating postconflict situations.

Background and Methodology

The observations in this chapter are based first and foremost on my practical experience as cofounder and director of the nongovernmental organization (NGO) Archis Interventions, which was active in postconflict situations from 2005 to 2013, mainly in Kosovo, Bosnia-Herzegovina, and Cyprus, in cooperation with local NGOs.[7] The chapter also draws on research undertaken in the framework of a postgraduate program at the Bauhaus Dessau Foundation in 2005–6, which critically examined the role of the international community in postconflict reconstruction, as exemplified in particular by developments in Mostar and Kabul.[8] The chapter may be read as a preliminary outline of a possible future research agenda inasmuch as it suggests initial approaches to a systematic study of how civil society activists (most specifically urban architects, planners, and researchers) might operate strategically in postconflict situations.[9] Several publications offer further insights into these issues and were taken into account as far as possible.[10] It must be said, however, that most of them address postconflict development almost exclusively from the political and social sciences standpoint and therefore fail, in my opinion, to pay sufficient attention to the significant role urban architects, planners, and researchers play in the design and concrete implementation of this process.[11] Hence, the position I defend here: namely, that more conscious reflection on planning, architectural, and research practices in urban contexts is imperative for social equity, economic recovery, and long-term peace. It is mainly the spatial designers engaged in local civil initiatives or NGOs who keep a lookout for concrete opportunities to apply their expertise to good effect in urban postconflict development. To my knowledge, no research to date has systematically examined the conditions under which the planning and design of (or research into) urban postconflict development takes place. The deliberations garnered from practice and compiled in this chapter therefore serve as preliminary pointers for a yet to be accomplished systematic and empirical research project. To this same end, there follows below a rough sketch of the structures within which architects, planners, and researchers operate, as well as some further reflections on their special role in urban postconflict situations. In conclusion, the potential themes of future practice-oriented research are discussed.

Governance and Urban Postconflict Development: The Role of NGOs

The postconflict process of rebuilding a city and restoring acceptable living conditions must be adapted as far as possible to the specificities of a locality which, for the reasons sketched above, is typically wracked by ambiguity and insecurity. In seeking to establish new forms of good governance, most aid and development programs resort simply to the principle of "copy and paste": namely, they reproduce the donor countries' political structures and notions of "civil society," then try to apply these unquestioningly to the postconflict situation in hand.[12] Thus, despite their good intentions, international NGOs often remain blind to, or ride roughshod over, local sensibilities and traditions. One widespread yet erroneous assumption, for example, is that a city's historically significant monuments may be used as a means of reconciliation.[13] Another is that the locals have no prior understanding of concepts such as "freedom" and "democracy" or, worse still, that the entire postconflict situation is a *tabula rasa,* a blank slate on which the donor countries can inscribe their own sociopolitical priorities in the name of aid, be these capitalism, the "free market," or whatever.[14] Often, even the term "human rights" is regarded as a universally valid political norm, and the specific and contextual history of each individual struggle for human rights is thereby overlooked.[15] Of course human rights are precious and worthwhile defending; yet they are not a neutral system of values but one pervaded always by political claims, which must necessarily be negotiated and adapted afresh in light of the respective local conditions. In brief, too little consideration is given to the particular circumstances of the locality in question, and certain actors' limited knowledge of the local culture further exacerbates this problem.

The result is a kind of "donor speak" that seeks to align everything in the aid locality with the donor countries' sociopolitical aims. All the local initiatives and the employees of international organizations use this jargon as their *lingua franca,* and unfortunately every plan and scheme must be adapted to it in the critical postconflict period. Donor countries are accountable to their own populations and cannot afford to lose sight of the political situation at home. Spatial designers accordingly need to be seen as dealing effectively with the overlapping problems of urban postconflict development, not least by devising strategic solutions for application to pilot projects. To create any "architecture of peace" of this sort, they must also have a clear understanding of the specific local form of political governance emerging from the postconflict situation in hand, and they must clarify their own position in relation to that. Thus, any practice-oriented research on urban postconflict development must consider the roles played within the new policy regime by international and local NGOs—for they are the main mediators between civil society and the ruling powers.

In addition to the international expansion of communications, transportation, and information systems; the intensification of economic interdependencies on the global market; and the increasingly seamless international circuits of production and labor, new forms of political regulation have emerged at a global scale. Bodies such as NATO, the IMF, the OECD, and the United Nations have made first attempts at a kind of global governance, with more or less success. They act at the international level wherever formal democratic institutions are lacking. They are often the major players in postconflict situations, organs of an international community of nation-states, which aspires to guarantee the reconstruction of postconflict locations as well as their integration in the global market. Frequently, they serve to replace or represent an absent (because disbanded or inoperable) state or institution; they may also play a major part in establishing institutions, postconflict, or even in nation building—as in Kosovo, for example, which until its declaration of independence in 2008 was under the auspices of the United Nations Interim Administration Mission in Kosovo (UNMIK). However, such bodies (and likewise NGOs) may have a detrimental impact on local administrations' decision-making procedures, simply because they payroll—and thus can define—the aid programs. Inasmuch as NGOs (ideally) operate independently of specific state or economic interests and address problematic issues that other national or international players may, for whatever reason, shy away from, they may also serve as important correctives. The dramatic increase in their number in postconflict situations in recent decades clearly attests this ambition.[16] Nonetheless, their role remains problematic and should be regularly and critically reviewed. Are they simply one more component in the hegemonic policy regime? Or do they truly represent the interests of civil societies?

NGOs may be broadly defined as civil society organizations that do not represent any nation-state. They are presumed to be financially and organizationally independent of state apparatuses and private business and to pursue solely the best interests of the community they elect to serve.[17] Ideally, the main tasks of an NGO should be:

- *Political advocacy*: to represent interests that have no voice in existing political structures
- *Setting agendas*: to identify relevant issues and bring them to the table in political negotiations and decision-making processes at both the local and international levels
- *Assuring expertise*: to mobilize knowledge-based and experience-honed skills so as to inform public debate and tackle and resolve problematic issues

- *Minding the gaps*: to develop projects that state and supra-state players neglect and/or to implement them if ever governments or the international community are unable to do so on organizational or political grounds.[18]

The potential of NGOs lies thus in their scientific, technical, and political expertise, and their familiarity with the problems both in their field and in local structures. To assert the latter assumes of course that international NGOs cooperate with local civil society organizations so as to successfully adapt their strategies to the local political, social, and cultural contexts. One vital aspect of their work is their ability to mobilize the public at both the international and local levels and to advance the goals and interests thereby articulated. In doing so, they make an essential contribution to the processes of compromise and consensus underpinning political decision-making, and since they pursue neither commercial nor (in the stricter sense of the term) political interests, they play an important role here as mediators.

In reality, however, things are not quite so straightforward. Very few NGOs can finance their work through donations alone, so most of them remain largely dependent on the financial support of national governments and international bodies such as the EU. Their only other alternative is to seek funding from private foundations set up by international corporations or wealthy benefactors (such as Aga Kahn, George Soros, etc.).[19] In addition, as they increasingly professionalize their expert workforce, they must find the funding to pay it, which is a further constraint. NGOs are accordingly obliged to adapt their approaches to accommodate the goals and programs laid down by their sponsors: and, possibly, also to compromise their programs in compliance with the donors' agenda. International NGOs have meanwhile become big business; they are frequently guided solely by self-interest, and their staffs indisputably rank among an elite corps of managers and functionaries.[20] Mary Kaldor calls them "the cosmopolitans": a community of like-minded, well-educated experts (including some of local provenance) who are employed by the United Nations, by an international or nongovernmental organization, or by foreign investors.[21] This too is a new form of global dominion, the "new divide," as Kaldor calls it. On one side are the generally impoverished local residents and migrants who are seeking a place in the new urban communities; on the other are the "global citizens" along with their allies, the local elite, most of whom have been educated in the Global North. Another problem is that NGOs are usually specialized in one particular area, such as health or education, and thus lack the skills required to tackle related issues in a locality and to formulate comprehensive overarching policies. And last but not least, there is the problem of the NGOs' nonelected and therefore undemocratic position within processes of political negotiation. This often leads to criticism by local stakeholders, who claim that international NGOs are interested solely in their own "business" and evade responsibility for their actions.[22] In truth, NGO employees are often merely passing through on limited contracts with little (if any) prior experience of the locality, may therefore cling all the more tightly to their professional "expat" circles, and hence may very possibly adopt a remote, paternalistic, or even condescending approach to the work in hand (and to local stakeholders).

The policies of NGOs operating in postconflict situations should therefore be consistently and critically examined. But room must be left nonetheless for further development; and one vital step here—if ever NGOs are to become strong enough to resist their donors' influence, gain independence, and find their own place within the policy regime system—is to support them in strengthening their contacts with one another and so foster their autonomy. To promote exchange and knowledge transfer was accordingly a major aim of the Archis network of initiatives and organizations involved in urban development in southeastern Europe.[23] And the strategy was found on the whole to be very helpful. Many participants in the Archis network had not previously been aware of each other's existence, were often surprised to find they were facing similar structural problems, and showed a keen interest in exchanging news and views on potential strategic solutions. Mostly, the workshop format was used for knowledge transfer; over time it fostered enduring working relationships across borders.[24]

It is only when local NGOs and initiatives pool their resources and build resilient networks that they can establish themselves long-term and internationally and thereby constitute a substantial political counterweight. Independent international collaboration and association also helps them formulate comprehensive political goals. However, they then also have to develop new forms of democratic politics. They must find new, more transparent, and hence more open ways to select and represent relevant issues and to develop decision-making processes. Experience has shown that "outside intervention" can succeed only when there is collaboration with local groups and support for political self-determination. Accordingly, sustained efforts must be made to integrate NGOs and other civil society groups in the international policy regime system as well as to strengthen their public profile. Research into the role of NGOs in urban postconflict situations is therefore vital, and it must encompass not only a critical assessment of their actual contributions but also guidelines for education and outreach programs, knowledge transfer, and exchange, so as to assure local activists a clearer understanding of the structures and aims of this particular policy regime.

The Role of Architects and Planners within NGOs in Urban Postconflict Situations

The architecture and urban planning disciplines can gain perspective on a situation only if they consider themselves part of the overall policy regime that goes under the name "governance." They must come up with new planning strategies that are applicable to a variety of social contexts and simultaneously ensure that new contexts are understood by, and accessible to, broader segments of the society or community in question. Once the contextualization necessary for planning has been assured (and this too may be considered a political project), fundamental principles come into play. This is strategic inasmuch as it responds to various social and cultural contexts while mediating between the special needs of individual social groups and the international power structure and its mechanisms. Yet it must also be cooperative insofar as it in turn provides various participants with new contexts in order to open up spaces whose effects go beyond local (and national) contexts. And planning in this regard must be communicative, too, because only through dialogue can participants be mobilized, and dialogue at not just the local but also the international level. There are numerous international stakeholders involved in any postconflict situation and this makes dialogue imperative. Here, NGOs can play an important role as mediators. Dialogue with the local population should at the least be brought to the attention of the international community, and internationally active NGOs are in a position to lend more weight to local voices. Thus, the support that the Archis network, and in particular the internationally distributed architectural magazine *Volume*, gave to Archis Interventions' local initiatives in

Prishtina (Kosovo) was extraordinarily important, as it aroused a great deal of interest among the local media, local politicians, and international development aid organizations in the city.[25] International visibility gives local actors a measure of protection, for they are then less likely to be put under pressure by criminally or politically motivated persons.

Planners and architects take a seductive "bird's-eye view," so to speak, for they need this overarching perspective in order to grasp the complex structures of an urban district or an entire city. Plans drawn to scale reflect in abstract form the built environment and go beyond individual perception at the 1:1 scale—and architects and planners mostly forget that their plans are virtually illegible for nonexperts. Also, the bird's-eye view may fail to detect the social relationships and power relations inscribed in urban spaces as well as how the city could or should be used in daily practice. Space is never neutral—and neither is the position of architect or planner. Every plan is the result of negotiations informed by power relations—and this is manifested in the plan. Architects and planners who regard themselves as "agents of change" and seek to make positive interventions in urban development know they depend on political "patronage." Such support should not be rooted in opaque relationships and agreements made behind closed doors, however, but must remain transparent and publicly accountable. Only then is it possible also to address the programs put forth by other political factions and include them in the negotiation process. Thus, any independent groups aspiring to intervene in urban space must accomplish a delicate balancing act in the political arena. For while their essential tasks include articulating the interests of excluded or overlooked segments of the population and mobilizing public opinion to scrutinize urban development, they must also adopt a position of their own within negotiation processes and be willing to cooperate, or possibly make compromises with, other political forces. In short, independent groups must be capable of criticizing the prevailing policy regime while simultaneously being a part of it. Critiques and public debates are not enough on their own, although they are certainly prerequisites of any successful intervention—for if sustainable change is ever to come about it is only ever thanks to assertive action; it is always a question of power. The regulation of urban development, particularly in postconflict situations, cannot be left to self-appointed bodies and local traditions but must be taken in hand by organs of the state. They alone can legitimately propose and enforce policy. However, no plan, no regulation, no urban development strategy can be carried out if there is no consensus in a society on its significance and purpose. Yet constraints must be imposed even here: if organs of the state (or the international institutions and organizations that support them) offer nothing but repression and corruption, they too lose their legitimacy; if they implement measures by means of coercion, it is right and proper to maintain a critical distance from them. But it is naïve to believe that an "architecture of peace" can exist independently of an "architecture of power."

Since architects and planners within NGOs in urban postconflict situations must always adapt their approach to the local context, it is unwise to make too many generalizations. The following basic principles are worth considering, nonetheless.

Architects and planners should:

- carefully clarify and communicate their own positions;
- not pursue commercial interests;
- address a broad variety of interest groups and seek to involve them, long-term, in the (urban development) projects foreseen;
- cluster interests and options for projects where success requires groups' cooperation;
- assure equity in all collaborations (advantages and profits must be equally shared);
- assure transparency (all goals and procedures must be publicly discussed);
- foster open negotiation by admitting different perspectives;
- mobilize knowledge and make it easily accessible to all; and
- plan and design the process, structure it through dialogue, and keep it open-ended.

As these principles show, the fundamental pillars of the work are communication, cooperation, and shaping processes. What does this mean specifically for architects and planners who want to intervene in urban development? On the one hand they are able to initiate important projects, since their professional expertise equips them to both anticipate potential pitfalls in urban development and publicly address them in good time. For example, they may direct attention to the social conflicts and health and safety issues that often ensue from unregulated construction (as described in reference to Archis Interventions in Prishtina).[26] They serve not only as initiators, however, but also—once again, thanks to their professional training—as mediators between state representatives, investors, and civil society. This role calls for clear communication as well as a capacity to foster cooperation among diverse stakeholders. At least initially, architects and planners should give a lot of thought not so much to the foreseen project itself but rather to the process as a whole, the crux of the matter being how best to devise and communicate the project and involve people in its implementation and long-term viability. And incidentally, it should not be assumed that a project takes the form of a plan or a building—even though every problem looks like a potential construction project, from the architect's standpoint. In reality, an urban problem may often be solved by other means: to name just a few examples, a space may be revitalized through public debate, by an economic strategy or a regulation, or by giving it a new function. Accordingly, when figuring out projects in a postconflict situation it always helps to ask a few basic questions:

- WHERE? Where is the space? Where can nondisputed, noncontroversial, "neutral" spaces be found?
- WHAT? What is it possible to create—perhaps a new space that will open up new perspectives?
- WHO? Who needs this space? Who will profit from it? Who are the partners involved in the process? Does it serve the public interest?
- HOW? Which tools and strategies are needed in order to create this space? How may cooperation be fostered? How may the process be shaped?

Toward Research on Urban Postconflict Development Strategies

It is imperative that future research on urban postconflict development explore and systematize the planning issues that arise in a variety of spheres, in light of their transferability (i.e., their applicability to a range of different contexts) and the potential strategic solutions outlined below. Further spheres of action may be identified in parallel. A conscious orientation to the practices of various actors in postconflict situations (architects, planners, and others) is crucial, as is critical reflection and supportive (i.e., constructive) criticism and analysis. The role of urban planning as a part of the policy regime able to shape contested spaces has been discussed at length in reference to divided cities.[27] Yet there is evidently a need for still more research into effective conflict resolution strategies that are developed on the ground in everyday practice, particularly those focused on the specific potential of architecture and planning. As mentioned earlier, those local civil society initiatives and organizations in which architects and planners are involved show an extremely keen interest in the systematic analysis and evaluation of conflict management and strategic urban development in times of social and political upheaval.[28] This played a pivotal role in Archis Interventions' project in Prishtina, the primary aim of which was to legalize the outcome of the largely informal construction boom that had taken place there after 1999. To address those parts of Prishtina developed without any formal planning or construction permits—approximately 70 percent of the total built environment—a comprehensive strategic concept was devised and, on the whole, the outcomes proved successful.

It was thereby essential to attract and maintain a high level of public attention by rolling out a well-coordinated communications strategy both locally and internationally: for example, by targeting local inhabitants, international political instances (such as the UNMIK, which was effectively the ruling body until 2008), and international development aid organizations.

In consequence, the legalization of informal buildings became a leading issue in the mayoral elections of 2007, and it proved possible in 2009 to hammer out minimum standards for legalization in cooperation with the city administration (as part of the Architecture Strategy). To explain essential issues such as the importance of fire escape routes and safety distance, a manual using simple language and graphics was produced and distributed to the general public.[29]

Implementation of the legalization process, which began only in 2011,[30] decisively influenced subsequent legislation on the legalization of informal buildings nationwide.[31] In addition, a Networking Strategy was rolled out, the major aim of which was to pool the knowledge and experience of other NGOs active in the region. Of particular importance for the Prishtina project was the involvement of Co-PLAN, a Tirana-based association that had initiated the integration and legalization of informal building in Albania in 2006 with successful outcomes. Expansion of the Archis network throughout the region as of 2008 further supported this process, not least through a series of workshops jointly organized by regional initiatives and organizations. The involvement of other local

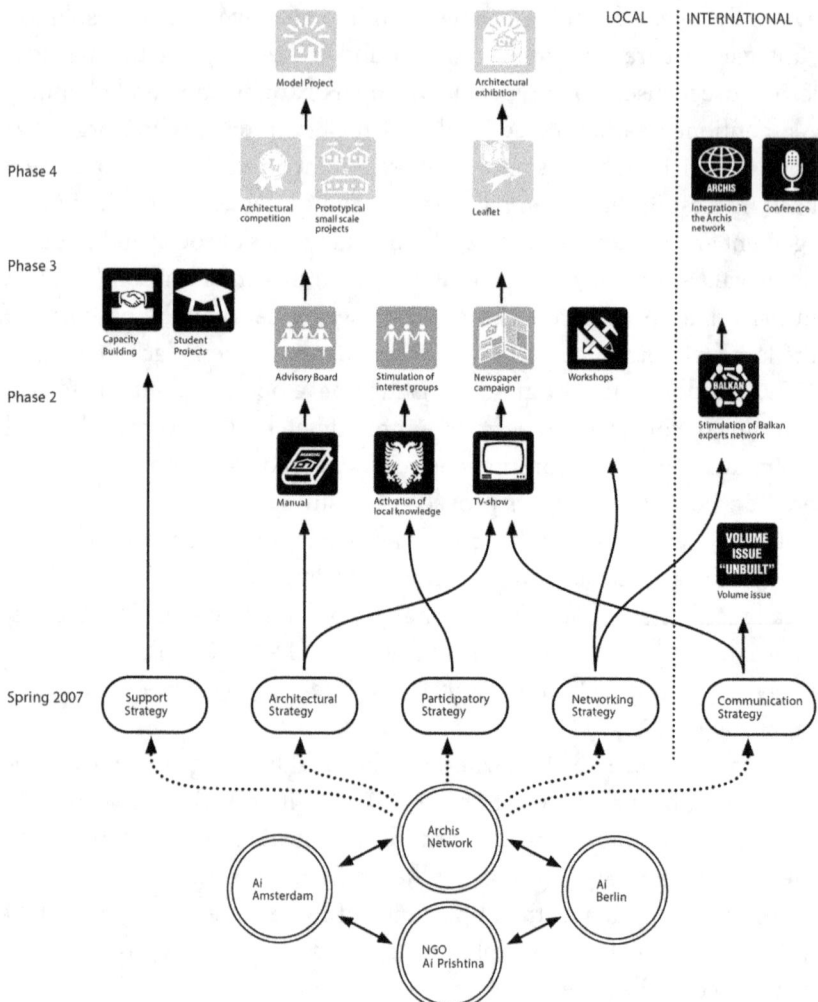

FIGURE 1.1. The strategic concept developed by Archis Interventions in 2006 combined different approaches in order to heighten public awareness of, and sensitivity to, environmental qualities and architectural values. It addressed diverse participants, local as well as international, and was designed to bridge the gaps between them. The combination of different strategies proved vital: most aspects of the strategic concept were successfully implemented. (Archis Interventions, 2014)

FIGURE 1.2. A public awareness campaign designed by Archis Interventions ran in parallel to the gradual regulation of informal construction in Prishtina (including the legalization of existing buildings), which started in October 2010. Public presentations and a media campaign raised public awareness of the most important aspects of this issue (safety regulations, public infrastructure and amenities, impact on the community, etc.)—and there was even an eight-part TV series produced by Visar Geci, a cofounder of Archis Interventions/Prishtina and a renowned TV star in Kosovo, in cooperation with Florina Jerliu and Kai Vöckler. Each of the eight episodes addressed a different aspect of informal building. Recorded on selected sites in Prishtina from August to December 2009, the TV series gave local citizens and officials a chance to express their opinions on the state of informal building in the city, in dialogue with Visar Geci. It was broadcast daily from July 9 to 16, 2011, by the cable channel KUJTESA. A summary of the series was broadcast on July 16, 2011, by the KTV channel. (Photograph by Kai Vöckler)

actors, architects, and planners, as well as the architecture faculty of the University of Prishtina was always a crucial aspect of this Support Strategy—and above all, that of the local populations most acutely at risk from informal building. Encouraging interest groups to speak out was therefore a major focus within the framework of the Participation Strategy.

The experience gained in Prishtina—in combination with analyses of postconflict development in cities such as Mostar (Bosnia-Herzegovina), Nicosia (Cyprus), Mitrovica (Kosovo), and Kabul (Afghanistan)—enabled

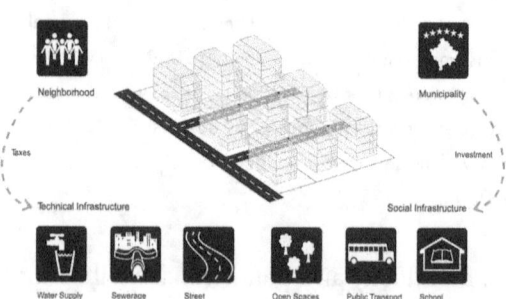

FIGURE 1.3. The *Manual on the Legalization of Structures Built without a Construction Permit* was developed in 2009 by Archis Interventions in cooperation with the Municipality of Prishtina. The municipality resolved to launch the legalization process on the basis of the manual after the mayoral elections in late 2009. (Archis Interventions, 2009)

us to pinpoint the major issues to be pursued in future research on urban postconflict development, which are discussed in further detail below.

Urban Vision

Planning in postconflict situations means much more than simply improving local security and living conditions, for it also holds the promise of a better future. Yet evidently, urban vision is often lacking. As experience in Afghanistan and Bosnia-Herzegovina has shown, the international aid community tends to concentrate on reconstructing major landmarks in historical city districts. While there is much to be said for restoring extraordinary buildings or neighborhoods that symbolize a city's identity, this focus on cultural heritage means that a city's current views on its postconflict future—which is to say, the views of the city's inhabitants—are often ignored.[32] Into this symbolic space, investor architects thrust "Dubai-style" office and retail blocks with mirrored blue façades, the modern epitome of the promise of prosperity and progress. These striking, solitary implants stand out from the overall urban development but do nothing to remedy the fundamental problems with which local inhabitants are faced: for example, the housing shortage which almost inevitably follows any period of conflict, owing both to the destruction of property and the massive wartime influx of rural migrants. But although barely viable megaprojects continue to be built by and on behalf of city administrations, universal implementation of a modernist *tabula rasa* urban vision does not work. Urban planning in Kabul after the turn of the millennium illustrates this only too well.[33] The Ministry of Urban Development (MoUD) had developed a concept for the "New Kabul Project," a satellite city in the northeast of the capital that was to house almost one million people in an area larger than that of the rest of Kabul at the time. How it would be financed and the necessary infrastructure provided was never clarified.[34] The legalization and upgrade of infrastructure in the existing anomalous settlements as well as the development of vacant lots within the city limits appeared to be a more pressing matter, one that UN-Habitat was in fact already taking action on. Yet in the absence of an urban master plan clearly oriented to future needs, issues such as the nascent investment architecture and its negative impact on community structures were consistently overlooked. Likewise conspicuous by its absence was strategic planning that might steer the city in flux by facilitating actions such as these: generating adequate responses to wartime demographic fluctuations; addressing the wave of illegal construction prompted by the massive influx of rural migrants; and setting realistic parameters for urban development, despite the still unresolved and largely disputed legal framework. Without taking all of these relevant cultural, social, and economic factors into account, drafting an urban vision for Kabul was doomed to failure. Strategic urban development must always allow for the locality's characteristic contrasts and contradictions.

Planning without a Plan

In the initial postconflict years local and international organizations concentrate on vital support, such as medical care, the allocation of accommodation and food, and the delivery of essential infrastructure (e.g., water supply). Urban development plans are repeatedly deferred in this phase, mostly because the city administration either does not yet exist or is not yet fully operational. The construction boom in the informal sector is fueled by the high demand for housing and the aforementioned investor/architect (office and retail) projects. A city's social fabric rapidly deteriorates in the absence of traditional planning tools: first and foremost, a master plan for coordinated urban development, but also building regulations and the attendant legislation on health and safety, especially if there is a lack of qualified personnel to use or enforce such tools (city planning department officers, civil engineers, health inspectors, etc.). It is often in the immediate postconflict period that ill-considered or illegal urban development encroaches on the existing infrastructure; it often takes many years of extraordinary effort to remedy such damage. Here, too, Prishtina is a prime example: immediately after the end of the conflict, Kosovo-Albanians embarked on a frenetic construction boom— they were by then the majority population given that almost all of the Kosovo-Serbs either had already left the city or were little inclined to invest in it under the new political regime—but at the time it was literally impossible to obtain a construction permit. The local administration (under UNMIK) had immediately set about drafting a master plan for comprehensive urban development, but several years were to pass before the plan was finished. In the meantime informal construction had gained the upper hand: approximately 70 percent of existing building infrastructure had been destroyed or remodeled in ways that prompted or exacerbated health and safety issues (for example, overly dense development in zones at risk of earthquakes; failure to provide escape and emergency routes; structurally unsound additions of up to three stories on existing buildings), as well as social discord (neighborhood conflicts) and infrastructural decline (the occupation of public space, destruction of recreational zones). All of this could have been prevented—in the interests also of those who were building—by enforcing a few basic regulations on minimum standards (which job would have fallen at the time to the international community, i.e., to UNMIK and the KFOR troops). Prishtina's situation had structural similarities with that in Kabul after 2001; there, too, the failure to impose a clearly coordinated strategy fostered rampant illegal construction, the impact of which on urban development was disastrous and later very difficult to remedy.

An urban postconflict strategy should seek ways to structure urban development in coordination with vital aid programs. This means addressing various standards and the problems they entail. Since planning institutions no longer exist, and basic data (on population size, for example) are unavailable, carrying out adequate or even anticipatory short-term planning is very difficult.[35] The question then arises as to whether planning without a master plan is feasible. Instead of following customary practice, highly complex planning operations have to develop a system of their own that allows for basic and variable uses, when these also cannot be foreseen or precisely determined in advance. One potential solution is the Project and Access Plan (PAP) proposed by Eberhard Knapp and applied in East Germany after the fall of the Berlin Wall.[36] Basically, the PAP principle is that any investor who proposes a building must simultaneously provide an urban planning proposal for its immediate vicinity. This "miniature master plan" ensures harmonious overall development even in the absence of a land-use plan or master plan— and it can be reconciled with a coherent formal master plan (or broader guidelines) after, say, five or seven years.[37] This planning provision was designed for investors and must accordingly be modified in the case of private, family-based construction activities.

Planning without a Neighborhood

Postconflict situations characteristically see a sharp rise in the urban population due to the influx of migrants from the countryside and returnee refugees. In parallel, habitual residents may leave the city.[38] The upheaval of conflict destroys the fabric of neighborhoods within certain sections of the city, and full or partial reconstruction is required. A lively, individual, and informal building activity develops which wholly ignores questions of collective needs: neither issues of technical and social infrastructure nor special design and its usage are addressed. The strategy for these new neighborhoods in the early development phase must therefore be to foster a sense of community and motivate individuals to look beyond their own four walls respectively their own lot. Neighborhood programs supported by the international aid community, such as UN-Habitat's urban community upgrade strategy, are mostly implemented too late; they would be more effective if rolled out at this early stage.

Planning without Ownership

Vacant lots or built properties are often illegally appropriated, at times because it proves impossible to establish who is the rightful owner or previously public land has been carved up and seized for private use.[39] On the one hand, the possibility of legal construction must be considered very early on (and thus without a master plan); on the other, thought must be given to alternative models of ownership or possession that allow for sustainable use but without the owners relinquishing the deeds to their property. The provision of a simple standardized tenancy agreement that clarifies basic rights and duties would probably be helpful. To develop this, however, would first require closer examination of ownership and restitution claims in various postconflict situations as well as the institution of an appropriate legal framework.[40]

Flexible Planning

The obvious failure of those city administrations and international organizations jointly responsible for urban postconflict development can be put down to their lack of understanding of planning and the role of the expert. Undeniably, plans are required in order to structure and regulate urban development. However, the traditional top-down approach that characterizes hierarchically structured planning—from the strategic master plan to land zoning to regulated building plans—entails a number of troublesome factors that are not generally taken into account. One is that planning is a notoriously tedious process: it may drag on for years—

and before it comes to an end, reality has usually outpaced it. Also, the city is regarded here as a coherent unit, an object that can be shaped and designed. That the city is always in flux, its form constantly shifting, is too often overlooked. Of course, it is necessary that planning goals are set, that planning be used as a regulatory force in urban development, but because circumstances change, there is also and always a need for flexibility. This is the paradox, especially in postconflict settings: on the one hand, urban planning establishes and fixes matters, but on the other, it must remain flexible. Planning accordingly needs to envisage the vagaries of the future but can do so only when it remains itself a process alive to the fact that the city is not just a built form to be (re-)structured but rather the sum of a million acts performed by different actors, among them the city administration. Such actors are guided by norms and values that may be useful for orientation. The challenge for planners, therefore, is to develop ways to cooperate with various actors—ways that are suited to the specific political and social circumstances. In this respect planning is always political, too.

If the traditional urban planning model is rejected, then new forms of cooperation and negotiation between private parties and governmental institutions must be developed. Master plans that attempt to treat complex layers of political and economic problems all in the same way (comprehensive planning) are meaningless. Instead, it is necessary to develop processual, participatory—and hence communication-based—planning models (collaborative planning). For this flexible sort of planning, it is crucial that new forms of collaboration be fostered and legalized. This is being discussed intensively in Western countries and has already become a feature of planning practice there.[41] In the postconflict situations discussed here, however, (Prishtina, Mostar, Kabul), this sort of planning is of limited use, for attention is all too fixated on the indisputably very challenging problems of reconstruction. UN-Habitat did try to involve a variety of local actors in a participatory planning process in Mostar, but the experiment was ultimately thwarted by the difficult political situation.[42] Cooperative efforts of this sort must remain sufficiently transparent as to be easily monitored by the public. The forces of civil society should therefore be encouraged to participate, for they can serve as an important corrective to the planning process. As in Archis Interventions' participatory project in Prishtina, the key to all of this is effective communication: public campaigns launched with the assistance of local media can foster public debate, assure knowledge transfer, and encourage people to get involved.

Legality in Lawless Contexts

As a rule, construction projects are undertaken without a building permit. This is possibly because the pressure to develop is high, city administrations still lack the capacity to provide services, and/or corruption makes permits unaffordable. Traditional tried-and-tested construction techniques are used for the most part, so the illegal buildings are basically viable.

However, the lack of supervision and monitoring by qualified personnel leads to problems, also of a structural nature: safety distances, emergency escape routes and lighting, and other health and safety measures are often completely neglected, and the construction methods and statics are unlikely to hold up in the long term. Simplifying construction regulations is therefore an option well worth considering: for example, one can highlight the importance of nonbureaucratic minimal requirements and communicate them simply, so laypeople too can understand them. The form, content, and presentation of minimal requirements must be given sufficient thought. Since an abstract set of rules generally cannot be enforced, a manual of the kind discussed above—which detailed steps to legalize informal construction in Prishtina—might well prove useful, especially if it offers very simple (perhaps cartoon-style) graphic descriptions of the most important basic principles and clearly conveys to contractors and builders both the urgent need for safety precautions as well as the commercial potential of quality buildings that withstand the passage of time. The transferability of basic principles to a variety of cultural contexts must also be taken into account.

Enforceability

In most cases construction regulations from the preconflict era are still in existence, but given the absence or dearth of adequately qualified personnel, they are not universally enforced. Even once the respective postconflict responsibilities of the international and local authorities have been clarified, the capacity to enforce complex laws and their numerous exceptions is limited. By simplifying construction legislation, it is hoped that monitoring will be made easier too; for it could then be carried out not only by technical experts but other authorized personnel. This is of paramount importance to any international military presence, for work of this kind falls within its mandate (which is itself a politically explosive issue). In summary, the fundamental prerequisites are minimum requirements presented in simple language and graphics, easily audited outcomes, and good communication. The latter is a primary facilitator. It depends on the broad inclusion of everyone involved in or affected by the project in hand, for example, through neighborhood initiatives, workshops, and participatory research; and also hinges on strategic use of the media.

All in all, we have established that a viable urban postconflict strategy should include an urban vision that articulates "images of tomorrow" as a development perspective. This perspective should encompass new forms of coordinating and implementing developmental measures and mediate between international and local levels and in this way (last but not least) generate architectonic value.

Conclusion

Experience and analysis have shown that within the conflict-ridden system of international politics, localized via the governance framework, civil society projects developed in cooperation with local, independent urban initiatives can successfully launch new kinds of cooperative and participatory planning that in particular help strengthen weakened civil forces. Positioning within a governance framework is of crucial importance: for an intervention to succeed, it must forge relationships with government institutions and the civil sector alike. In initiating independent, nongovernmental, noncommercial participatory projects, architects and urban planners play an important role. They not only bring their technical expertise to the table but also serve as mediators; by deploying strategies for target-audience empowerment, networking, and clear communication, they ensure that urban developments are facilitated by a broad coalition of interests and are monitored with the requisite level of transparency and public accountability.

There is nonetheless a need for further practice-oriented research into the role of architecture and planning in contested spaces. Building on the above palette of responsive and remedial strategies, the future focal research themes should include refining and systematizing the tools to implement these strategies; examining their transferability (adaptability) to a broad variety of cultural contexts; monitoring outcomes in order to assess the (non)viability of past projects; and (not least, in light of the latter) revising and devising new planning models. The expertise thus gained could also be pooled and widely disseminated. This would both improve public understanding of planning processes and assure professionals in the field vital support. Simultaneously, it would help clarify spatial designers' significant role in steering urban postconflict development and also bring that role to international attention.

Notes

1. See Kai Vöckler, "Politics of Architecture," in *SEE! Urban Transformation in Southeastern Europe*, ed. Kai Vöckler (Vienna: Lit Verlag, 2012), 14–18.
2. The Albanian spelling of Prishtina (Priština in Serbian) is used here. This is in accordance with historical reality: 90 percent of the population of Kosovo speaks Albanian. The prewar and postwar population of Prishtina (Kosovo) barely altered in number (ca. 200 000), but certainly in composition. While in 1981 there were about 60,000 Kosovo-Serb inhabitants, by 2011 there were only 500. See Kosovo Agency of Statistics (2011), accessed June 15, 2021, http://ask.rks-gov.net/en/kosovo-agency-of-statistics/social/demography-and-migration (in Albanian).
3. Several major international organizations working in Kosovo have reported a high level of migration from rural to urban centers (e.g., ILO and IPEC 2005, and UNDP 2005). See Zana Vathi and Richard Black, *Migration and Poverty Reduction in Kosovo* (Development Research Centre on Migration, Globalisation and Poverty, February 2007), 6–8, accessed June 4, 2021, https://pdfs.semanticscholar.org/3eb1/23d94df5f49864b316cf254c5cfc52f9cea0.pdf.
4. There are no reliable statistics for Kabul (Afghanistan), but it is estimated that the population of approximately 500,000 people in 2001 has meanwhile grown to over 2 million. See estimates of the Central Statistics Organization, Islamic Republic of Afghanistan, accessed June 4, 2021, http://cso.gov.af/en/page/demography-and-socile-statistics/demograph-statistics/3897111.
5. On Kabul (Afghanistan), see Jolyon Leslie, "City of Contest," in *UN Urbanism: Mostar Kabul*, eds. Regina Bittner, Wilfried Hackenbroich and Kai Vöckler (Berlin: Jovis, 2010), 94–99. On Prishtina, see Kai Vöckler,

Prishtina Is Everywhere: Turbo Urbanism: The Aftermath of a Crisis (Amsterdam: Archis, 2008). Includes a coauthored supplement on postconflict development.

6. See Babar Mumtaz and Kaj Noschis, eds., *Development of Kabul: Reconstruction and Planning Issues* (Lausanne, Switzerland: Comportment, 2004); Sultan Barakat, ed., *After the Conflict: Reconstruction and Development in the Aftermath of War* (London: Tauris, 2005); Jon Calame and Esther Charlesworth, *Divided Cities: Belfast, Beirut, Jerusalem, Mostar, and Nicosia* (Philadelphia: University of Pennsylvania Press, 2009); Frank Gaffikin and Mike Morrissey, *Planning in Divided Cities* (Chichester, UK: Wiley-Blackwell, 2011); Vöckler, *Prishtina Is Everywhere*.
7. Ole Bouman and Kai Vöckler founded Archis Interventions in 2005; see http://archis.org. On its activities in southeastern Europe, see http://archis.org/projects/archis-see-network/.
8. See Bittner, Hackenbroich, and Vöckler, *UN Urbanism*.
9. The work in this chapter references earlier articles by the author, in particular those published in the international architecture magazine *Volume*: see Kai Vöckler, "Stateless Urbanism," *Volume* 11, Cities Unbuilt (2007): 146–47; "Politics of Architecture," *Volume* 26, Architecture of Peace, special insert "SEE: Archis Interventions in Southeastern Europe," (2010): 1–7; "Four Strategies to Counter the Division of Cities," *Volume* 40, Architecture of Peace Reloaded, special insert "The Good Cause: Architecture of Peace—Divided Cities" (exhib. cat., Munich Architecture Museum, 2014): 28–31.
10. For example, Annika Björkdahl and Stefanie Kappler, *Peacebuilding and Spatial Transformation: Peace, Space and Place* (London: Routledge, 2017); Giulia Carabelli, *The Divided City and the Grassroots: The (Un)making of Ethnic Divisions in Mostar* (Singapore: Palgrave Macmillan, 2018); Susan Forde, *Movement as Conflict Transformation: Rescripting Mostar, Bosnia-Herzegovina* (Singapore: Palgrave Macmillan, 2019).
11. Recent exceptions include Arta Jakupi, *The Effect of the International Community Presence in the Urban Development of Post Conflict City. Case Study: Kosova* (PhD diss., Bauhaus University Weimar, 2012), https://e-pub.uni-weimar.de/opus4/frontdoor/deliver/index/docId/1831/file/Arta+JAKUPI-+The+Effect+of+the+International+Community+Presence+on+Urban+Development+of+Post+Conflict+City_pdfa.pdf; Socrates Stratis, ed., *Guide to Common Urban Imaginaries in Contested Spaces: The "Hands-on Famagusta" Project* (Berlin: Jovis, 2016); Mirjana Ristić, *Architecture, Urban Space and War: The Destruction and Reconstruction of Sarajevo* (London: Palgrave Macmillan, 2018). See also note 7, above.

12. See John E. Trent, *Modernizing the United Nations System: Civil Society's Role in Moving from International Relations to Global Governance* (Farmington Hills, MI: Barbara Budrich Publishers, 2007).
13. For example, reconstruction of the Stari Most (Old Bridge) in Mostar, Bosnia-Herzegovina, did nothing to reconcile the opposed communities there. See Kai Vöckler, "Politics of Identity—The Example of Mostar, Bosnia-Herzegovina," NECE conference paper, 2010, www.bpb.de/system/files/pdf/2G5U1B.pdf; see also Emily Gunzburger Makaš, *Representing Competing Identities: Building and Rebuilding in Postwar Mostar, Bosnia-Herzegovina* (PhD diss., Cornell University 2007), https://uncc.academia.edu/EmilyMakas.
14. All aid organizations (not NGOs) funded by their own governments represent the geopolitical interests of their home countries. I am referring here to those Western organizations that fail to be transparent about their interests. For a critique of development aid, see James C. Scott, *Seeing Like a State: How Certain Schemes to Improve the Human Condition Have Failed* (New Haven, CT: Yale University Press, 1998); Michael Herzfeld, "Developmentalism," in *Anthropology: Theoretical Practice in Culture and Society*, ed. Michael Herzfeld (Oxford: Blackwell, 2001), 152–70; Hubertus Büschel, "*Geschichte der Entwicklungspolitik*," in *Docupedia-Zeitgeschichte (November 2, 2010)*, http://dx.doi.org/10.14765/zzf.dok.2.591.v1.
15. See Michael Walzer, *Thick and Thin: Moral Argument at Home and Abroad* (Notre Dame, IN: University of Notre Dame Press, 1994).
16. From 1991 to 2015 the number of internationally networked NGOs (INGOs) equipped with a headquarters and permanent staff and active in more than one country steadily increased from 4,620 to 8,976. Union of International Associations, *Yearbook of International Organizations* (2017). https://www.globalpolicy.org/component/content/article/176-general/31937.html. There is no reliable data on either local civil society organizations (CSOs) or informal initiatives. See also Trent, *Modernizing the United Nations System*, 179–80. On Afghanistan, see David F. Mitchell, "NGO Presence and Activity in Afghanistan, 2000–2014: A Provincial-Level Dataset," *Stability: International Journal of Security and Development* 6(1).5 (2017): n.p., http://doi.org/10.5334/sta.497.
17. See Ulrich Brand et al., eds., *Nichtregierungsorganisationen in der Transformation des Staates* (Muenster: Westfälisches Dampfboot, 2001).
18. The deliberations presented here are the outcome of discussions with local partner organizations and initiatives within the Archis network.
19. The Aga Khan Foundation (AKF) is a nongovernmental development aid organization that was founded in 1967 by Karim Aga Khan IV, primar-

ily to support initiatives in mainly Muslim countries. The Open Society Foundations (OSF), formerly known as Open Society Institute (OSI), were founded by the American billionaire George Soros and are mainly active in Eastern Europe. One example of an organization whose work in the field of development aid is funded by business enterprise (in this case, by banking) is the ERSTE Foundation, set up by the Austrian ERSTE Group. It is mainly active in Central and Eastern Europe and was a primary supporter of the work of Archis Interventions. Critical discussion here of the relationship of NGOs to their donors is in part based on experience gained in said context.

20. See Linda Polman, *War Games: The Story of Aid and War in Modern Times* (London: Penguin, 2010).
21. Mary Kaldor, "Cosmopolitanism Versus Nationalism: The New Divide?," in *Europe's New Nationalism: States and Minorities in Conflict*, eds. Richard Caplan and Jon Feffer (New York: Oxford University Press, 1996), 42–58.
22. This is why Archis Interventions, on principle, takes action (intervenes) in situations solely at the initiative or invitation of local stakeholders, such as CSOs or informal project groups.
23. The network could not have been built without the generous support of the ERSTE Foundation.
24. Documented and discussed in Vöckler, *SEE! Urban Transformation in Southeastern Europe*.
25. See Vöckler, *Prishtina Is Everywhere*, 129–35.
26. See Vöckler, *Prishtina Is Everywhere*.
27. Gaffikin and Morrissey, *Planning in Divided Cities* (note 5); Vöckler, "Four Strategies to Counter the Division of Cities," note 8.
28. As SEE discussions with local initiatives and organizations revealed, this is the case not only in the field of urban postconflict development, but also in instances of social upheaval in general, including those ensuing from political shifts or natural disasters. See Vöckler, *SEE! Urban Transformation in Southeastern Europe*.
29. *Manual on the Legalization of Structures Built without a Construction Permit*, Archis Interventions in cooperation with the Municipality of Prishtina with the support of the Association of Kosovo Municipalities and Co-PLAN, Tirana, March 13–15, 2009, http://www.seenetwork.org/files/2010/11/16/3/Archis%20Interventions_Prishtina_Manual_2009.pdf.
30. The process of legalization in Prishtina: March 2009, workshop to create the *Manual on Legalization*; July 2009, city council resolution to start the process of legalization on the basis of the manual after the mayoral elections in late 2009; October 2010, announcement of legalization process. (Every owner had four months to submit applications.) Start of the legalization

process: November 2010, workshop on evaluation of the legalization process (Archis Interventions, with the Municipality of Prishtina); June 2011, started issuing legalization permits; October 2011, public debate on the topic of recurrent problems in the legalization process (Archis Interventions, with architects from Prishtina and city representatives).
31. For details of this, see Florina Jerliu, Wilfried Hackenbroich, and Kai Vöckler, "Post-Conflict Planning: Archis Interventions in Prishtina, Kosovo," in Vöckler, *SEE! Urban Transformation in Southeastern Europe*, 52–71.
32. See note 14, above.
33. See Wilfried Hackenbroich and Kai Vöckler, "The Re-Urbanisation of Kabul by the International Community or: What Can We Learn from Kabul?" in Bittner, Hackenbroich, and Vöckler, *UN Urbanism*, 79–99.
34. See the interview with the deputy minister at the Ministry of Urban Development and Housing, Dr. Qiamuddin Djallalzada, "What 'Post-War Country' Really Means," in Bittner, Hackenbroich, and Vöckler, *UN Urbanism*, 100–8.
35. An example: in 2005 official sources such as the city planning authority estimated the population of Prishtina at 500,000 but provided no data to back this up. In 2006 the local planners and architects at an Archis Interventions workshop drew on the city waterworks map of legal and illegal connections to extrapolate data on the number and size of households and concluded that the population was ca. 250,000–300,000. The census of 2011 put the population at ca. 200,000 (the drop being in part due to the mass migration of Kosovo-Serbs). See also note 3, above.
36. Eberhard Knapp, "The Need for One 'Urban Vision' and Many 'Masterplans,'" in Mumtaz and Noschis, *Development of Kabul*, 101–9.
37. Knapp, "Need for One 'Urban Vision.'"
38. As in Prishtina (Kosovo) or Kabul (Afghanistan). See notes 3–5, above.
39. There is no reliable data on informal building. Illegal land appropriation for housing construction was common in Kabul after 2001. See Jurjen van der Tas, "Social Services, Access to Land and Transportation as Core Sectors for the Future Growth of Kabul," in Mumtaz and Noschis, *Development of Kabul*, 67–72; Hackenbroich and Vöckler, "Re-Urbanisation of Kabul?," 79–99; Anthony Fontenot and Ajmal Maiwandi, "Reconstructing Kabul: Past, Present and Future," *Volume* 40, Architecture of Peace Reloaded (2014), 30–39.
40. As conversations with international aid workers have revealed, they and local actors have ample knowledge of these topics but conclusive research and analysis have not yet been conducted—and remain unlikely, unless a framework for cooperation between different development aid organiza-

tions is put in place and likewise with the international NGOs. Since in both cases our sources either spoke strictly "off the record" or wished to approve reports prior to publication, we can assume there was some concern that surveys would involve critical evaluation of their own projects. Future researchers should take note.

41. See Patsy Healey, *Collaborative Planning: Shaping Places in Fragmented Societies* (New York: Palgrave, 1997). For an overview, see Thomas Kruger, "Alles Governance? Anregungen aus der Management-Forschung für die Planungstheorie," *RaumPlanung* 132/133 (2007), 125–30. On this, see also Sven-Patrick Marx, "Stadtplanung zwischen Umbruch und Kontinuität," in *Strategieorientierte Planung im kooperativen Staat*, eds. Alexander Hamedinger et al. (Wiesbaden: VS Verlag für Sozialwissenschaften, 2007), 87–101.
42. See the interview with Aleksandr Stular, who worked for UN-Habitat in Mostar from 2004 to 2007 ("Mostar was a very specific case"), in Bittner, Hackenbroich, and Vöckler, *UN Urbanism*, 157–64.

2

IVAN ŠTRAUS

War Diary and Design Intentions of an Architect in Postwar Sarajevo

ARMINA PILAV

This chapter explores the role of architects during and after the war in Bosnia and Herzegovina (1992–96), including their relations to the practices of architects in socialist Yugoslavia (1945–92). I will analyze the documentation and design activities of architect Ivan Štraus (1928–2018) and examine his short collaboration with American architect Lebbeus Woods (1940–2012), which started during the war in Bosnia and Herzegovina. Štraus's long and varied life as well as his professional experience allows us to consider the roles played by different generations of architects in Bosnia in the making of the complex and contested post-Yugoslav architectural environment.

Since the first, massive antiwar demonstrations in March 1991, Sarajevo has been an example of shifting political and material realities in which architecture and urban space acquire new forms and meanings. Successive wars fought on the territory of Socialist Federative Republic of Yugoslavia, including the most brutal one in Bosnia and Herzegovina between 1992 and 1996, destroyed more than just significant architectural achievements. Fragmented and biased postwar architectural education systems also erased the names of many architects who shaped the socialist landscape between the end of World War II and 1992.[1] Meanwhile, the destruction of Yugoslavian modernism continues through postwar design practices. Following the end of the war in Bosnia and Herzegovina in 1996, many past modernist achievements have been neglected by the state and city offices involved in postwar reconstruction, or they have been poorly maintained and left unprotected from vandalism, particularly antifascist memorial complexes such as Partisan Cemetery in Mostar, designed by architect Bogdan Bogdanović.

In 2014 I did several interviews with architect Ivan Štraus in his home in Sarajevo.[2] This text is guided by one of the statements he made during our meetings: "Architecture makes sense only as the practice of the present."[3] That same year he became a member of the Serbian Academy of Sciences and Art, showing clearly his autonomy as an architect, as he could choose to be both a member of the Serbian Academy and an architect from Sarajevo. This decision by Štraus and the Serbian Academy to proclaim him a member transcends the Serbian aggression against Bosnia and Herzegovina because in his diary from the war he describes Serbian military forces destroying buildings that he had designed as well as documenting the destruction of Sarajevo. My main questions to Štraus did not focus on any particular architectural projects he designed prior to 1992. Instead, I was interested in understanding how he experienced the transition from one political system to another, how he dealt about the military destruction of his own buildings, and, later, how he reacted to the new approaches to reconstruction brought about by the new political order in a destroyed city inhabited by a traumatized society.

A relevant figure in relation to the work of Ivan Štraus is American architect Lebbeus Woods, who visited Sarajevo in 1993. Woods's engagement with the Yugoslavian territory started in 1991 with his exhibition "Zagreb-Free-Zone" at the Museum of Arts and Crafts in Zagreb, Croatia.[4] Following this exhibition he came to Sarajevo and gave a public lecture by invitation of the Architects Association of Sarajevo. In November 1993 he returned to a Sarajevo under siege on the invitation of theatre director Haris Pašović. During the siege access to the city was controlled and limited; to reach the urban area, he assumed the role of a journalist, taking advantage of the fact that media workers could more easily access the city. Woods brought with him a copy of his freshly printed pamphlet *War and Architecture*, which marked the beginning of his professional relationship with Ivan Štraus.[5] He presented the book in the destroyed building that had housed the Olympic Museum in Sarajevo, which was at that moment the world's most famous war city. Following their first meeting, Štraus and Woods remained in contact, exchanging architectural drawings regarding the reconstruction of the destroyed *Elektroprivreda* Building designed by Štraus in 1978.[6]

Ivan Štraus's *Architect and Barbarians* diary was written in 1991 and

1992, almost simultaneously with Woods's pamphlet.[7] It documents the dissolution of Yugoslavia and the beginning of the war in Bosnia and Herzegovina through the prism of the destruction of architecture during the first months of the siege of Sarajevo.[8] The observations Štraus presented in the diary about the destruction of the city were soon confirmed by Woods, who during his second stay in Sarajevo toured the city with local architects and saw its architectural and cultural destruction (fig. 2.1). Woods articulated his reactions to the devastation verbally and visually. (For example, on his blog where he recorded his observations on destruction of the city and sketched possible solutions.[9])

Štraus's diary and the attempt to reconstruct the *Elektroprivreda* Building by intersecting his prewar design with Woods's concepts led my interest in his work.[10] He was one of those rare architects in Sarajevo who, after the war, had the opportunity to participate—in the role of main architect—in the reconstruction of a building he had designed back in 1978.

In order to understand the processes and changing practices of architects under the unstable political systems created during and after the

FIGURE 2.1. Štraus (center right) and Woods (in the red hat) in the destroyed Olympic Museum in 1993. (Lebbeus Woods official blog: https://lebbeuswoods.wordpress.com/2008/02/06/the-reality-of-theory/)

war, I relied on multiple sets of documents. In addition to interviews with Štraus, I examined materials researched and produced by architects in reaction to destructive transformative processes, including the above-mentioned diary and reports on the urban and architectural destruction published in *Warchitecture* magazine in 1993, as well as interviews, archival photos, sketches, and drawings.[11] Introducing cross-media analyses of the architects' practices and productions during the war expands the domain of architectural analytical tools into the design method itself. The investigation highlights the ways in which "architecture is no longer understood as a practice that inevitably brings about the construction of an artifact, but as a way of thinking, observing and analyzing the present and the society in which we operate; of identifying and asking questions while marking a new territory on which to act; of looking for or inventing suitable tools; and finally, of responding generously and concisely."[12]

In this reading, the production of war architecture becomes part of the wider domain of actions that lead to forced and unpredictable spatial transformations, which are often dangerous, may introduce substandard building methods, and are influenced primarily by military operations and citizens' survival practices. Citizens aiming to protect and normalize their lives will change their living spaces by transforming accessible materials around them: rubble, destroyed cars, furniture, and other objects. Architects might be familiar with the subject of war destruction either through personal experiences or popular media coverage. However, in very rare cases they are trained to work and operate in war-destroyed cities. Whether they are working in war zones or in postwar cities, their work is mainly focused on providing humanitarian aid facilities and aiding postwar reconstruction without any critical attachment to context and without knowing the architectural production prior to the war destruction. Camillo Boano, architect, urbanist, and educator, confirms the above statement from his own experience, in his interview with Isabelle Doucet for the journal *Candide, in which he* reflects on his working experience in several cities in Bosnia and Herzegovina: "In the early 1990s, I started working in a conventional conflict area in the Balkans, including Sarajevo and Mostar where conflict was of macro dimension. I was working for the UN, NGOs and what is now called the humanitarian system, where the intervention, whether in water and sanitation, housing, or refugee assistance was completely devoid of any critical thought."[13] Wars are human-made disasters that affect emergent spatial conditions.

However, addressing urban destruction does not form an integral part of the disciplinary discourse in architecture. The military siege of Sarajevo is now a historical event that marks the beginning of the twenty-first century for its citizens. In architectural discourse it is the moment when urban war became public on a planetary scale, spatially and virtually, through migration of Yugoslavian citizens to Western Europe and Americas, displacement and destruction both brought to the fore through the Internet and media technologies.

Architect of the Future Present: Ivan Štraus

A Yugoslavian and Bosnian architect of Slovenian and Montenegrin origin, Ivan Štraus designed and built some of the most important architectural symbols of Sarajevo, the city where he worked and lived until the last days of his life.[14] Among the many buildings he built there are schools, hotels, residential and cultural buildings, and churches. He also participated in many international competitions in collaboration with other renowned architects, such as Zdravko Kovačević and Halid Muhasilović. Štraus developed various projects in other Yugoslavian cities and in the African states of the Non-Aligned Movement. His most significant buildings are the General Post Office and the Ministry of Transport and Telecommunications buildings in Addis Ababa (fig. 2.2), codesigned with Kovačević in 1969. He also built the Unis Towers in 1986, which quickly and strikingly were renamed *Momo and Uzeir* by Sarajevo citizens—once a symbol of Yugoslav "brotherhood and unity" and now a sign of Sarajevo's forced multiculturalism.[15] Other famous buildings he designed include the Hotel Holiday (1983), also in Sarajevo, and the Museum of Aviation (1989) in Belgrade.

However, his most significant project is the *Elektroprivreda* Building (fig. 2.3), for which Štraus made his first design proposal in 1972. The building was, and today still is, the headquarters of the company of the same name that oversees power distribution in Bosnia and Herzegovina. In the 1990s the building became a source of inspiration for Lebbeus Woods as well as a focus of his own experiments on the theme of radical reconstruction (fig. 2.4).[16]

An architecture critic and theorist from Sarajevo, Nedžad Kurto describes the work of Ivan Štraus as the result of an independent, contemporary design process in which the architect developed a new exercise

FIGURE 2.2. General Post Office and the Ministry of Transport and Telecommunications in Addis Ababa, codesigned by Štraus and Zdravko Kovačević in 1969. (Photograph by Brook Teklehaimanot Haileselassie, 2010)

FIGURE 2.3. *Elektroprivreda* Building after the postwar reconstruction. (Photograph by Zoran Kanlić, 2014)

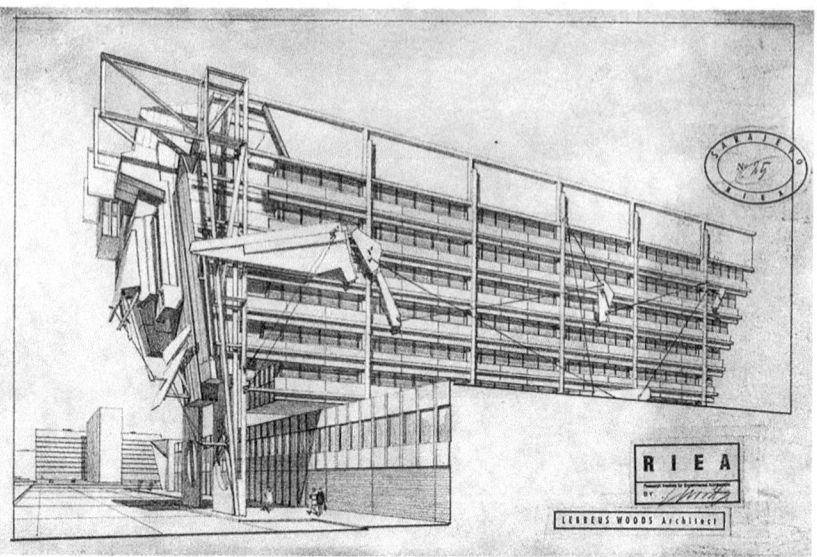

FIGURE 2.4. Proposals for *Elektroprivreda* Building reconstruction by Lebbeus Woods. (From https://dprbcn.wordpress.com/2009/11/23/electroprivreda-reconstruction-and-freespace-designed-by-lebbeus-woods/)

of architectural production for every new building design, without any side influences, while also referencing existing architectural forms and the context in which the buildings were situated in the city.[17] In fact, some of Štraus's works, like the 1983 Olympic Press Center in Bjelašnica, were destroyed during the war in Bosnia and Herzegovina and never rebuilt. During our conversations, Štraus told me that since his design practice started in 1952, he had been interested, for example, in using vivid colors on the façades of his buildings—the most important example of this attention to color would be the yellow façade of the Hotel Holiday Inn in Sarajevo. During our first interview in November 2014, he mentioned that despite his wish for design expression with vivid colors, for the prewar façade of the *Elektroprivreda* he had to use military colors: light and dark brown or dark green. The reason? During that period architects could only import construction materials (for example, aluminum for the façade of the *Elektroprivreda*) through the state military company UNIS. The imported materials were limited to the colors list for camouflage that the Yugoslavian military agencies used for their purposes. Another example of Štraus's interest in design processes is found in his dedication to interiors, which emerged when I talked to him during our visit to the *Elektro-*

privreda Building (fig. 2.5).[18] Before the war, buildings designed by Štraus—such as public buildings, halls, amphitheaters, and meeting rooms—had hosted the artworks of many of Sarajevo's artists, such as Jagoda Bulić, Ismet Mujezinović, and Miroslav Šutej. Now, due to war destruction, various works have been destroyed while others await restoration, some of which are inside the depository of the *Elektroprivreda* Building.

Along with an extensive design practice, Štraus also wrote books and articles for architectural magazines and journals. In 1963 he was one of the founders of *ARH* magazine, the last issue of which focused on war destruction in Sarajevo. *Warchitecture* was printed in 1993, thirty years after the magazine's founding.[19] The issue is extremely relevant to this study because it shows the adaptive role of the architects during the war in Sarajevo and documents processes of city destruction. Andrew Herscher, an architect and associate professor of architecture at the University of Michigan, argues that there is great value in the engagement of architects during war, from both a human and a professional point of view. In the introduction to the text *Wararchitectural Theory,* he writes: "The term 'warchitecture' emerged in Sarajevo as a name for the catastrophic destruction of architecture during the 1992–1996 siege of the city. Blurring

FIGURE 2.5. Portrait of Ivan Štraus in front of *Elektroprivreda* Building façade after the postwar reconstruction. (Photograph by Zoran Kanlić, 2014)

the conceptual border between 'war' and 'architecture,' the term provides a tool to critique dominant accounts of wartime architectural destruction and to bring the interpretive protocols of architecture to bear upon that destruction. Reflection on 'warchitecture' can therefore open up new ways to examine and understand violence against architecture and to connect this violence with emergent discussions of war, violence, and modernity in and across other disciplines."[20]

During the war Sarajevo and its surrounding quarters suffered extensive damage under military operations, including shelling and sniper fire from Mount Trebević and the surrounding hills, which transformed urban and intimate spaces such as the neighborhoods of Grbavica and Dobrinja into "loc[i] of disruption."[21] A short time before the war started in Yugoslav territory on June 7, 1991, Ivan Štraus published the book *Architecture of Yugoslavia from 1945 until 1990*.[22] In issue 23 of *ARH* (1992), Štraus gave an interview to Selma Arnautović that he included in the published version of his diary, *Architects and Barbarians*.[23] Her first question was related to *Architecture in Yugoslavia*, which she described as marking the close of the modernist Yugoslavian architectural cycle. She stated that its end was the beginning of a new war and asked Štraus how he saw the future in the context of such an enclosing past.[24] Štraus replied:

> I am tied in a nostalgic way to this past construction period that was forty-five years long, so my view of the future of architecture is burdened with that nostalgic atmosphere. My feeling should not surprise anyone. The buildings will be constructed again, but many fewer, since the state or little states will be exhausted. Just to have a roof overhead will be the priority, as it was after WWII; there will be no place for real architecture. Only here and there, when the ruling regimes decide to build monuments to themselves, as in the times of so-called single-mindedness. At the same time, Europe will far surpass us—even now we are behind—and not only in the field of architecture. [. . .] While Europe is working on advanced technical development to take the lead in innovation in the world, we are dealing with distributing the colors on the new flags, with designs for future emblems and costume jewelry. We will be busy with folksongs that people will sing while standing with their right hands over their hearts. A terrible primitive and pure perspective for all, even for the architecture in this region.[25]

In this quote and in other parts of *Architects and Barbarians*, Štraus made an effort to trace and explain—first to himself and then to future readers—the importance of the role of the architect and of taking a firm position in times of political crisis, as during war destruction.

Changing the Role of the Architect: Writing the Diary

After the war began and following the destruction of the cities of Vukovar and Dubrovnik in Croatia, Štraus's diary took a different form. He began to explore two "parallel themes" that described the opposite processes of construction and destruction of cities. Štraus wrote: "My way of constructing, my wish to build, was with the aim to serve humans and their needs in life; war destruction is the exact opposite way of thinking and doing—to deprive humans of their habitat, as well as of the spaces they live and work, and even during the war in Bosnia people were killed in their homes."[26] The diary is divided in two main thematic sections. The first part is autobiographic and focuses on Štraus's career as an architect, his awards for design competitions, and his built projects. Štraus described how interstate political disputes began to influence every domain of the architectural discipline, such as design competitions, publishing, architects' meetings, and national awards nominations.[27] The diary also includes correspondence among Yugoslavian architects, who shared concerns related to urban destruction and put forward the idea that the architectural field and its actors should continue a united and independent conversation. The second part of the diary, based on first impressions of the war in Yugoslavia gathered from colleagues, newspapers, radio, and TV news, describes the transition of Bosnia and Herzegovina from peace to war in 1991–92.

Day after day, Štraus recorded the changes in the city caused by the movements of military vehicles, equipment, and soldiers: he wrote of the first barricades and checkpoints on the streets; of the destruction of buildings; of the new organizations of citizens in the city; and of the life of his own buildings. According to the diary, in May 1992, when the Serbian Army began bombing Sarajevo, the city underwent a violent transformation of its architectural materiality and urban image. On June 8, 1992, at three a.m., Štraus went to his balcony and saw one of the Unis Towers he had designed on fire.[28] On June 10, 1992, he wrote that since his apartment was still intact, and thanks to its position in a neighborhood of low hills, he could see from his living room and terrace huge areas of the city under bombardment.²⁹ Soon after, Štraus, his family, and neighbors moved to an underground shelter where he continued to write his diary. Radio broadcasts became his source to learn which public buildings had been destroyed each day.

The situation was also very difficult in the countryside; many people were killed or expelled from their cities. Instead of focusing on these topics, Štraus decided to write about architecture, his field of expertise, and he kept working incessantly on his diary. Today, this document offers analysis and proof of how military strategies against Sarajevo city and its inhabitants were aimed to destroy public life and the urban resources necessary for everyday life, such as water, gas, and electric power supplies. Instead of documenting, for example, his career as a successful Yugoslavian architect, Štraus's diary recorded everyday devastation, detailing how and when the buildings in Sarajevo were destroyed. He also unintentionally introduced the term "systematic destruction of the city," which describes an organized and planned destruction of public buildings and the public works infrastructure necessary for the everyday needs and survival of local citizens.³⁰ Among these were post offices and phone communication systems, power distribution buildings such as *Elektroprivreda* (fig. 2.6), water supplies, and hospital facilities.

The 1993 special issue of *Warchitecture* also includes a complementary text and map entitled "Project: Map of Sarajevo City Destruction," created by Sabahudin Špilja and Borislav Ćurić.³¹ In the text the authors observe that "architecture, whatever it may be (good or bad, expensive or cheap, representative or not) is a material medium that most directly (with exception of human victims) and most convincingly reflects terrible war destruction consequences."³² In urban war conditions architects are forced to change their traditional role and become new actors responding with different tools. Architects and designers have to redraw, extract, build, and develop other tools for the redevelopment of ruins and city streets. They have to juxtapose reality and imagination even as they witness the processes of unmaking architecture and the city, learning from the everydayness and the transitional spaces made by the violent military destruction, and observing the inhabitants' nonviolent spatial reactions. One can view Štraus's work as a product developed by both a civilian and a professional: he produced fast observations from a distance, redrawing and recoding modernist housing plans, extracting forms

FIGURE 2.6. Façade of the destroyed *Elektroprivreda* Building. (Photograph by Zoran Kanlić, ca. 1992–96)

and meanings, and selecting relevant cases of the destruction of public buildings; he also listened to the radio and the sounds of destruction and translated them into writings on architecture. As this example illustrates, under such conditions and while living in fear, architects' observations create transitional images of architectural forms. An architect's observation of a building may show it having different forms at the distance of only some hours: for example, if it is under constant bombardment. In these architects' works the traditional building form is missing, and geometry is replaced with asymmetry, imprecision, and irregular forms.

Building Again in Postwar Sarajevo

The prewar generation of architects within Yugoslavian territory had a certain autonomy in designing during the socialist political system. Before the dissolution of socialist Yugoslavia in 1991, architecture and its design methods were defined as something that served society and the state. Architects also gained authority and autonomy under the single-party political system, but at the same time they had to respect urban planning and building regulations in the city in which they operated.

Both urban planning and architectural design practices worked under the procedures of state, regional, and city legislation, and projects were organized through public, state-owned architecture bureaus of differing sizes and expertise. The apparatuses were generally located in the major Yugoslav cities of Skopje, Zagreb, Belgrade, Sarajevo, Ljubljana, and Podgorica as well as in smaller urban centers. What is interesting is how easily recognized are buildings developed by different Yugoslav architects according to their form and adopted aesthetics. For example, even today, those observing the Sarajevo urban landscape can clearly recognize which buildings were built by Juraj Neidhart and which by Ivan Štraus. During our interview Štraus argued that the architect should be concerned with "the present of the city" rather than trying to imagine how it should look in the future. City reconstruction includes several parallel, socio-spatial processes as well as individual and collective experiences of its architecture. Construction from prewar periods, destruction caused by the war, and reconstruction organized after the war are processes related to the collective imagination of the formation and disappearance of the city.

Following the end of the war in 1996, the reconstruction of public buildings in Sarajevo was slow. Even as we enter the third decade of the twenty-first century, many public buildings are still under reconstruction (for example, the Olympic Museum). On the other hand, new constructions by private investors have advanced on an everyday basis. According to local newspapers, the construction boom in Sarajevo happened in 2008–9.[33] In 2008, in his statement for the magazine *Slobodna Bosna/ Free Bosna,* Said Jamaković, director of the Planning Institute for Development of the Canton of Sarajevo, predicted that the construction market in Sarajevo would grow until 2011, when residential and commercial buildings on offer would exceed local demands.[34] Jamaković's statement confirms that the Planning Institute followed private investors' interests and the commercial real estate market even when they knew that the city did not need all these new square meters. As of this writing, the government of Bosnia and Herzegovina and the local government in Sarajevo have not built any new buildings of public interest and ownership.

On the other hand, today Sarajevo looks and is publicly represented as a renewed city. However, some of the architectural and urban elements both destroyed and created by the war are still present in the central and peripheral areas of the city. They include half-destroyed buildings such as the former Maršal Tito barracks, the Olympic Museum, the school in the neighborhood Ali Pašino, the observatory building, and the bobsled on Mount Trebević; earthworks created during the war still stand near the houses above Vraca neighborhood and many others.

Postwar Sarajevo has been overbuilt intentionally and to generate profit for the private building sector, outside of any urban planning process or general plan containing redevelopment guidelines that would determine new urban development zones. Each municipality of Sarajevo is allowed to decide where and what to build on its territory, relying on regulatory plans. Therefore, in Sarajevo today architecture and urban development are measured in millions of square meters built by private local and international investors, who apparently, as a result of their economic power, are allowed to be architects and urbanists. Several articles that describe the postwar construction boom in Sarajevo omit the architects' names and opinions and instead highlight politicians' statements, investors' names, building locations, square meters, and monetary investments. This phenomenon actually reflects the ambiguous position that the postwar generation of architects occupies today in Bosnia and in the post-Yugoslavian territory. These designers exercise their architectural knowledge and creativity in very fast, real-time design processes that are computer based, often working in anonymity and guided by the private real estate development rather than accurate urban analysis. Many projects relying on these working methods have been realized in the urban space: for example, the Tibra neighborhood in Sarajevo is the site of a high-rise dwelling complex where the buildings lack adequate infrastructure and are built so close together that they do not admit enough daily light in the apartments.

With the above described tendencies of postwar urban (re)development in mind, I wanted to center my conversations with Štraus around his way of understanding and technically practicing (re)constructing, even when it meant rebuilding the same architectural project.

Un-Doing Architecture and Collaborative Design Failure: Cutting and Reconstructing

As a consequence of the systematic destruction of 1992–96, two public buildings with significant material damage designed by Štraus were rebuilt. The first building was *Elektroprivreda*, which he reconstructed with nearly the same team of people who had participated in the design phase and the construction team in the late 1970s. The second project was the Unis Towers, entirely burned during the war, whose reconstruction started in 2000. In this case, however, Štraus was excluded from the renewal project for political reasons.

Redesign, reconstruction, and renovation of *Elektroprivreda* happened in parallel with Štraus and Woods's exchange of several letters and drawings on the same building and can be listed as a failed attempt of a collaborative postwar redesign practice. From my preliminary investigation on the case and from my conversation with Štraus, interesting intersections and juxtapositions of two different approaches emerge. Their considerations regarding the reconstruction of the destroyed building differed to the point that they promoted divergent approaches. In the case of Woods, this was a radically new proposal, while in the case of Štraus, he recommended building again in the same architectural form. Besides the *Elektroprivreda* Building, Woods proposed several other scenarios for postwar reconstruction in Sarajevo, focusing on public buildings and small urban areas and following the three principles described on his personal blog: "First Principle: Restore what has been lost to its pre-war condition; Second Principle: Demolish the damaged and destroyed buildings and build something entirely new; Third Principle: The post-war city must create the new from the damaged old."[35]

These principles are presented as well in the pamphlet *War and Architecture* and in his book *Radical Reconstructions*.[36] According to Štraus's statements, reconstruction of *Elektroprivreda* started with the additional destruction and removal of the ruined parts of the building up to the second floor (fig. 2.7). Only the prewar concrete structure was kept. Before the reconstruction Štraus and his team of engineers and technicians made new architectural and structural drawings for the building reconstruction.

On my request to discuss the process of building reconstruction, Štraus replied:

> It is very difficult to explain. Edhem Bičakčić [at that time the general director of *Elektroprivreda*], his collaborators, my team group, and I agreed to remove everything that was above the second floor due to the damaged structural stability of the building. We literally agreed to cut off ruined parts of the building and those architectural

FIGURE 2.7. Composition by the author of the photos showing the cleaning of the ruined parts of the *Elektroprivreda* Building. (Photograph by Zoran Kanlić, 2000)

elements that stood atop one another due to the destructions caused by rockets, special tank shells, and other destructive weapons. After the building was cleared of debris, and with the nondestroyed concrete construction of the first and the second floors still standing, we had to rebuild the demolished floors in raw concrete. In addition, and while we were building the concrete structure in accordance with investors, I had time to negotiate adding some sculptural elements on the façade of the new building. They had been originally designed in 1978 but never developed as part of the prewar project. The reconstruction process actually gave me the opportunity to build a fountain with falling water symbolically representing the water and turbines that produce electricity.[37]

Woods's visions for the reconstruction of the *Elektroprivreda* Building and his thoughts about war and architecture represent his methodology to work with local unfinished architectural designs and postwar reconstructions. During our conversation Štraus remembered his first meeting with Woods, during the war. Their exchange of ideas continued through correspondence after the meeting, exchanges that, according to Štraus, were accompanied by drawings integrating both the prewar project of *Elektroprivreda* and Woods's visions for radical reconstruction. As Štraus stated: "I even made a certain kind of intersection of our drawings. I partially transferred his drawing on my drawing. I sent it to him by mail and wrote: "Lebbeus, don't be surprised, this is not your drawing, this is my drawing, we could have built something of your proposal, but dimensions should be reduced, because we cannot overconstruct it."[38] According to Štraus, Woods's work was the gesture of an architect who wanted to "do us a favor." Štraus was probably referring to Woods's engagement to contribute to repairing the damage to the city after the war. In Štraus's view, Woods wanted to try to build something different. Even if Štraus had been interested as an architect in other approaches and possibilities for city reconstruction, he stated: "I would have not been happy if the board had accepted Woods's proposal."[39] Over time, their initial idea to collaborate on the *Elektroprivreda* reconstruction process had changed, probably related to the aesthetics and the final image of the building that would follow after the intersection of their drawings.

Eventually, *Elektroprivreda* was rebuilt following Štraus's postwar design, which technically integrated some parts of the prewar building not visible in the façade, as was the case with Woods's proposal for the reconstruction. Štraus also mentioned that Lebbeus did not come to Sarajevo after the war to show his idea to the company's board of directors. He stated: "I tried to show it to the people in the top positions in the *Elektroprivreda* firm. I think I didn't have enough words to present someone else's project. Maybe it would have been more successful if Lebbeus was present at the meeting to explain his vision to them. At the same time, I think that it was not necessary, and the result would have been the same. They would have just removed his drawings."[40]

Both Štraus and Woods believed that once destroyed, the prewar building could not be rebuilt in the same way and using the same principles. In our conversations, Štraus explained: "During the reconstruction we cannot build the same buildings. We can correct some things, and some parts of the building can be constructed better than they were at first."[41] Woods and Štraus do not diverge in their thinking on this, and their approaches could partially intersect in Woods's third principle: "The post-war city must create the new from the damaged old. Many of the buildings in the war-damaged city are relatively salvageable, and because the finances of individuals and remaining institutions have been depleted by war and its privations, that salvageable building stock must be used to build the 'new' city. And because the new ways of living will not be the same as the old, the reconstruction of old buildings must enable new ways and ideas of living. The familiar old must be transformed, by conscious intention and design, into the unfamiliar new."[42] Yet despite a similar theoretical stance toward postwar reconstruction, their design concepts for the postwar *Elektroprivreda* could not be more different aesthetically and in architectural form, as we can observe in figures 2.3 and 2.4.

Štraus's comments on the postwar reconstruction of Sarajevo twenty years after the war are also worthy topics. Given this, did he believe the city in 2014–15 was what its citizens needed? Or could postconflict rebuilding have embraced a broader spatial experiment with regards to urban architectural forms and their aesthetics, perhaps following Woods's suggestions and Štraus's experimentations? Štraus gave many interviews and wrote articles about investigating possible postwar reconstructions of Sarajevo. These interviews were published in local and international newspapers such as *Sarajevo Notebooks* and Paris's *Liberacion*.[43] As an example, in 1996, immediately after the war, he published an article entitled "Invitation for the European Experts" in the magazine *Business*.[44] He argued that reconstruction in Sarajevo was possible only if professional and immediate assistance was provided by notable figures, and that this could provide a unique basis for the discussion of contemporary architectural tendencies: "Three years after the total siege and destruction of Sarajevo, a motto is circulating more and more: 'Urgent reconstruction of the city!' However, in practice, behind the word 'urgent' often hide disorganization and improvisations as well as negligence. Considering my knowledge of architectural practice and the bad life experiences of others in similar situations, such as war, earthquakes, fires, and so on, I think that Sarajevo as a whole and its central urban area should be observed as two separate objects of reconstruction in the years to come."[45]

In my view, his idea for territorial separation in the reconstruction process is related to the fact that all important governmental and public buildings, such as theaters and hospitals, are located within the central urban area, while on the outskirts of the city are located collective and individual housing areas that might require different reconstruction approaches in relation to their inhabitants. Štraus ended this article with several recommendations for postwar reconstructions. He suggested that reconstruction begin with the prewar public governmental, commercial, and cultural buildings and services. These buildings were among the first destroyed in the war, with the aim of disrupting everyday "normal" life in the city. For the new constructions, he invited architects to look for exceptional architectural and construction creativity to realize new spatial and design values for the city.

Conclusion

My analysis of the role of the architect during and after the war, using the specific case of the reconstruction of Sarajevo's *Elektroprivreda* Building, reveals the material and political complexity present during and after war destruction. By comparing Camillo Boano's critique of the "way of doing" in contested cities with the experiences of an architect from Sarajevo and Lebbeus Woods's engagements with the subject and with that architect, we can see that war is an urban and architectural subject. Architects should be able to—and should feel the responsibility to—respond to war destruction with professional integrity as well as humanity. Ivan Štraus observed postwar reconstruction as an opportunity to correct architectural failures and urban design mistakes made before the war. He and many other Sarajevan architects argued to start the reconstruction with public buildings such as hospitals, schools, and governmental facilities in order to restore public functions to postwar Sarajevo. This was only partly accomplished, since architectural postwar reconstructions, new constructions, and urban development have been driven by corrupt and contested governmental systems, real estate markets, and private interests. Numerous state-owned properties were sold out to private owners or to other states.[46] With this act, the Bosnian government promised in vain to invest in public buildings such as university campuses, for example.

If we read carefully and collectively into the image of contemporary Sarajevo, we might notice the architectural intersections of different political systems, governing practices, and spatial conditions belonging to the Bosnian territory of the last thirty years. Designers such as Štraus and Woods recognized that it is utopian to think that prewar urban development and architecture can be rebuilt exactly as they were before the conflict. This is true not only because of the political reasons described above but also because of environmental issues related to the building sector as well as technological changes in construction principles and practices across the industry. Finally, and looking back at the life and working experience of Štraus and Woods and Boano's reflections, it is important to recognize that architecture should be thought of and practiced transformatively, using both critical thinking and the material production (of space) while reinventing the roles as well as the tools of the architect.

Notes

1. Here I am referring to my own education in architecture in Sarajevo from 2000–2006, during which the achievements of Yugoslavian architects and urbanists were not taught; in some cases their names were just shortly mentioned as designers of certain buildings. We did not study modernist projects of any kind, the organization of architectural practice, or schools of architectures during Yugoslavian times.
2. I conducted two interviews with Ivan Štraus in his home for my research on the role of the architect during the war in Bosnia and Herzegovina. I visited him first on November 23, 2014, and we had long conversation about his path in becoming an architect. Following the first visit, we met two more times: once on December 15, 2014, to continue our interview on the war and postwar experience in Sarajevo; and again when we visited *Elektroprivreda* Building together on December 18 of the same year. That day we also filmed Štraus with filmmaker Guillermo Gutiérrez and took photos of him with photographer Zoran Kanlić while he was explaining the prewar design and postwar reconstruction of the *Elektroprivreda*.
3. Ivan Štraus in conversation with the author during the first meeting in his home on November 23, 2014.
4. The exhibition was organized by the Zagreb Museum for Arts and Crafts in April 1991, on the invitation of the Croatian Association of Architects and its president at the time, Andrija Rusan.
5. Lebbeus Woods, *War and Architecture* (New York: Princeton Architecture Press, 1993).
6. "Elektroprivreda" stands for "electric power industry." The office building housed the control facilities for electric power distribution.

7. Ivan Štraus, *Arhitekti i Barbari/Architects and Barbarians* (Sarajevo: Međunarodni centar za mir/International Center for Peace, 1995).
8. On September 1, 1991, Ivan Štraus started a diary as the symbolic beginning of his retirement. As he writes in the diary's introduction, the purpose of the informal writing was to remember and to describe his forty years of work as public architect in the design bureau *Arhitekt*.
9. Lebbeus Woods's official blog, accessed July 2019, https://lebbeuswoods.wordpress.com/2008/02/06/the-reality-of-theory.
10. During our first interview on November 23, 2014, Ivan Štraus verbally explained to me the drawings' intersection process. He did not have any prints with him. Instead, he told me that they could be found in the *Elektroprivreda* archive. I tried to find these drawings in their offices in November 2014 but was unsuccessful.
11. *Warchitecture,* special edition of *ARH* magazine, focusing on war destruction in the city. Published by the Association of Architects Sarajevo, October 1993.
12. Giovanna Borasi, ed., *The Other Architect: Another Way of Building Architecture* (Leipzig: CCA, Spektor Books, 2015), quotation from the introduction.
13. Camillo Boano, "Disruptive Design: On Design Gestures, Breathing and Non-Doing," guest editor Isabelle Doucet in conversation with Camillo Boano in London, May 2016, *Candide* 10 + 11 (December 2016), 114–15.
14. Ivan Štraus completed his studies in Sarajevo under the mentorship of Muhamed Kadić, one of the exponents of the Prague Architecture School. He died at the age of ninety in Sarajevo on August 25, 2018. Many journals and TV programs announced his death, reminding us of his very productive life as architect.
15. Within the Yugoslavian context and prior to war, Bosnia and Herzegovina was a territorial artifact of the different ethnic and religious groups of Yugoslavia, who lived in near proximity in Bosnian cities and villages. This is represented in many cities within urban spaces, as is the case of Sarajevo, where mosques, churches, and synagogues are located in the same part of the city and in walking distance of each other. During the Socialist Republic of Yugoslavia, this coexistence was known as "brotherhood and unity" without specific focus on religion. After the war in Bosnia and Herzegovina, however, the narrative has been changed by both local and international mainstream politics into generic "multiculturalism," which, in my opinion, is used as a tool for postwar propaganda to promote tourism or to build a narrative for postwar ethnic reconciliation, avoiding the war trauma experienced by all humans involved in the Yugoslavian conflict.

16. Lebbeus Woods, *Radical Reconstruction* (New York: Princeton Architectural Press, 1997).
17. I assume that Nedžad Kurto in his analysis is referring to side influences from architects who lived in other Yugoslavian cities and states who were designing during the same period as Štraus. The statement was republished in Štraus's diary, *Architects and Barbarians*, 5.
18. As mentioned above, we visited the *Elektroprivreda* Building together on December 18, 2014.
19. *Warchitecture*, special edition of *ARH* magazine, 1993.
20. Andrew Herscher, "Wararchitectural Theory," *Journal of Architectural Education* 61.3 (January 2008): 35–43.
21. Boano, "Disruptive Design," 114
22. Ivan Štraus, *Arhitektura Jugoslavije 1945–1990* (Sarajevo: Svjetlost, 1991).
23. The interview is in Bosnian (my translation). It was republished in Štraus's diary, *Architects and Barbarians*, where I read it. He decided to include it in the published diary because he found it had a certain resonance with his interview with Selma Arnautović and the political, conflictual, and architectural events during 1991–92.
24. Štraus, *Architects and Barbarians*, 63.
25. Štraus, *Architects and Barbarians*, 63.
26. Štraus, *Architects and Barbarians*, 5.
27. He dedicated a few pages to the award "Borba" for best architectural achievements in Yugoslavian territory, which changed its name and territorial coverage due to the processes of war in Croatia and the dissolution of the country. Until December 1991 it was issued for twenty-six years by the Yugoslavian association of architects for the best Yugoslavian architecture. In 1972 Štraus himself received the "Borba" award for the most successful achievement in Bosnia and Herzegovina for the neighborhood "Sun" in Sarajevo.
28. Štraus, *Architects and Barbarians*, 98.
29. Štraus, *Architects and Barbarians*, 98.
30. Štraus, *Architects and Barbarians*, 104.
31. Sabahudin Špilja, Borislav Ćurić, "Project: Map of Sarajevo City Destruction," *Warchitecture*, special edition of *ARH* magazine, 1993, 81–83.
32. Špilj and Ćurić, "Project: Map of Sarajevo City Destruction," 82.
33. The magazine *Start* in 2008 published an article entitled "Sarajevo Goes in the Sky," while *Slobodna Bosna/Free Bosnia* in 2008 published very similar article entitled "Sarajevo Is Growing in the Sky." In 2009 around 1.4 million new square meters were built. This number surpassed even the construc-

tion operations of Socialist Yugoslavia, when the neighborhood Ali Pašino was built in the years 1974–79, with a residential area of five hundred thousand square meters.
34. Said Jamaković, "Sarajevo Is Growing in the Sky," *Slobodna Bosna/Free Bosnia* (August 2008): 29.
35. For detailed reading, visit Lebbeus Woods's official blog, accessed July 2019, https://lebbeuswoods.wordpress.com/2011/12/15/war-and-architecture-three-principles/.
36. Woods, *War and Architecture*; and Woods, *Radical Reconstruction*.
37. Ivan Štraus, in discussion with the author in his home in December 2014. This was our second interview during which we discussed in detail the *Elektroprivreda* reconstruction related to the architectural project and rebuilding process.
38. Štraus, interview with the author, December 15, 2014.
39. Štraus, interview with the author, December 15, 2014.
40. Štraus, interview with the author, December 15, 2014.
41. Štraus, interview with the author, December 15, 2014.
42. To read more on Woods's three principles, visit his official blog, accessed June 15, 2021, https://lebbeuswoods.wordpress.com/2011/12/15/war-and-architecture-three-principles/.
43. Štraus, interview with the author, December 15, 2014.
44. Ivan Štraus, "Poziv stručnjacima Europe/Invitation to European Experts," *Business* (April 1996): 74.
45. Štraus, "Poziv stručnjacima Europe," 74.
46. This was the fate of several buildings on the university campus, which before the war was the military campus of the Yugoslavian National Army, located between the neighborhoods Marijin Dvor and Pofalići. The campus buildings were preplaced by the construction of the American Embassy.

3

NORMALIZING WAR

The Aesthetics of National Resilience

GABRIEL SCHWAKE

Civil defense infrastructure is a state-led development intended to protect and guard the civilian population during natural and human-made disasters. Like other national interventions in the built environment, it is inseparable from the actual sociopolitical narratives, and it is therefore often used to express and reinforce them.[1] In Israel architecture and urban development have long functioned as a political tool used to establish territorial control and merge fragmented groups of Jewish immigrants into a unified society.[2] On the other hand, since the 1970s the local economy has been undergoing an intense process of liberalization and privatization.[3] In this process, several key national projects were forwarded from the jurisdiction of the state to the profit-driven logic of the free market. Subsequently, the allocation of civil defense infrastructure turned into a privately developed national project, promoted and encouraged by the state yet funded mostly by private capital. This became evident in the early 1990s, which saw a significant increase in the need for civil defense infrastructure. The conclusions of the first Gulf War, the growing threat of missile and rocket attacks, and changes in the regional power balance brought larger portions of the Israeli civil population under the immediate threat of violent attacks.

The privatization of the local economy and the increasing threats of violence against civil society transformed the Israeli civil defense perspective. Instead of "providing" the civilian population with protection through public construction, the state began "enabling" it by relying on the private sector. The construction of civil defense infrastructure was promoted through its commodification, while its aestheticization was used as a means to normalize its presence. This chapter hence focuses on changes in the Israeli understanding of civil defense and how they were manifested in the built environment. It concentrates on the design competition conducted by the National Center of Israeli Resilience as a next step in the privatization of civil defense, which began with the creation of "protective spaces" in the 1990s. This case represents a final stage in the efforts to normalize the ever-lasting presence of war in civilian everyday life in Israel, intending to blur its violent and brutal aspects by turning them into an aesthetical spatial experience.

Aestheticizing Violence

Various regimes have tried to transform war and violence into an aesthetic experience as a political tool. The references that immediately come to mind are the totalitarian regimes of the twentieth century, such as fascist Italy, Nazi Germany, and Soviet Russia.[4] The urge of these regimes to aestheticize violence was of a Kantian nature, which identified the aesthetical with the moral and the sublime.[5] Thus, these ideologies transcended the state's monopoly on violence by portraying it as an aesthetic experience.[6] The fascist version of aestheticization was meant to define the nation as a sublime entity that one should fear and admire equally. It is through this dual mechanism that the individual would aspire to be part of a greater cause, which is the state.[7]

However, the aestheticization of politics and war is not always of a sublime or transcendent nature. While the fascist version of aestheticization is done for the sake of admiration, other versions focus on its more general appeal. Kant bases his theory and critique of aesthetic politics on the differentiation between the sublime and the good. While the first is an absolutely transcendent experience, the latter is more toned down but nevertheless pleasing. He mentions "flowers, free designs, lines aimlessly intertwined in each other" as objects that "signify nothing, do not depend on any determinate concept, and yet please."[8] Aestheticization could therefore be used as an instrument to beautify an object, turning one's perception of it into a pleasing experience. In this sense, aesthetics is also claimed by Paul de Man to be "a seductive notion that appeals to the pleasure principle . . . that can displace and conceal values of truth and falsehood."[9] In contemporary postmodern society, everyday life is conceived as an aesthetic experience meant to enhance the consumerist aspect of the culture.¹⁰ In a society focused on an aesthetic everyday life, the aestheticization of war and violence is therefore not done for the sake of evoking admiration but rather for the sake of normalizing them and merging them into civilian everyday life.

The aestheticization of war for the sake of normalization is a recurring theme in the Israeli built environment. The signs of perpetual war were, and still are, an integral part of Israelis' day-to-day existence. The first and most obvious example is the remains of Arab Palestinian houses and ruins that are evident all across the Israeli landscape and in all major cities. The initial and most common tactic of normalizing their existence was to transform such sites into recreational parks; later attempts would include converting former Palestinian houses into picturesque artists' quarters and villages.¹¹ Israeli planners and architects were thus concerned with hiding and disguising the traces of war through their aestheticization, although the presence of war was evident through the status of the Israel Defense Force (IDF) as a fundamental part of local culture. Alongside its combatant role, it played a crucial part in the formation of a local identity and even participated in the physical development of the state by establishing so-called frontier settlements.¹² Accordingly, for a long while the slogan of IDF's education corps was "the nation builds the army builds the nation," and the local public apparatus was significantly affected by the military mindset.¹³ Although the military facilities, fences, barriers, and guard posts were spread across the rural landscape, inside populated areas defense and security measures were reduced to a minimum. These were almost nonexistent in major cities and mostly consisted of checkpoints, guard posts, and security fences in peripheral areas.

However, since the early 2000s growing threats against the whole of Israel's civilian society have meant an increased presence of defense and security measures in the public everyday life, concurrent with a huge effort to normalize their existence through commodification and aestheticization.

Erasing Boundaries between the Home and the Front

The concept of civil defense is an integral part of the development of the modern nation-state. Historically, unarmed civilians have been, and still are, victims of ongoing wars and conflicts worldwide. Yet the modern nation-state is based on a dual obligation between the government and the people, where the former becomes responsible for the safety of the latter in return for the latter's obedience. By promising personal security to individuals, the modern state has been able to expand its control and to interfere with almost every aspect of the everyday life of its citizens.[14] In other words, unlike premodern states, which relied on despotic power, modern nation-states secure their citizens' allegiance and participation in the nation-building project under the pretext of "caring for the people."[15] Ensuring the safety and wellbeing of its citizens, whether from foreign military attacks or natural disasters, was not only a responsibility of the modern state but an integral part of its sovereignty.[16] Hence, the wartime division between "home" and "front" was fundamental.

The development of modern warfare increased the role of the modern state in securing the protection of its citizens. By the beginning of the twentieth century, new weapons included long-distance air bombardments, mortars, and missiles, which brought larger segments of the civilian population into the battlefield, turning them into passive participants while blurring the division between home and front. The intensification of conflicts in the last century meant that boosting national sentiment became an integral part of war.[17] This task was usually manifested in the work of propaganda ministries or in nationwide drills designed to prepare civilians for large-scale enemy attacks (fig. 3.1).[18] Furthermore, states also invested in preparing their people for natural disasters. Although in many cases this too fell under the responsibility of military defense forces, by the 1970s it had become an independent discipline that is usually labeled as civil "protection," in contrast to civil "defense."[19] Though the collapse of the Eastern Bloc countries in the early 1990s decreased the international atomic scare, new concerns were raised within a decade. The attacks on civilian targets on 9/11 and the West's responding "War on Terror" revived the issue of civil defense, as the preparation of society for violent attacks returned to public focus.[20] With the reemergence of security threats, national defense merged once again with civil protection: home became the front.

In Israel the notion of civil defense has transformed significantly from the state's inception to the present.[21] In 1951 the young Israeli government passed the Civil Defense Law, which ordered the formation of the Civil Defense Service (Hagana Ezrahit, or Haga), whose purpose was the regulation and maintenance of alert systems and public "neighborhood shelters."[22] These shelters were public facilities and thus were built on

FIGURE 3.1. Duck and cover drills, United States. (Stills from the short film *Duck and Cover*, 1952)

public land. They usually occupied open public spaces, where shelters were dug under playgrounds and community gardens. Consequently, the sloping roof of the entrance to the local underground shelter turned into a recognizable item in many neighborhoods and parks (fig. 3.2). The use of shelters was restricted to emergency situations only, while all other unrelated uses were officially prohibited. In the early 1970s, however, the Israeli government began compelling the construction of private shelters, which became a mandatory feature for all new buildings. The communal neighborhood shelters were therefore replaced by shelters shared by all apartments in a building or by shelters for single-family houses. These shelters were frequently located on the ground floor, near the entrance to the building, or behind the kitchen in case of private houses. With the ongoing conflict in the region, the use of these shelters was mainly limited to the northern border area, which was occasionally targeted by rockets and mortars fired from southern Lebanon. The shelters in other Israeli cities, however, remained relatively unused.

Beginning in the 1990s, the Israeli perspective on civilian protection infrastructure shifted. During the First Gulf War (1991–92) the entire Israeli population was targeted by the Iraqi Scud missile system. Due to

FIGURE 3.2. Children playing near an entrance to a shelter, Kibbutz Misgav,1970. Moshe Milner. (Governmental Press Office–Israel)

a deficit of—and a lack of maintenance of—communal shelters, as well as their maladaptation to unconventional warfare, the IDF ordered families to designate an area in their homes as a "sealed room" that could be used in case of missile attacks. Unlike previous wars, in which the military was engaged in open combat while citizens were spared from it, in the Gulf War, Israeli citizens bore the brunt of the military campaign. This made the Israeli administration aware of the increased risks of both conventional and unconventional weapons. In response, the understanding of civil defense transformed yet again, leading to the establishment of the IDF Home Front Command, which is currently in charge of civilian preparation, assistance, and protection during a conflict or crisis. The new measures imposed by the Home Front Command have radically reshaped the local built environment.

This change in civil defense policies led to the birth of the Merhav Mugan (protective space).[23] The protective space is an integrated, small-scale shelter that is designed to provide immediate protection for the users of a specific building, which became mandatory in all new projects during the mid-1990s. It is usually a room of 9 square meters that is built with 30–45 centimeter reinforced concrete walls, a special steel door, a window one meter square with a protective steel shield, and a ventilation system.[24] In order to enable and encourage the construction of these shelters, planning regulations do not calculate the areas of protective spaces in the overall allotted surface area for construction. Protective spaces thus constitute additional untaxed real estate that can be sold to future buyers.[25] Structural demands require protective spaces to be built one on top of the other with continuous walls reaching the building's foundations, so all new buildings come with so-called protective towers that are surrounded by continuous walls of reinforced concrete, with one-by-one-meter windows running top to bottom (fig. 3.3).

The early 2000s reinstated two main threats on Israeli civilian society. First came a concern with earthquakes, which significantly increased following fatal quakes in Turkey and Greece at the turn of the millennium. Israeli planning law did oblige all buildings constructed after 1980 to follow building codes for earthquake protection; however, all structures built prior to 1980 had minimal chances of enduring such an event. Official estimates calculated that a medium-scale earthquake would lead to severe destruction of the built environment.[26] Second was the concern of missile and rocket attacks, mainly from Gaza and Lebanon, which

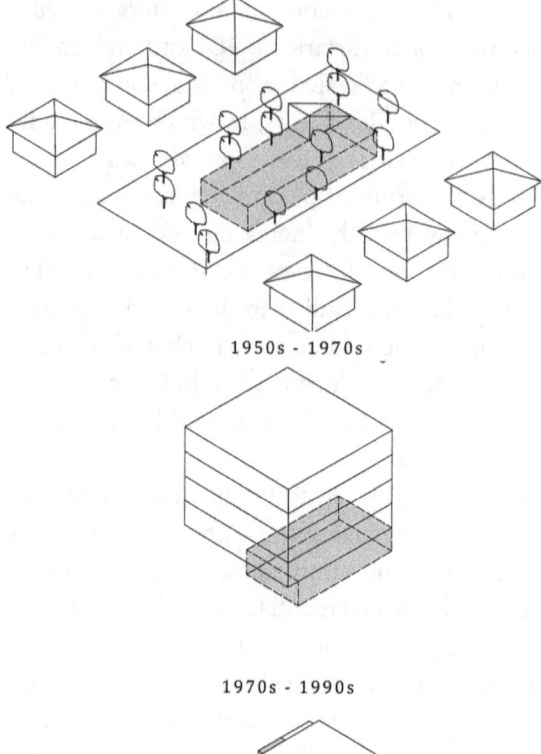

1950s - 1970s

1970s - 1990s

1990s - Present

FIGURE 3.3. The evolution from shelters to private protective spaces. (Author's drawing)

now threatened almost all of the Israeli population, putting them under the immediate and constant danger of bombardment. These concerns, together with growing national anxiety regarding the Iranian missile program and nuclear project, increased the overall demand for protective spaces and civil preparation.

To meet the challenges of natural and man-made disasters, the Israeli government promoted new actions. In 2007 it established the National Emergency Management Authority (NEMA, or *RACHEL* in Hebrew), a unit under the jurisdiction of the Ministry of Defense, whose task is to coordinate between the different relevant agencies in a time of crisis. At the same time, a new national outline plan, titled TMA 38, tried to jointly address the threat of both earthquakes and missile attacks.[27] In order to retrofit existing buildings that lacked protections for both scenarios, the state encouraged structural adjustments and the construction of protective spaces by expanding the existing building permits. The plan ratified the demolition of existing buildings and the construction of bigger and better-prepared ones, or allowed the expansion of existing dwelling units by adding external protective "towers" and the construction of two to three new upper floors.[28] In the latter case, the "towers" that primarily functioned as shelters from missile attacks would also serve as part of the anti-earthquake support, literally tying the threats of war with those of nature. Yet the successful realization of these projects rested on the economic interest of private entrepreneurs, as the state hoped to tie concerns for civil defense with the interests of investors, fueling the local real estate market.

The burgeoning construction of civil defense infrastructure was therefore enhanced by the constant presence of the threat of wars and natural disasters. The commodification of these measures enabled vast construction projects and eventually led to a situation where the fear of missiles, rockets, and earthquakes was omnipresent in the civilian everyday life. It was in the midst of this lasting anxiety that the idea for the National Center of Israeli Resilience was born. It was envisioned as a tool to prepare the civilian population to endure different disaster scenarios, enabling them to cope with the transformation of their homes into a battle front.

Design Competition for the National Center of Israeli Resilience

The notion of "resilience" concerns people's physical abilities and emotional strength to withstand natural and man-made disasters. Though seemingly part of the general "urban resilience" discourses, the name chosen for the National Israeli Center has also a very hawkish interpretation. The Hebrew name is *HaMirkaz LeEitanut Yisraelit*, and the word *"eitanut"* or *"eitan"* strongly connotes the word "power": other possible translations include terms like "might," "firmness," "strength," and "solidity." Being (nationally) resilient, in the Israeli interpretation, not only indicates the state's ability to sustain and survive disasters but also its heroic and defiant character. This dual interpretation of populist buzzwords and militant mindset promoted the idea for the National Center of Israeli Resilience.

The concept for the Center for Israeli Resilience came from a joint effort by the Home Front Command and the National Emergency Management Authority. The central idea concerned the formation of a training center that would prepare the civilian population for the different damaging scenarios of wars and natural disasters. The facility would have different simulators producing various emergency situations and a training school for emergency personnel, but it would also include a heritage center for the commemoration of war casualties and victims of national disasters. The training school was supposed to serve as a multidisciplinary compound for the instruction of civil servants in order to improve their operational effectiveness in various emergency settings. The execution of this initiative was forwarded to the Ministry of Defense's Department of Construction and Engineering, which together with the Israeli Association of United Architects (IAUA) promoted a design competition open to all licensed Israeli architects.[29] According to the "terms of building's design and content" stated in the competition brief, the main inspirations for the center came from similar establishments in countries like Japan and Turkey.[30] However, since those references are predominantly civilian—that is, not affiliated with military operations but more concerned with natural disasters—the Israeli Ministry of Defense sought to give this institution a more civilian-like appearance.

The civilian-like approach to the design of the Center of Israeli Resilience was part of a larger rearrangement and rebranding effort led by the Ministry of Defense. Although military and defense institutions have the central role in Israeli society, it cannot be said that military architecture in Israel is concerned with questions of performance and monumentality. Beside rare examples like Zvi Hecker's brutalist Officer Training School (*Bahad* 1), Israeli military architecture and the buildings of the Ministry of Defense are usually an outcome of technocracy-driven projects mainly focused on utilitarian and budget-minded issues. The main military bases, for example, are mostly situated in former British camps and Arab villages in what was known as Mandatory Palestine, reusing their outdated buildings and facilities while adapting them to changing needs through a series of improvisations and alterations. Newly built bases are mainly replicas of the same model, using identical layouts and prefabricated elements. This practice was somewhat changed when the military began vacating or optimizing some of its bases that were located in city centers.

In this reorganization process, which included the construction of alternative compounds or the readjustment of existing ones, a greater emphasis was placed on the architectural quality of the new buildings. In an interview with Haaretz newspaper from 2016, the chief architect of the Ministry of Defense claimed that the military's new inspiration was civilian architecture.[31] The objective was to turn the military environment into a quasi-civilian one while blurring the difference between combatant and civilian realms and incorporating the former into the latter. The term used was "*leazreah*," which translates as "to make civilian," but also "to naturalize someone" (i.e., turn him/her into a citizen of a certain country), or to acclimatize someone to a new environment. This aesthetic turn in the planning and construction of new military compounds is inspired by the architecture of high-tech offices and public institutions, masking the battleground environment with a more pleasant appearance.[32] The new military aesthetic was therefore conceived for the sake normalization rather than for the sake of admiration.

Launching an open design competition for the Center of Israeli Resilience was part of these normalization efforts. In most cases the Ministry of Defense chooses architects from its preapproved pool of planners. Or, in the case of a BOT (build, operate, transfer) project, where the ministry puts the entire project into the hands of a private developer, an architectural firm is chosen by the developer that is managing the construction of the site. By opening the project to a larger professional audience, the Ministry of Defense sought to broaden the project's societal impact and to involve architects whose design approaches are considered to be less militarily inclined. This was implicitly stated in the competition brief, which specified that "the Ministry of Defense is interested in contacting a large number of planners," all in order to come up with a building concept that would properly relate to both "civilian and military environments."[33] The proposed building was therefore imagined not only as a space for training and disaster preparation but also as possessing a "unique architectural design, which will reflect its designation," hoping that a unique design would appeal to a larger public.[34]

This attempt to produce a civil appearance in the new military-led center was evident in the formulation of the competition brief. In the evaluation guidelines used by the competition jury, the "planning" criteria (which included the "building's envelope," its "aesthetics and design," the "coherency of the architectural language," and a "hierarchy of the circulation and spatial division") comprised 40 percent of the total score (10 percent each).[35] Other criteria included the building's integration in the surrounding environment (10 percent), its usability and flexibility (20 percent), its sustainability (20 percent), and the economic feasibility of the plan (10 percent). The emphasis was therefore on the building's performance and user experience and not on economic and practical considerations. In all other military-funded projects (which are conducted as tenders and not competitions), the main criteria are always cost efficiency and maintainability, while the questions of design, aesthetics, and user experience are usually disregarded.[36] In addition, more than half of the twelve jurors were nonmilitary architects, enhancing civilian involvement once more. At the same time, evidently the competition brief was prepared according to the common formula of the Ministry of Defense, employing the jargon of the military operation order that uses terms such as "mission," "objective," and "means."

The location of choice for the new center was in the Home Front Command headquarters at Rehavam Base in the city of Ramleh. Although officially part of a military base—which is usually a gated and isolated compound, disconnected from the nearby civilian environment—the intention here was to create a clear and easy connection to the site. It was emphasized that the key elements of the design proposals should accentuate the center's accessibility to the nearby "urban" layout and the adjustment of the building to fit its surrounding. This meant presenting to the jury large plans, sections, and diagrams that would explain the building's integration into the surrounding (urban) landscape, as is done for any other "regular" public building.

The socially oriented approach was enhanced through collaborations with civilian institutions established prior to the competition. Cooperation with the IAUA, for example, enabled the Ministry of Defense to use the association's network and publication platform to significantly enlarge the competition's outreach. Other partnerships included the WIZO Academy of Design and Education in Haifa, which dedicated a group of its architecture students from the public buildings design studio to the cause.[37] The students, under the supervision of their tutors and architects from the Home Front Command, were given a specific design task that was similar to that of the competition. During the studio sessions the students were presented with the plans of the Home Front Command, they visited its headquarters, and they were addressed by several high-ranking military architects and engineers. In this collaboration the Ministry of Defense hoped to introduce various military activities to civilian society and to ignite an academic discussion around the spatial relations between military bases and their civilian surroundings. The military's PR campaign, validated through the collaboration with WIZO and IAUA, was thus part of a much larger normalization strategy designed to promote a more amicable image of the military among the people of Israel and to incorporate a military presence in everyday social life.

These PR efforts eventually produced a relatively high number of entries for a military-led competition, especially when compared to similar architectural competitions in Israel.[38] By the end of the deadline some thirty architectural firms and offices had submitted their proposals. The success of the competition is also indicated by the submissions made by Israeli-Arab architects, who usually refrain from collaborating with the IDF or are prohibited from doing so by the Ministry of Defense due to security clearance issues. Finally, most entries were submitted by small- and medium-size offices and almost none by the large-scale firms that are usually commissioned for this kind of job by the Ministry of Defense while refraining from participation in small, open, and unpaid competitions.

The evaluation of competition entries and the announcement of winning proposals were also designed to appeal to the broader civilian population. The competition jury consisted of twelve members: seven were civilian architects, while the remaining members were professional military engineers and architects and not high-ranking combat officers. The jury's deliberations were relatively short, and they mainly focused on issues of design and aesthetics, while only secondarily discussing the questions of feasibility, maintenance, and construction schedule. In the end, the jurors' choices were quite consistent, and the majority of them shortlisted the same entries.[39] Unlike the standard press release the ministry typically issues, the announcement of the winning proposals was done at the opening of the competition's exhibition, which was held at the gallery of the IAUA in Jaffa. Until then, the results had been kept confidential—only the finalists were mentioned in the press. The exhibition, which took place in August 2016, showcased all competition entries as well as selected student projects from the WIZO studio. The event was open to the public and endorsed by the IAUA and the Tel Aviv Municipality; as such it served the further promotion of the nonmilitant image of the project.

The top five entries provided the aesthetic experience the Ministry of Defense was seeking to promote. The proposal of Auerbach Halevy Architects, which received an honorary mention, sought to design the new center as a mediator between the military environment and the civilian one. The second honorary mention was given to Goshen Architects; their proposal revolved around an inner courtyard that was intended to symbolize life and hope as an abstraction to the concept of resilience. The third prize was given to the Eliav Architects, whose design focused on creating a reachable public building that would function during leisure hours. The proposal of Peri Davidovich Architects consisted of layers of networks that were meant to create the required brightness and transparency.[40] All of these finalist entries proposed well-designed architectural products that might have been mistaken for art museums or galleries (figs. 3.4–3.5). The performative aspect of these projects was clearly focused on creating a pleasing aesthetical and spatial experience. Proposals that did refer to the notions of power, security, strength, and stability were deliberately ignored by the jurors.[41]

The winning entry also matched the competition's demands for aesthetics and architectural coherency.[42] The proposal of Ran Blander Architects was a highly aesthetics-oriented submission with a strong emphasis

FIGURE 3.4. Proposal for the Center for Israeli Resilience by Eliav Architects. (Ministry of Defense, Israel)

FIGURE 3.5. Proposal for the Center for Israeli Resilience by Peri Davidovich Architects. (Ministry of Defense, Israel)

on architectural performance and user experience. Compared to other entries, the winning proposal was a bit toned down yet still a very effective public building, whose conception was also properly explained in the submission documents, plans, perspectives, and sketches.[43] The overall profile of the winning office also pleased the jurors. On the one hand, it was a medium-sized firm with relevant knowledge and expertise that would enable the completion of such a project, while on the other, it was a relatively young and popular design studio, which additionally validated the project from a civilian point of view.[44]

The inner arrangement of the various functions and the proposed hierarchy were also designed with the idea of a "broader public appeal" in mind. The proposal consisted of an inner "core" that included an information point, an area for interactive learning, an open courtyard, and a "remembrance and heritage wall." All other functions, which included the managerial offices, training school area, and instruction rooms, were situated around the glassed inner core and designed as sealed volumes, whose appearance can be described as a trendy version of protective spaces (fig. 3.6). The core is basically the leitmotif of the project, and in order to emphasize its value, the project team used elaborated schemes that explained the core's role in the building's circulation system, functions'

FIGURE 3.6. Rendering of the central area for the Center for Israeli Resilience by Ran Blander Architects, winner of the design competition. (Ministry of Defense, Israel)

distribution, interior-exterior connections, and even the project sustainability concept (fig. 3.7). Above all, the open and glassed core provided the aesthetic and user-oriented experience that the competition brief was looking for. The praises given to the winning entry in a special issue of the *Architecture of Israel Quarterly* magazine emphasize the proposal's success in creating a highly aesthetical architectural product. The article highlights the use of "light architectural language" and the "experiential course" of the building, which "exposes the visitors to founding heritage event . . . preparing them for the reality of real emergencies."[45] Through this innovative design, the architects managed to create a new image, even a new typology, for military/public buildings by merging the necessity of civil protection and defense with architectural aesthetics that operate on a more human level. At the same time, this design approach enables the normalization of war, leading to the preservation and assimilation of violence in the civilian everyday life by sugarcoating it with an aesthetic spatial experience.

As of 2021, it has become clear that the design of the wining proposal will remain on paper. The main obstacle was funding; while the Ministry of Defense was willing to allocate half of the needed funds, the other half depended on the goodwill of private donors willing to cover the remaining costs. In this sense, the privatization of civil defense infrastructure is impacting not only the construction of protective spaces but also

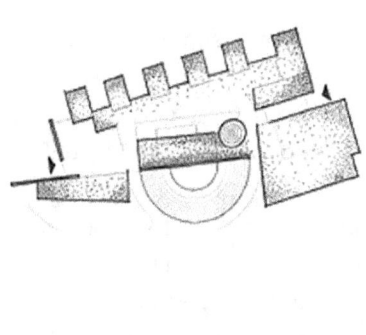

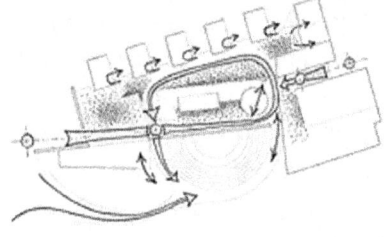

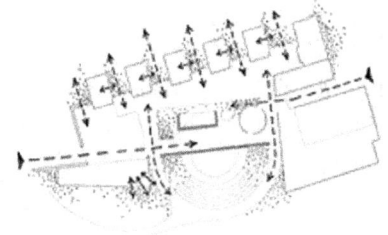

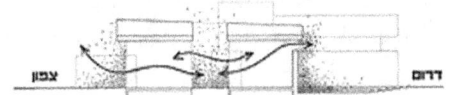

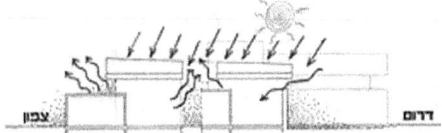

FIGURE 3.7. Explanatory schemes by Ran Blander Architects. (Ministry of Defense, Israel)

the development of training facilities. While the supply of civil defense relies on its commodification, the flagship project of the Home Front Command, whose purpose is to empower civilians and give them the needed tools to handle different disaster scenarios, eventually depended on the generosity of private donors.[46] However, though the center was not built according to the winning design, the competition itself did promote the overall naturalization of the military presence in Israeli society. Following the Center of Israeli Resilience competition, the Ministry of Defense organized two additional design competitions. First was the open competition for the Israeli Air Force Museum, and second was a closed competition for the campus of the military colleges in Jerusalem. Both focused on similar issues such as user experience and architectural quality as well as connection to and integration with the neighboring civil environment. Thus, by contributing to the normalization of military presence and war infrastructure through their aestheticization, the design competition for the National Center of Israeli Resilience achieved its main objective.

Conclusion

The proposed National Center of Israeli Resilience reflects several cultural and societal changes in Israel. First and most obvious is the privatization of the civil defense mechanisms, which was forwarded to the hands of entrepreneurs and the profit-driven market. Shifting from providing civil defense to enabling it, the new mechanism endorsed populistic terms like "national empowerment" and encouraged popular discourse about "resilience," "stability," and "adaptability." The notion of the National Center of Israeli Resilience is therefore a direct continuation of the protective spaces approach. But while protective spaces were conceived in order to fulfill much-needed civil defense measures, the Center of Israeli Resilience was intended to give those measures an aesthetic framework to incorporate the threat of violence into civilian everyday life. While the former commodified the presence of war, the latter was meant to normalize it. Simultaneously, the new civil defense approach was aligned with the growing hawkish perspective of Israeli society, which is focused more on managing the conflict instead of trying to resolve it. The normalization of the presence of war is therefore a sort of coping mechanism in Israeli society, which has accepted living under the constant threat of violence and is now seeking innovative architectural solutions to disguise this pessimistic condition.

During the 1948 war, Israeli prime minister Ben-Gurion coined the expression, "The whole country is a front line; the whole people are an army."[47] Seventy years later, with the changing relationships between the front and the home, Ben Gurion's quote is still relevant, especially in a grim reality in which almost every household has its own private shelter. However, while Ben Gurion's words were spoken with a sort of admiration for the assimilation between the civilian society and the military apparatus, the current efforts to aestheticize military infrastructure are an attempt to turn it into a pleasing and desirable object. The design-oriented discourse that accompanied the competition for the National Center of Israeli Resilience and the wide appeal to a large number of young architects indicates how alluring the aestheticization of war can be, normalizing the constant transformation of the home into a front.

Notes

1. Lawrence Vale, *Architecture, Power and National Identity* (London: Routledge, 2008); Henri Lefebvre, *The Production of Space*, trans. Donald Nicholson-Smith (New York: John Wiley and Sons, 1991).
2. Baruch Kimmerling, *Zionism and Territory: The Socio-Territorial Dimensions of Zionist Politics* (Berkeley: Institute of International Studies, University of California, 1983); Elisha Efrat, "Changes in Israel's Urban System after Forty Years of Statehood (1948–1988)," *Eretz-Israel: Archaeological, Historical, and Geographic Studies* (1991): 19–26; Rafi Segal, David Tartakover, and Eyal Weizman, *A Civilian Occupation: The Politics of Israeli Architecture* (London: Verso, 2002); Oren Yiftachel and Sandy Kedar, "Landed Power: The Making of the Israeli Land Regime," *Teoria U'Bikoret* 16 (2000): 67–100; Zvi Efrat, *The Israeli Project* (Tel Aviv: Tel Aviv Museum of Art, 2004); Baruch Kimmerling, *The End of Ashkenazi Hegemony* (Tel Aviv: Keter, 2001).
3. Yael Hason, *Three Decades of Privatisation* (Tel Aviv: Adva Center, 2006); Daniel Gutwein, "The Class Logic of the 'Long Revolution,'" *Iyunim Bitkumat Israel* 11 (2017): 21–57.
4. Susan Sontag, *Fascinating Fascism* (New York: Vintage Books, 1974).
5. Immanuel Kant, *Critique of the Powers of Judgment* (1790) (Cambridge, UK: Cambridge University Press, 2001); Hannah Arendt, *Lectures on Kant's Political Philosophy* (Chicago: University of Chicago Press, 1982); François

Debrix, "The Sublime Spectatorship of War," *Journal of International Studies* 34.3 (2006): 767–91.
6. Josef Chytry, *The Aesthetic State* (Berkeley: University of California Press, 1989).
7. Debrix, "Sublime Spectatorship of War."
8. Kant, *Critique of the Powers of Judgment*.
9. Paul De Man, *The Resistance to Theory* (Minneapolis: University of Minnesota Press, 1986), 64.
10. Mike Featherstone, *Consumer Culture and Postmodernism* (London: Sage, 1996).
11. Walid Khalidi, *All That Remains* (Washington, DC: Institute for Palestine Studies, 1992); Yosef Jabareen and Hakam Dbiat, *Architecture and Orientalism in the Country* (Haifa: Technical Institute of Israel, 2014); Gabriel Schwake, "Post-traumatic Urbanism," *Cities* 75 (2018): 50–58; Saree Makdisi, "The Architecture of Erasure," *Critical Inquiry* 36 (2010): 519–59.
12. Yair Douer, *Our Sickle Is Our Sword* (Tel Aviv: Yad Tevenkin, 1992).
13. Orna Sasson-Levy, "Where Will the Women Be? Gendered Implications of the Decline of Israel's Citizen Army," in *The New Citizen Armies: Israel's Armed Forces in Comparative Perspective*, ed. Stuart A. Cohen (New York: Routledge, 2010), 173–95; Baruch Kimmerling, "Militarism in Israeli Society," *Teoria U'Bikoret* 4 (1993): 123–40; Erez Tzfadia, "Militarism and Space in Israel," *Israeli Sociology* 11.2 (2010): 337–61.
14. Michael Mann, "The Autonomous Power of the State: Its Origins, Mechanisms and Results," *European Journal of Sociology* 25.2 (1984): 185–213; Michel Foucault, *Discipline and Punish: The Birth of the Prison*, trans. Alan Sheridan (New York: Vintage Books, 1995).
15. Michel Foucault, "Space, Knowledge, Power," in *Rethinking Architecture—A Reader in Cultural Theory*, ed. Neil Leach (London: Routledge, 1997), 367–80.
16. Robert M. MacIver, *The Modern State* (Oxford, UK: Oxford University Press, 1926).
17. James M. Landis, "Morale and Civilian Defense," *American Journal of Sociology* 47.3 (1941): 331–39.
18. Anthony Rizzo, dir., *Duck and Cover* (New York: Archer Productions, 1952).
19. David Alexander, "From Civil Defence to Civil Protection—and Back Again," *Disaster Prevention and Management* 11.3 (2002): 209–13; Kelly Charles, "Limitations to the Use of Military Resources for Foreign Disaster Assistance," *Disaster Prevention and Management* 5.1 (1996): 22–29.
20. Jon Coaffee et al., *The Everyday Resilience of the City* (Basingstoke, UK: Palgrave Macmillan, 2009); Armina Pilav, "Before the War, War, After the War," *International Journal of Disaster Risk Science* 3.1 (2012): 23–37.

21. Antonio Missiroli, "Disasters Past and Present," *Journal of European Integration* 28.5 (2006): 423–36; Lawrence Vale and Thomas J. Campanella, eds., *The Resilient City: How Modern Cities Recover from Disaster* (Oxford, UK: Oxford University Press, 2005); Coaffee, *Everyday Resilience of the City*; United Nations International Strategy for Disaster Reduction, *2009 UNISDR Terminology on Disaster Risk Reduction*, accessed June 8, 2021, https://www.unisdr.org/files/7817_UNISDRTerminologyEnglish.pdf.
22. Israeli Civil Defence, Home Front Command (IDF, HFC), *Shelter Maintenance Instructions* (Ramleh: IDF, 2006); Government of Israel, *1951 Civil Defense Act*, https://www.nevo.co.il/law_html/law01/125_001.htm.
23. Sheli Cohen and Tal Amit, "Public Shelters to Protective Space: The Privatisation of Civil Defence," in *Living Forms: Architecture and Society in Israel*, eds. Sheli Cohen and Tal Amit (Tel Aviv: Am Oved, 2007), 124–43.
24. IDF, HFC, *Shelter Maintenance Instructions*.
25. IDF, HFC, *Shelter Maintenance Instructions*.
26. State Comptroller of Israel, *Resistance of Buildings and Infrastructure in Earthquakes* (Jerusalem: Office of the State Comptroller, 2011).
27. Government of Israel, *National Outline Plan 38* (Jerusalem: State of Israel, 2012).
28. State Comptroller of Israel, *Resistance of Buildings and Infrastructure*.
29. Department of Construction and Engineering of Israel, *Open Architectural Competition* (Tel Aviv: Ministry of Defence, 2016).
30. Department of Construction and Engineering, *Open Architectural Competition*.
31. Naama Riba, "The Next Objective of the IDF: An Architectural Revolution," *Haaretz*, October 10, 2016, https://www.haaretz.co.il/gallery/architecture/.premium-1.3092731.
32. Riba, "Next Objective."
33. Department of Construction and Engineering, *Open Architectural Competition*, 2.
34. Department of Construction and Engineering, *Open Architectural Competition*, 2.
35. Department of Construction and Engineering, *Open Architectural Competition*, 7.
36. Senior IDF-Architect, *IDF Competitions*, anonymous interview, June 13, 2019, Tel Aviv, Israel.
37. WIZO is the acronym for Women's International Zionist Organization.
38. Midlevel IDF-Architect-II, Center for National Resilience, *anonymous interview*, July 18, 2019, Ramat Gan, Israel. (Both architects I spoke with regarding the competition wished to remain anonymous.)
39. Senior IDF-Architect, *IDF Competitions*, interview, June 13, 2019.

40. Rachel Ben-Aharon, "National Centre of Israeli Robustness," *AIQ* 106 (2016): 89–95.
41. Senior IDF-Architect, *IDF Competitions*, interview, June 13, 2019.
42. Senior IDF-Architect, *IDF Competitions*, interview, June 13, 2019
43. Senior IDF-Architect, *IDF Competitions*, interview, June 13, 2019; mid-level IDF-Architect-II, *Center National Resilience*, interview, July 18, 2019.
44. Senior IDF-Architect, *IDF Competitions*, interview, June 13, 2019; mid-level IDF-Architect-II, *Center National Resilience*, interview, July 18, 2019.
45. Ben-Aharon, "National Centre of Israeli Robustness," 94.
46. Department of Construction and Engineering, *Open Architectural Competition*, 2.
47. Moshe Naor, *Social Mobilization in the Arab/Israeli War of 1948* (New York: Routledge, 2013), 47.

4

SCARS OF WAR AND RECONSTRUCTION IN LEBANON

DEEN SHARP

On a hellishly hot Sunday in July 2016, I waited on a narrow strip of pavement alongside the George Haddad Highway in front of an outlet of the French bakery chain Paul. The highway links to the Fouad Chehab Ring Road, forming part of an open-trench road that encircles the Beirut Central District (BCD). Since 1994 this trench has delineated the territory of the Lebanese Company for the Development and Reconstruction of the Beirut Central District SAL (in French, SOLIDERE: SOciété LIbanaise DE REconstruction). A joint-stock company, Solidere is the centerpiece for the national reconstruction project that followed the end of the civil war in Lebanon. Constructing this infrastructural trench around the BCD was one of the first tasks that Solidere's sponsors undertook. At the time of its inauguration, Solidere was one of the largest single inner-city and waterfront renewal projects in the region. It turned the whole of the BCD—1.8 million square meters and an additional 608,000 square meters of reclaimed land on the seafront—into a corporation. This enabled investors not only to buy property in the BCD but also buy shares in the land bank, Solidere, on the Beirut stock exchange as well as those in Kuwait and London.

Paul was the meeting point for the tour "'Beauty under Stress': Practicing Public Space in Beirut Central District," organized and guided by Rania Sassine, an architectural consultant, lecturer, and former employee of Solidere International, under the auspices of the Arab Center for Architecture.[1] At ten a.m. sharp, the tour began by effortlessly crossing the George Haddad Highway, a feat made possible because of the sparse Sunday traffic. Crossing the highway on a weekday is a dangerous

FIGURE 4.1. Jean Nouvel in Beirut. The graffiti reads, "Our revolution, for us and for all of you." (Author photograph, 2016)

proposition, and entering the downtown area—now also known as Solidere—by foot is no easy task. Sassine later told me, "I started, if you noticed, by crossing the highway . . . to highlight one of the wrong design decisions of Solidere, to cut out the rest of the city."[2] Sassine added, "I always call Solidere 'paradise in a box.'"

Solidere has facilitated the construction of a high-quality rebuilt urban fabric in the BCD, which includes its own electricity, fiber-optic network, and a tunnel that connects the area straight to the airport highway. It features buildings designed by some of the world's most prominent architects, including Zaha Hadid, Herzog & de Meuron, Norman Foster, Jean Nouvel, and Steven Holl. This exclusive, physically connected, and high-end urban core, with its pristine but empty streets, now stands in stark contrast to the rest of Beirut and Lebanon more broadly. Outside of the paradise of the Solidere box lies a corroding urban landscape. Electricity cuts and water shortages are constant, a garbage crisis has left rotting rubbish along the streets and created open dumps, public space has been privatized, building regulations are widely ignored, architectural heritage has been replaced with rapidly constructed buildings, and traffic has ground to a halt.

In addition to showing tour visitors how Solidere is cut off from the rest of the city, Sassine told me that she also wanted to demonstrate how this separation creates a distinct atmosphere. "I call it a sensation tour. You note the difference in smell and acoustics, in texture, of being on this unfriendly highway and then getting onto this very narrow street [in Safi, located inside the BCD]," Sassine explained. "[In the BCD] there

FIGURE 4.2. Rania Sassine conducting the "'Beauty under Stress': Practicing Public Space in Beirut Central District" tour. (Author photograph, 2016)

are flowers, little noise, and shade from the planted trees; it is like in a second, life has changed radically . . . [Safi] has all the ingredients for success in terms of sensation, materials, and quality of life."

In Lebanon a furious and continuing debate has raged over how the reconstruction, with Solidere as its core, has been undertaken. In 2019 *The Economist* reported that nearly twenty-five years after the start of the reconstruction, "few projects arouse Lebanese passions as much as the rebuilding of Beirut."[3] The article notes that while some in Lebanon claim that the reconstruction process resulted in Beirut's revival, others argue it allowed tycoons and politicians linked to warring factions to dispossess owners of their prime real estate. The accompanying urban form that Solidere produced has equally caused distress among the people of Beirut. As Lebanese scholar and urban planner Mona Fawaz told *The Economist*, "Reconstruction destroyed downtown [Beirut] as a space for mixing. It finished the work of the war."[4] Fawaz articulates a widely shared view in Lebanon that the reconstruction process did not contribute to peace-building or the establishment of a postwar era. Rather, it perpetuated certain forms of violence following the active fighting of the war years. The idea that reconstruction can perpetuate conflict demands we reconceptualize our understanding of this process.

In the context of the built environment, the English word "reconstruction" is conventionally understood to be "the act of rebuilding a devastated area in the *aftermath* of war" (emphasis added).[5] This usage assumes that reconstruction happens after the act of destruction and is distinct from it. In this chapter I argue that the reconstruction of the BCD that began following the halt to active fighting in 1990, with Solidere at the forefront, cannot be comprehended independently from the previous rebuilding efforts, most significantly those that started in 1977 and 1983. I reframe the concept of reconstruction by showing how the Solidere project was rooted in the multiple attempts to rebuild within the various phases of the civil war and how the reconstruction processes were also entangled in continued violent struggles for power within the country.

To fully understand how the reconstruction facilitated the continuation of conflict, it is integral to consider how the construction of the built environment, as well as its destruction, can be undertaken to pursue certain forms of violence. In the first part of this investigation, I explore how the Lebanese Civil War produced a military urbanization in which the city was planned and built as part of the conflict. I then contend that the reconstruction was an extension of this militarized urbanization. The reconstruction has been a point of contention for many in the country because it perpetuated struggles by competing factions for power. Through archival research of the various and competing reconstruction plans, I trace the processes back and highlight how they were deeply embedded within the dynamics of the civil war rather than merely arriving after the fact.

In the context of a region currently suffering from extensive conflict, the experience of reconstruction in Lebanon has become all the more important. In Syria, Iraq, Yemen, Libya, and Gaza (Palestine), large-scale reconstruction projects are planned or are underway. Understanding the processes and complexity of reconstruction in contexts of conflict has perhaps never been more vital.

The Construction of War

The conflict in Lebanon was not a military contest between two hostile groups with clearly demarcated battle lines. Rather, analysts have broadly understood this war as a highly complex and brutal series of violent "events" that consisted of four different phases: 1975–77; 1977–82; 1982–83; and 1984–90. Even within these different phases of the conflict there were further incidents. As Robert Fisk notes when describing the fighting circa 1975–76, these events were "a series of horrors rather than battles: Black Saturday on the Ring motorway, the Palestinian massacre of Christians in Damour, the Christian massacres of Palestinians at Karantina and Tel al-Za'atar."[6] The multiple, overlapping battles of the Lebanese conflict entangled a wide range of actors and spaces and resulted in the deaths of an estimated 130,000 people.[7]

Little accurate data is available on the impact of the war on the built environment or on the effect the conflict had on many other sectors of Lebanese social life. The government's Department of Statistics did not function during the war years, and many records were destroyed. The appraisals by international institutions frequently stressed how difficult it was to gauge what was needed for reconstruction.[8] A commonly cited assessment by the United Nations estimated that the damages from the civil war amounted to US$25 billion (around US$42 billion in 2018) in destroyed infrastructure and property alone.[9] The World Bank reported that 800,000 people, or 160,000 households—almost one quarter of the population—had been displaced and sought shelter in existing dwellings or on state-owned or private land and were living "in unhealthy and overcrowded conditions."[10] While international organizations tried to assess the amount of destruction that the war had caused, it is integral to stress that the damage was not only undertaken through the destruction of the built environment. Equally integral to warfare was the role of competing militias and how they organized the built environment and delivered basic urban services.

The construction and reformulation of urban space was critical to the conduct of urban conflict. This warfare produced a highly fragmented urban landscape in Lebanon—specifically in Beirut—that has continued to impact urbanization processes and urban forms to the present day. "I compare Beirut to an extremely crowded room full of people that turn their back to each other, packed with solitary islands; all these buildings are very solitary, they do not communicate with one and other," the noted Lebanese architect Bernard Khoury said.[11] Not only were regions and neighborhoods turned into enclaves, but wooden panels replaced glass windows, steel slats substituted wooden doors, and open streets transformed into fortified compounds.

Several scholars have noted that the civil war produced a particular urban project in Beirut that killed any prospect of an open and plural city.[12] As the Lebanese state's sovereignty receded, militia territories—often associated with sectarian identities—proliferated. War and violence transformed Beirut into an enclaved city. The urban question was integral for militias that wanted to shift rural communities to the city to facilitate the creation of a religiously homogenous geographical space.[13] Historian Fawwaz Trablousi describes this process, writing that "when the militias finally 'cleansed' their territories and came to control 'their own people' and run their affairs, pressure on the individual to define himself/herself in terms of a unique social and cultural sectarian identity reached its climax."[14]

Voluminous scholarship has documented, as Joanne Nucho has detailed, how networks of urban infrastructures, institutions, and services reproduced particular notions of sectarian belonging and community.[15] The state was no longer the principal provider of basic urban services; it was replaced by numerous sectarian political and religious organizations. Militias used the provision of basic urban services as a strategy to control and intimidate both their "own" population and "others."[16] Michael Davie, for instance, has written on how competing militias wrestled to takeover pumping stations, water towers, and distribution valves allowing access to water only to areas under their control and under conditions based on their own political goals.[17] A similar process was also undertaken with the provision of electricity and other basic urban services, including garbage collection, telephone service, postal delivery, and health services. Hiba Bou Akar has noted how land and apartment sales and access to housing, as well as zoning and planning regulations and infrastructure projects, have all become entangled in the competing geopolitical territorial contests of various politico-religious organizations.[18]

As a result, even in the context of large-scale urban destruction during the war years, Lebanon continued to urbanize. Khoury stated: "Beirut did not stop its development during the war years; in fact, development was accelerated by the fact the center of the city was voided out. . . . Beirut grew in the absence of any master plan, or any sort of regulating mechanism."[19] The construction sector was one of the few parts of the economy that continued to grow and develop throughout the years of the conflict. Construction and land parcellation, including the real estate market, were all active in the war years.[20] A World Bank report notes that in 1974, before the civil war, construction represented US$141 million, an estimated 4 percent of national GDP; by 1988 this had grown to US$328 million, equaling 10 percent of GDP.[21] Beyond the construction that created sectarian enclaves and the new housing needed for those displaced by the war, the absence of government supervision meant that developers were keen to exploit land beyond permitted or appropriate legal restrictions.[22] The civil war clearly showed that urbanization was part of the conduct of the war, and as I detail below, the processes of reconstruction were equally significant.

The "Reconstructions" of Beirut: 1977, 1983, and 1991

The Lebanese Civil War lasted for fifteen years, but it was not continuous. At various stages lulls in open conflict meant both the government and citizens thought the war was over and the reconstruction phase could begin, only for fighting to start once again. The reconstruction process that began in 1991—and placed Solidere at its forefront—was the third significant attempt to rebuild. Yet the Solidere phase cannot be understood independently from the multiple previous—and competing—rebuilding efforts, most significantly those that started in 1977 and 1983. The Solidere project, focused on the rebuilding of downtown Beirut as the centerpiece for national reconstruction, did not simply arrive in Lebanon after the Ta'if Peace Accord nor with the project's inauguration in 1994. It was the result of intensive, complex, and (at times) violent social struggles.

Solidere and the broader reconstruction of Lebanon that emerged following the end of the last stage of the civil war (the so-called War of Liberation) and the signing of the Ta'if Accord should be understood as a reorganization of socio-spatial life for one political coalition led by the principal sponsor of Solidere, the Saudi-Lebanese billionaire Rafik Hariri, to gain power over another group, comprised primarily of his Syrian-backed rivals and other prominent elites competing for social power. Who controlled the reconstruction process and how it was undertaken were of immense sociopolitical and economic importance to factions both within and outside Lebanon. The choices, means, and methods by which particular infrastructure, housing, governmental, and financial institutions were reconstituted were of great significance. This is evident in the intense internal wrangling between Lebanese factions over the political, institutional, and spatial formulation of the reconstruction plans I examine below. Externally, there was often a rapid deployment of financial assistance by various interested parties, including international institutions led by the World Bank and nation-states looking for influence, including the United States, Italy, and France.

Although these reconstruction plans aimed to revitalize Lebanon as a whole, they consistently focused on the BCD, which had taken on contradictory roles during the civil war. On the one hand, its position as the metropolitan and commercial center of the nation was reduced due to the decentralization that occurred as various political-sectarian groups created their own respective centers, such as Jounieh in the north and Saida in the south. On the other hand, rival militias viewed the BCD as crucial both tactically and symbolically, and it remained a central site of conflict.[23]

Lebanese elites formulated a number plans to rebuild the BCD throughout different episodes of the war and in so doing emphasized the importance of this area to the formation of social power within the country. Indeed, over the course of the civil war, three series of distinct (but overlapping) master plans for the downtown area of Beirut were formulated.[24] The first series (1977–86) was centered around a 1977 plan that French organization l'Atelier Parisien d'Urbanisme (APUR) made with the newly established Council for Development and Reconstruction (CDR). The second series of plans (1983–91) is notable for the involvement of Rafik Hariri's corporation Oger Liban and the realization by many in Lebanon that the intensification of conflict meant that a larger rebuilding plan was warranted in the downtown area. Finally, the third series (1991–94) produced intense public debate as Lebanon entered the so-called postwar period, and the nation shifted its focus from war to reconstruction. In the next section, I investigate each of these plans, emphasizing their significance for the formation of what would eventually result in the Solidere project.

The APUR Plan, 1977

The Lebanese government's first full attempt to start the reconstruction process occurred in 1977. In December 1976 then-president Élias Sarkis had installed his banker friend, Salim al-Hoss, as prime minister and established a "colorless cabinet of technocrats."[25] This technocratic government quickly started to formulate plans for reconstruction as hopes began to solidify that the fighting had stopped. Perhaps most notably, they created the CDR, which had profound consequences for how the reconstruction was undertaken and how Solidere was formed in 1991. The Hoss government gave the CDR the authority to bypass parliament, and it acquired financial and administrative independence, reporting directly to the Council of Ministers. Through a complex institutional arrangement, the CDR was even able to bypass the Council of Ministers, receiving sweeping powers for planning, financing, implementing, and monitoring the reconstruction process. These powers included activities normally associated with the Finance Ministry, such as borrowing; line ministries, including project executions; and development banking, such as credit programs.[26] In 1977 the CDR began the active rebuilding of the Port of Beirut and lent money for reconstructing housing, industry, hotels, and hospitals.[27] It represented a remarkable power-grab by Sarkis and his technocratic partners in an increasingly violent struggle for the power over the Lebanese state.

The first reconstruction plan for downtown Beirut announced by President Sarkis was the Beirut Central District Plan of 1977–86. When opposing groups called a cease-fire in 1977, many in Lebanon thought that this marked the beginning of a transition into a postwar period. A reconstruction plan, which included a damage assessment, was carried out by APUR in collaboration with the Beirut Municipality. The APUR-led plan of 1977 entailed a damage assessment showing that the most severe destruction (wherein more than 80 percent of an average building was razed) was concentrated in the most economically important part of the city, if not the nation: the northern tip of the downtown area surrounding the port and the souks (markets). Another ring of destruction surrounded this northern tip, with damage estimated to be at 30–50 percent, while the rest of the downtown area had less than 30 percent damage.[28] Importantly, compared to later plans, the 1977 plan favored preservation over reconstruction.

APUR envisaged that property owners would largely be responsible for the repairs. However, for those areas in downtown Beirut that suffered more extensive damage, namely Ghalgoul and Saifi, either the government or private firms would be responsible. Significantly, the plan introduced the concept of several small-scale real estate corporations (*sociétés foncière*) to finance reconstruction in those areas. The shares would be distributed according to previously existing legislation from 1964, which stipulated that real estate owners would hold 75 percent of the shares and the government would hold 25 percent.[29] These partnerships between proprietors, legal tenants, and interested investors were based on the principle of exchanging property ownership or tenancy rights for shares in a company, while the monetary capital was provided by investors for similar shares. The provisional laws for the financing of real estate companies would provide the basis for the 1991 law that formed Solidere.

In December 1978 the CDR began to implement the Lebanese Lira (LL) 22 billion (approximately US$2.5 billion in 2019 dollars) national reconstruction project. It consisted of a rehabilitation program for roads and the Port of Beirut, a waste management study, and the rebuilding of housing, industrial sites, hotels, and hospitals. The 1978 reconstruction project was framed around the idea that the private sector was to be the principal generator of productive activity, able to provide basic social services, and in this way decentralize the economy away from Beirut and finance the reconstruction mainly from external sources. The Israeli invasion of southern Lebanon in 1978 and the escalation in fighting between Christian militias and Syrian forces stopped these plans. However, the 1977 APUR plan remained partially in use until 1986.

The Oger-Gemayel Plan, 1983

In 1983 a ceasefire and the appointment of Amin Gemayel as president instigated a new set of reconstruction plans. These plans included a proposal for the redevelopment of the northern littoral between Beirut and Jounieh (the Linor Project). This was a region where Gemayel wanted to assert his authority due to its strategic importance. During the war the area had been the site of intense and anarchic development; as a result, Jounieh had established itself as a notable Christian metropole and a competing urban center away from Beirut.[30] The Reagan administration in the United States strongly supported Gemayel. Reagan had agreed to the enlargement of the multinational force in Lebanon and had taken a more active role in asserting American power in the country. The administration formed the US Businessmen's Commission on the Reconstruction of Lebanon, which issued a report, *The Reconstruction of Lebanon* (1984), outlining opportunities for US enterprises in the rebuilding effort.[31] The author of the report, John Law, notes that in 1983 the US Agency for International Development "was busy helping on a number of infrastructural projects."[32] In addition, the World Bank approved a US$50 million loan to the government of Lebanon to assist them in urban redevelopment and the reconstruction of the port; telecommunications, water, and sewage systems; and sanitation facilities.[33] However, half of this loan was never disbursed, and the project was cancelled in 1985.

This second set of reconstruction plans is notable for the insertion of the Saudi-Lebanese contractor Rafik Hariri into the process. Hariri, who acted in part as a representative for the Saudi king in peace negotiations between Lebanese warring factions, would emerge as the central figure in Lebanese social life following the cessation of active fighting. In 1992, soon after the civil war had ended, Hariri was elected prime minister under controversial circumstance. Paul Salem argues, "Never has one individual wielded such a combination of public and private power in modern Lebanon as has Rafiq Hariri."[34] I contend that Hariri's role in the reconstruction of Beirut was an important component of the accumulation of this unprecedented social power in Lebanon.

This set of reconstruction plans included the 1983 and 1986 plans by Dar al-Handassah (DAR), commissioned through Hariri's corporation Oger Liban and funded by Hariri directly. Although Hariri himself kept a relatively low profile when he first entered the Lebanese theater, the Oger Liban trucks that cleared rubble from the streets for free bore advertisements that read, "Project of Cleaning Beirut, courtesy of Rafiq Hariri, Oger Liban 1982."[35] Hariri first established his presence in the country through his involvement in the reconstruction of the urban fabric, utilizing his corporation to undertake rubble removal and provide funding for rebuilding damaged buildings. The reconstruction was therefore a geopolitical and ideological project as much as it was one of urban development.

Prominent figures in Lebanon have accused Oger Liban of destroying many significant buildings in the downtown area (including Souk al-Nouriye, Souk Sursok, and parts of Saifi) during its "cleanup" operation.[36] It is important to note that it was during the "peaceful" years between 1983 and 1992, as Lebanese architect Assem Salam has shown, that the most extensive demolition of the downtown area occurred.[37] However, Hariri's efforts to reinvent downtown Beirut were soon brought to a halt, since the reconstruction of this area was not a priority for President Gemayel. Lebanese architect Henri Eddé notes that Gemayel was more concerned with constructing a vast new underground computer center, a tennis court with clay (*brique pilée*) imported from the United States, and a new palace in his hometown in Bikfaya.[38]

But by the end of 1983 the civil war had flared up once again. Incidents included the infamous bombing of the US Embassy and the US Marine headquarters, as well as the assassination of the president of the American University of Beirut (AUB). Fighting also broke out in the Mountain War (*harb al-jabal*) in 1984. Plans for reconstruction were once again shelved. But the return of fighting resulted in Hariri entering political life in Lebanon more forcefully. It also marked a turning point in the plans for the downtown area.

Charbel Nahas, who worked as the head of the general studies department at Oger Liban in this period, argues that the renewed conflict created a different logic in people's relation to the city.[39] In the opening phases of the war, people had sought to return to their downtown properties as soon as possible. By 1984 another logic emerged: "In 1983–84 it was absolutely different; no one was of a mind to come back—on the contrary—because alternative new centers had developed in the west, east, etc."⁴⁰ Many in Lebanon perceived that a larger scale of rebuilding and a new program were required for the reconstruction of the downtown area: "A much more ambitious approach needed to be put in place to justify the recentralization of the city."⁴¹

In their work at Oger Liban, Nahas and his colleagues discussed with Hariri the reconstruction in Europe after World War II and the broad legal set up of the operation: "And we diverged very seriously. He had at the time the idea of having a private development area, while the previous proposals of a series of real estate companies [developed in the 1977 plan] . . . were not supposed to be operational but were supposed to [facilitate] the distribution of land rents. . . . It was not supposed to be a private development in any way."⁴² During this period downtown Beirut would transform into the upmarket, private development and joint-stock corporation that we are familiar with today. The previous attempts for reconstruction that had sought to wrestle power away from certain groups were built upon and expanded.

The Solidere Plans, 1991

The third set of plans for downtown Beirut, which would result in establishment of the joint-stock corporation Solidere in 1994, came soon after the War of Liberation ended. As soon as the fighting halted, Hariri led a rapid political, legal, and economic mobilization under the premise of urban reconstruction. Between 1991 and 1994, a heated public debate concentrated on the plans proposed for Beirut and the scheme to turn the entire BCD into a real estate corporation. Following the signing of the Ta'if Accord and the eventual cessation of the conflict, Hariri took full charge of the rearrangement of social life in Lebanon through the reconstruction of downtown Beirut. The CDR appointed the engineering firm Dar al-Handassah (DAR) to create a new plan for the downtown redevelopment.⁴³ In the summer of 1991 prominent Lebanese architect Henri Eddé designed a new master plan, financed by Hariri and launched by DAR. The proposal became known as the Eddé Plan. Alongside the master plan, the CDR agreed to a new US$6.9 million study for Lebanon, funded by the Hariri Foundation and created by the American engineering firm Bechtel in partnership with DAR.⁴⁴ This plan culminated in the document *Horizon 2000 for the Reconstruction and Development of*

Lebanon, which envisaged a US$12 billion national reconstruction with Solidere at its center.

The Eddé Plan was based on the APUR plan and expanded many of the power grabs that plan had sought to put in place, such as extending the powers and role of the CDR even further and deepening the corporate takeover of the BCD. The Édde master plan created a spectacular new vision for the downtown area: it envisaged a mixed-use city center including commercial, residential, governmental, tourist, and cultural buildings alongside the implementation of modern infrastructure. The city center was to be rebuilt around three major north-south axes, the most prominent of which was a boulevard ten meters wider than the Champ-Élysée. Most buildings would be ten to twenty stories high, and the centerpiece was to be a forty-story World Trade Center. In the Normandy Bay area, the plan envisaged an artificial island with bridges that would connect it to the rest of downtown in the style of the Ponte Vecchio in Florence.

The master plan stated that because of the increased destruction since the creation of the APUR plan, the zone imagined for real estate corporations would be expanded to all rights holders.[45] In parallel to the Édde Plan, parliament passed Law 117 in 1991 under controversial circumstances—there were widespread allegations of MPs taking bribes. Law 117 provided a legal framework for a real estate company to be involved in the reconstruction of the BCD area.[46] Soon after this, further demolition of the BCD occurred, even though, as Saree Makdisi notes, the reconstruction plan had yet to be approved or defined: "Not only were buildings that could have been repaired brought down with high-explosive demolition charges, but the explosives used in each instance were far in excess of what was needed for the job, thereby causing enough damage to neighboring structures to require their demolition as well."[47]

Many people mobilized against the plans for the BCD in Beirut. They included tenants and apartment owners, competing political factions, numerous funding agencies, urban planners and architects, the intelligentsia, political and religious leaders, displaced groups and semi-governmental institutions. Scholars and urbanists heavily criticized the Eddé Plan.[48] Saree Makdisi noted that the 1991 plan was "unanimously denounced as an outrageous rebuilding project to follow the virtually total demolition of whatever structures remained in the city centre."[49] Much of the scholarship and broader criticism around the plan focused

FIGURE 4.3. Stop Solidere. (Author photograph, 2013)

on the proposal for a single real estate corporation and the conflicts of interest it produced between the public and private sectors.[50] However, there was also significant support for this master plan throughout Lebanon. Supporters argued that a single private company was the only viable option in the context of a fractured government, wide-spread distrust of the public sector, and inadequate public funds.[51] Furthermore, supporters viewed the transfer of property rights from owners to the real estate company as the only way to reclaim properties from squatters and initiate the reconstruction of an area that was estimated to have some 250,000 property-right claimants.

The controversy around Eddé Plan, however, caused enough public opposition for it to be revised. Henri Eddé resigned over what he stated was his naivety regarding Hariri's intentions and his own wish to protect his client, "*qui était l'Etat*" [that is, the state].⁵² A new master plan for BCD was formulated under the auspices of Angus Gavin, formerly of DAR and the London Docklands Development Corporation (LDDC), and the French urbanist Jean-Paul Lebas, who had worked on the La Defense Project in Paris. Gavin and Lebas's new master plan for downtown Beirut consciously bolstered "the historical fabric of the city" and drew explicitly from the New Urbanism design movement and Kevin Lynch's *The Image of the City* (1960).⁵³ But while the physical form of the reconstruction may have been adapted to respond to certain critiques, the economic model underlying the reconstruction was not. Najib Hourani argues that rather than adjust to the criticisms and concerns over the finalization of the BCD, the new plan "deepened rather than tempered, the commodification of space in the Beirut city center."⁵⁴

Solidere's Legacy

In September 1994, at the Beirut Festival, the Lebanese elite gathered in Martyrs' Square in the heart of the BCD for the inauguration of the government-sponsored joint-stock corporation, Lebanese Company for the Development and Reconstruction of the Beirut Central District SAL (Solidere). At the inauguration the president and speakers drawn from the country's religious and political elite took turns in endorsing and singing the praises of Solidere's foremost supporter and majority shareholder, Prime Minister Rafik Hariri. In the context of a country recovering from a brutal series of civil wars, such broad consensus of agreement by the Lebanese political and social elite was rare. The rise of Hariri and his Solidere project was remarkable given the violence of the war and the fractured country. Hariri's Solidere-led reconstruction project produced a new economic order focused on luxury real estate. As a number of scholars have detailed, the Solidere-led reconstruction was part of an intricate set of flows of rents created through compensation, treasury bills, high interest rates, tax avoidance, and real estate speculation.⁵⁵

By the end of the 1990s, Lebanon's national debt was among the highest in the world, with much of this debt created by Lebanese banks directly or indirectly associated with Hariri. The reconstruction of Beirut was central to Hariri's ability to accumulate social power in the highly fractured and often violent social context of postwar Lebanon. Solidere and the broader urban reconstruction that pivoted around it were integral to the profound concentration of social power that Hariri had accumulated in Lebanon by the early 1990s.

The formation of Solidere, and with it the Second Lebanese Republic, was also a violent process. Saree Makdisi details how the election of Hariri in 1992 was followed by the strengthening of the "repressive apparatuses of the state."[56] Old censorship laws previously ignored were enforced; the death penalty was brought back for political and civil crimes;

FIGURE 4.4. Solidere. (Author photograph, 2016)

widespread allegations circulated regarding the torture and abuse of prisoners in Lebanese jails. In 1993 a ban was placed on street protests of any kind. In 1996 a military curfew was introduced in Beirut and other cities to prevent strikes planned by the General Labor Confederation. Lebanon under Hariri, Makdisi argues, "witnessed both an astonishing increase in the activities of repressive state apparatuses as well as an increase in the state's role in those forms of public planning that—as opposed to health care, education, and low-income housing—are calculated either to yield immediate private profits or to improve the infrastructural conditions for the generation of private profits."[57]

Solidere was also directly associated with violence. Bahij Tabbara, who created the legal framework for Solidere, stressed that the real estate corporation was not an ordinary business: "The concept was to force the tenants and land owners to form a stock exchange company against the value of their share; it was a kind of expropriation, but it was not a real expropriation. The tenants were forced into a company."[58] Many of the property rights holders supported the creation of Solidere, as property rights over the years had become fragmented into thousands of different claims. Many other property owners did not agree with the formation of Solidere and were often violently dispossessed of their claims.

The Association of Owners Rights in the Beirut Central District formed and campaigned against the actions of Solidere. The preparation for the creation of Solidere resulted in the large-scale destruction of much of the BCD, causing much more damage than had been caused by targeting through active conflict between militias. In 1996 a building in Wadi Abu Jamil (plot 999 Mina el Hosn) collapsed, killing fifteen people who were squatting in the building and seriously injuring eight others. At the time, many media outlets accused Solidere of weakening the foundations of the building, but no one was prosecuted.[59] Makdisi notes that when the family of fifteen squatters was killed inside the building, "many people's worst fears were confirmed: there would literally be no space in the revitalized and gentrified cosmopolitan city center for such destitute and 'undesirable' migrants."[60]

From the time Solidere was formed, and the broader reconstruction in Lebanon was organized around it, the initiative was a source of severe tension within the country. As Najib Hourani has argued, Solidere is one example of "illiberal and anti-cosmopolitan forces" that illustrate how the reconstruction process has been utilized by Lebanese

FIGURE 4.5. A poster by the Association of Owners Rights in the Beirut Central District that reads "Woe to a nation that rips out its heart and does not revolt!" Circa 1993. (Source: Archives of the Arab Center for Architecture; copyright: Association of Owners Rights in the Beirut Central District)

elites "to turn reconstruction into the reproduction of their own nation-fragmenting power."[61] As many people in Beirut lament, no space for the Lebanese people themselves has been created in the newly constructed downtown area.

The reconstruction in Lebanon was never aimed at rebuilding a social contract or establishing a postconflict era; rather it was part of an accumulation of social power by one faction at the expense of others. Reconstruction, therefore, is not necessarily the mark of a postwar era. It too is driven by conflict among competing groups that can result in sociopolitical and economic violence against civilian populations. The lesson to be learned from reconstruction in Lebanon is that rebuilding can play a central role in sustaining conflict situations rather than creating new social contracts that would work toward creating circumstances supporting peace. The built environment can be weaponized. Infrastructure, walls, and buildings all can be constructed through communities, can encircle them, can exclude, and/or divide. This construction and organization of the built environment can be as violent as the dramatic instances of the destruction of the urban fabric.

FIGURE 4.6. Solidere's empty streets. (Author photograph, 2013)

Postscript

The proposition that what is good for Solidere is disastrous for Lebanon has been powerfully articulated in the country's more recent troubles. In March 2020, as COVID-19 began to spread across the world, the Lebanese government failed to repay a $1.2 billion bond. This was the country's first-ever sovereign default, and it precipitated a remarkable economic downfall. The Lebanese lira suffered hyperinflation, losing over 80 percent of its value. The economic crisis also resulted in many people's dollar deposits in Lebanese banks being frozen. These deposits have become known as "Lollars," US dollars stuck in the banking system, a computer entry with no corresponding currency. In the context of this economic collapse, which the World Bank has stated ranks among the top three most severe crises episodes globally since the mid-nineteenth century, Solidere's share price has sky-rocketed.

In July 2019 a share in Solidere was worth US$6, significantly below the value of a share (US$10) when the company was launched in 1994 and the downtown area had yet to be rebuilt. But since the economic collapse of Lebanon, Solidere's share price has risen to US$24, in part because the corporation allowed transactions in Lollars. The rise in Solidere's share price, it should be stressed, occurred in a context in which the BCD was severely damaged following the August 4, 2020, explosion at the Port of Beirut. Indeed, the debate over Solidere and reconstruction in Lebanon more broadly has been given renewed significance in the context of the August 4 explosion that sliced through the downtown area and east side of the city. The blast ruined hundreds of buildings, killed over two hundred people, and displaced thousands more. Beirut is confronted with the question, yet again, of what it means to reconstruct.

Notes

1. Sassine is an architect and the former head of the master planning unit at Solidere International. This was the third tour that Sassine had conducted of downtown Beirut that was undertaken through her own initiative.
2. Rania Sassine, recorded interview with the author, Beirut, July 13, 2016.
3. "Anti-cementism in Lebanon: Beirut Is Still Arguing over Its Post-war Reconstruction," *The Economist*, July 11, 2019.
4. "Anti-cementism in Lebanon."

5. *Oxford English Dictionary*, 3rd ed., 2009.
6. Robert Fisk, *Pity the Nation: Lebanon at War* (Oxford: Oxford University Press, 1990), 78.
7. According to the Peace Research Institute Oslo (PRIO), Battle Deaths Dataset, version 3, the Lebanese Civil War resulted in a total of 131,104 deaths, accessed June 9, 2021, https://www.prio.org/Data/Armed-Conflict/Battle-Deaths/The-Battle-Deaths-Dataset-version-30/.
8. World Bank, "Lebanon Stabilization and Reconstruction: Vol. 2," report no. 11406-LE, March 1, 1993, World Bank Group Archives, https://documents.worldbank.org/en/publication/documents-reports/documentdetail/213051468055439952/sectoral-annexes.
9. World Bank, "Lebanon Stabilization and Reconstruction," report no. 11406-LE.
10. World Bank, "Republic of Lebanon Recent Economic Developments and Emergency Rehabilitation and Technical Assistance Needs in Selected Priority Sectors," World Bank Group Archives, 1991, 29.
11. Bernard Khoury, principal, DW5 Architects, recorded interview with the author, Beirut, July 11, 2016.
12. Nasser Yassin, "Violent Urbanization and Homogenization of Space and Place: Reconstrcuting the Story of Sectarian Violence in Beirut," *World Institute for Development Economics Research*, no.2010/18 Working Paper, 2010; Éric Verdeil, "Reconstructions manquées à Beyrouth : La poursuite de la guerre par le projet urbain," *Les Annales de la recherche urbaine* 91.1 (2001): 65–73.
13. Maha Yahya, "Forbidden Spaces, Invisible Barriers: Housing in Beirut," (PhD diss., Massachusetts Institute of Technology, 1995), 110.
14. Fawwaz Tarabulsi, *A History of Modern Lebanon* (London: Pluto, 2007), 233.
15. Joanne Randa Nucho, *Everyday Sectarianism in Urban Lebanon: Infrastructures, Public Services, and Power* (Princeton, NJ: Princeton University Press, 2017), 6.
16. Yahya, "Forbidden Spaces, Invisible Barriers," 107.
17. Michael Davie, "La gestion des espaces urbains en temps de guerre: Circuits paralleles a Beyrouth," in *Reconstruire Beyrouth: L es paris sur le possible*, ed. Nabil Beyhum (Lyon: Maison de l'Orient Méditerranéen, 1991), 157–93.
18. Hiba Bou Akar, *For the War Yet to Come: Planning Beirut's Frontiers* (Stanford, CA: Stanford University Press, 2018).
19. Khoury interview with the author, July 11, 2016.
20. World Bank, "Lebanon Stabilization and Reconstruction," report no. 11406-LE, 34.
21. World Bank, "Republic of Lebanon Recent Economic Development," 3.

22. Henri Eddé, *Le Liban d'ou je viens* (Paris: Buchet-Chastel, 1997), 116.
23. It was during the two-year war, known as the Battle of the Hotels (*ma'arakat al-fanadiq*) in downtown Beirut that the infamous Confrontational Lines (*khutut at tammas*, or the "Green Line") were created.
24. There is considerable confusion in the literature concerning the different master plans due to the negotiated approach to planning in Beirut, the existence of competing plans, the lack of clear dates on the plans, and the many different names used for each plan.
25. William Harris, *The New Face of Lebanon: History's Revenge* (Princeton, NJ: Markus Wilener Publishers, 2006), 167.
26. The powers that were devolved to the CDR were documented by the World Bank, whose officials were critical of the moves; see, for instance, "Assessment Study Entitled the Council for Development and Reconstruction," World Bank Group Archives, 1990.
27. World Bank, "Assessment Study Entitled the Council for Development and Reconstruction."
28. Cited in Nicole Tannous, "Re-envisioning Beirut: A Critique of Populism and Neo-liberalism in Modern City Planning" (Master's thesis, California State University, 2015).
29. Omar Kabbani, *The Reconstruction of Beirut* (Oxford: Centre for Lebanese Studies, 1992).
30. Eddé, *Le Liban d'ou je viens*, 105.
31. Johnathan Law, *The Reconstruction of Lebanon* (Washington, DC: US Businessmen's Commission on the Reconstruction of Lebanon, 1984).
32. Law, *Reconstruction of Lebanon*, 131.
33. World Bank, "Project Completion Note, Lebanese Republic, Reconstruction Project, Loan 1476-LE," World Bank Group Archives, Washington DC, 1995.
34. Paul Salem, "Framing Post-war Lebanon: Perspectives on the Constitution and the Structure of Power," *Mediterranean Politics* 3.1 (1998): 13–26.
35. Hadi Makarem, "Actually Existing Neoliberalism: The Reconstruction of Downtown Beirut in Post-Civil War Lebanon" (PhD diss., London School of Economics, University of London, 2014), 178.
36. Saree Makdisi, "Laying Claim to Beirut: Urban Narrative and Spatial Identity in the Age of Solidere," *Critical Inquiry* 23 (1997): 667; Makarem, "Actually Existing Neoliberalism," 180; Assem Salam, "The Reconstruction of Beirut: A Lost Opportunity," *AA files* 27 (1994).
37. Salam, "Reconstruction of Beirut."
38. Eddé, *Le Liban d'ou je viens*, 107.
39. Charbel Nahas, recorded interview with the author, Beirut, July 18, 2016.
40. Charbel Nahas, recorded interview with the author, Beirut, July 18, 2016.

41. Charbel Nahas, recorded interview with the author, Beirut, July 18, 2016.
42. Charbel Nahas, recorded interview with the author, Beirut, July 18, 2016.
43. According to Omar Kabbani, officially the Lebanese cabinet requested the CDR to draw up plans for the reconstruction of Beirut, and the CDR in turn commissioned DAR.
44. Nassar Shammaa, who later would become the head of Solidere, joined the Hariri Group after working for the Bechtel Group.
45. "Il devenait inévitable d'élargir, à tout le Centre, les zones prévues d'intervention de Sociétés Foncières regroupant tous les ayant-droits" (DAR 1991).
46. Lebanese MP Najah Wakim notably claims in his book *The Black Hands* [*al-ayādī as-sawwad*] that forty deputies voted in favor of Law No. 117/91 after they obtained bribes ranging from US$50,000 to 100,000 in cash, as well as interest-free loans to subscribe to Solidere's initial public offering in 1994. See Najah, *The Black Hands* (Beirut: Sharikat al-matbu'at lil-tawzi, 1998).
47. Makdisi, "Laying Claim to Beirut," 672.
48. Nabil Beyhum, Assem Salaam [Salam], and Jad Tabet, eds., *Beyrouth: Construire l'Avenir, Reconstruire le Passe?* (Beirut: L'Urban Research Institute, 1995); Angus Gavin and Rami Maluf, *Beirut Reborn: The Restoration and Development of the Central District* (London: Academy Press, 1996); Kabbani, *Reconstruction of Beirut*; Samir Khalaf and Philip Khoury, eds., *Recovering Beirut: Urban Design and Post-War Reconstruction* (London: Brill, 1993); Salam, "Reconstruction of Beirut."
49. Makdisi, "Laying Claim to Beirut," 672.
50. Kabbani, *Reconstruction of Beirut*, 15.
51. Kabbani, *Reconstruction of Beirut*, 12.
52. Eddé, *Le Liban d'ou je viens*, 126.
53. Gavin and Maluf, *Beirut Reborn*.
54. Najib Hourani, "Transnational Pathways and Politico-Economic Power: Globalisation and the Lebanese Civil War," *Geopolitics* 15.2 (2010): 290–311.
55. See, for instance, Hannes Baumann, *Citizen Hariri: Lebanon's Neo-liberal Reconstruction* (London: Hirst, 2017).
56. Makdisi, "Laying Claim to Beirut," 697.
57. Hourani, "Transnational Pathways and Politico-Economic Power," 290.
58. Bahij Tabbara, former Minister of Justice and Hariri's private lawyer. Note based on an interview with the author, Beirut, February 6, 2018.
59. Wakim, *The Black Hands*; Giorgio Tarraf, *Beirut: The Story of a City Destroyed by Peace* (Master's thesis, Lebanese American University, 2014).
60. Makdisi, "Laying Claim to Beirut," 700.
61. Hourani, "Transnational Pathways and Politico-Economic Power," 290.

5

"SIMPLE PLANS" AND COMPLEX LIVES

A Dialogue about Planning and Designing
Emergency Settlements

CHARLIE HAILEY, INTERVIEW WITH
PER IWANSSON AND HANS SKOTTE

On May 13 and 14, 2018, in Lund, Sweden, I had a conversation with Per Iwansson, a Swedish architect and planner working on refugee camps, and Hans Skotte, Norwegian architect and planner focused on postwar reconstruction. Conducted exactly twenty-six years after Iwansson's work in Kenya, our conversation focused on his and Skotte's experiences of planning and designing emergency settlements in Kenya, Mozambique, Sierra Leone, Bosnia, and Sri Lanka.[1]

Cast across a wide range of locations and laced with multivalent topics, our dialogue's main objective was to understand how the efficacies of design — how the process works, what it offers, what it can do — relate to the exigencies of refugee camps and conflict-driven settlements. A key question stood out: What is the relevance of very "simple plans" done in "haste" for life in these settlements?[2] By no means rhetorical, this question is at the core of the difficulty of design in emergency situations, a struggle that is not taken lightly by professionals like Iwansson and Skotte. This question must be asked at each stage of the design and planning process.[3] How it is asked will change with each new location and each new set of conditions. The responses to this question have profound implications for the displaced populations of each densely settled camp.

The term "simple" occurs at the critical intersection of efficacy, identified by Iwansson as "relevance," and urgency, which he refers to as "haste." The simplicity of the plans for camps like Kakuma and Hagadera in Kenya was, in part, a function of the exigency of their situation; planning refugee settlements requires time, but one does not always have it. Iwansson had less than two weeks to survey the site for Hagadera and plan the camp's layout, and then only another two weeks for implementation before the arrival of refugees.[4] For Iwansson, the "simple plan" served as a starting point that included a degree of control at the outset but acknowledged that changes would occur over time. This strategy ties what Iwansson calls "simple plans" in early versions of the United Nations High Commissioner for Refugees (UNHCR) guides to emergency settlements.[5] Those models for settlements were rendered as diagrams that could be readily adapted to specific site conditions, and their simplicity and openness to interpretation did not lay down the heavy-handed functionalism of quantitative control at the micro scale but instead provided a wider organizational framework for living areas, roads, and services.[6]

However, the simple plan can be linked to principles that risk becoming ends in themselves if those principles do not take into account local conditions and if they remain unchanged throughout the design process.[7] For Iwansson, the simple plan, rather than an end in itself, is a first step in the camp's short-term development and plays a longer-term role in the process of a camp's transition from temporary condition to more permanent settlement.[8] After his experience at Dadaab and as a part of his efforts at Kakuma, Iwansson proposed a set of "adjustments" rather than overarching principles. In the context of the situation's urgency, these points of adjustment track along the process of site planning but also acknowledge the role of improvisation. In contrast to fixed principles, and thus open to change, this series of adjustments bears the simple plan through the rapid process from initial surveying toward the goal of housing.

The dialogue below explores simple plans in three parts, based on Iwansson's experiences with the Walda, Kakuma, and Hagadera camps in Kenya, along with Skotte's additional experiences in Bosnia and Herzegovina and Sri Lanka. The first part of the interview focuses on the preliminary situation in the camps and the challenges of implementation and orientation in the early stages characterized by urgency. The second section investigates how those initial design proposals might bridge between emergency conditions and more durable solutions. The third part looks closely at what Iwansson has called "created spontaneity" to understand how the simple plans relate to the complexities of context and refugee life.

Urgency and the Challenges of Implementation

From the outset, camp planners must contend with an architecture of scarcity. In Iwansson's case, the rudimentary design tools available at the earliest phase of the design process, including site surveys and schematic design, mirrored the camp's own lack of resources and its architecture of necessity. Here, simplicity was a function of the return to basic tools and a makeshift office where the preliminary work was carried out.

> **PER IWANSSON:** I had a portable T ruler, and I could actually fold the legs of the T so that I could put it in a fairly small pack. I also had a few triangles and a pen. When I first arrived in Kenya, I wasn't quite sure of the situation. I thought I could easily get tracing paper, and I did find [. . .] flimsy, thin paper in Nairobi, but I realized that when I'm in field conditions, I need something more solid, so I sought out thicker tracing paper. There was another thicker, older type of tracing paper [like velum] that I got from a colleague who came down from Geneva. In Walda camp I worked at a ramshackle table with only a little cover from the sun. In Dadaab it was only slightly better; the table was also a ramshackle table, but in Walda there had been boards with lots of slots between them, making it quite difficult to draw [. . .] After I did the drawings in the field, I went into Nairobi where I could sit in an office for a day or two and finalize the drawings. I could also copy and distribute them to people.

The use of simple tools reflected the deployment of fundamental concepts—basic, elemental design principles that remain despite advancements in technology in the three decades since the Kenyan camps at Kakuma and Dadaab were laid out. Main axes in each direction are one of these concepts. In Hagadera, for example, they serve as public corridors that connect the blocks, and a central market further links the two main sections of the camp. The grid is another basic tool for organization, which, Iwansson acknowledges, poses a normative risk. At the same time, he sees its straight lines as practical solutions for basic surveying and for implementation in urgent situations: its lattice is a tool for orientation and wayfinding—critical aspects within a settlement, particularly in places with such high densities as these camps and with the necessity for care provided by humanitarian workers who may not otherwise be able to navigate a camp's dynamic context. The blocks of the grid remain open for self-settlement and do not prescribe how each lot is organized. They are key elements for Iwansson's idea of "open-ended urban design," which Skotte identifies here and will be further discussed in the last section.

> HANS SKOTTE: The amazing thing is that this is how the camps that today house two or three or four hundred thousand people came about. And although there are new tools for designing and planning today, the principles of an open-ended urban design, which allows for urgency, unpredictability, and the uncertainty of how the inhabitants will alter their surroundings, still remain the same. In many camps, the basic design is a grid, a military layout, systematically controlled.
>
> PI: The camps that I designed and others I've seen are according to this military-like grid. There are reasons for it. At Hagadera I had started out drawing the layout for the camp in a much different way, with flowing curves, but it was impossible to implement at the pace of one thousand [incoming] refugees a day. The surveyor said to me: "Look, we can implement a lot of straight lines, including street lines. We can hire refugees and then three men in a row form a straight line; they cut through the bush, and we let the bulldozer follow." We had several teams who were cutting bush, and we knew they had to go about one kilometer, [thus] we could learn how long it took. The form was a very simple grid.
>
> One thing I could see was that it is very difficult to administer health or any other social services when camps are settled spontaneously. In Walda there was a very high infant mortality rate, so they were desperate to try to stop that. There was a woman, a British nurse, who was part of the UNHCR staff. She was tasked with putting in place mother and child feeding centers, which supplied extra food, milk, and milk substitutes. This center would also teach mothers how to use what was being provided. At the time, about 40,000 people were living in the camp. To set them up, she had simply gone out from the field office in one direction and found a site, and then she'd gone out in another direction, and then a third direction; but, in the end, she had placed the three centers right next to each other. She didn't realize this until she had been there longer. With planning, we could redistribute the centers. This is the basics

FIGURE 5.1. Grading roadbed and laying out water pipes at Hagadera, Dadaab, Kenya, 1992. (Photograph by Per Iwansson)

of town planning—that there is a public space and there is private space in a system of blocks. The quality of any kind of town relies on the quality of its public space, its streets and its markets, what they consist of and what they can offer.

HS: What you're talking about now, to some extent, we could also see it in Bosnia, and you can certainly see it in Kakuma: that camps are examples of the very basics of urban structure.

Designing as Bridging

Bridging between theory and practice is a core component of the design process. Developing principles and concepts into a design that fits a need and its sociopolitical and environmental contexts proves particularly difficult in refugee camps, where numerous displacements are at play.[9] I asked what the role of design is in bridging the multivalent conditions that characterize the refugee camp as a complex political situation: power, money, financing, actors who are from outside (including consultants and aid workers), and the refugees themselves, who in many cases are required to remain inside the camp. Can design itself serve as a bridge? Or is it too much to ask of the process, whether its outcome is an urban design or a simple shelter? How can design facilitate the temporal bridging that occurs between a camp's early stages and its longer duration? In answer to these questions, three modes of bridging emerged from our discussion: between the planner as outsider and local authorities as well as refugees, between temporary shelter and permanent housing, and between short-term mentalities and longer-term thinking. Each mode will frame the relevance of the simple plans to the complex situations of the refugee camp.

*Bridging between the Planner as Outsider and
Local Authorities as Well as Refugees*

Those who seek to help with emergency response after war and disaster are inherently outsiders. They are outside the situation in multiple ways: they have not directly experienced the events leading up to displacement, in terms of the difficulty of thinking about long-term solutions when they are struck by the urgency and immediacy of the short term, and in their position of power. In Kakuma and Hagadera, like most UNHCR camps, humanitarian aid workers and offices are positioned in restricted compounds. Whether located at the center of the camp or along the periphery, these administration areas are physical manifestations of this "outsider" condition.[10] At the same time, bridging occurs professionally with connections made between external and local planners. These interactions are not without difficulties: Iwansson witnessed a breakdown in the dialogue between fieldwork and broader organizational logistics at Walda, particularly with the disconnect between Kenyan contractors and the implementation of the camp. Skotte noted the challenges of bridging between the expertise of consultants and local officials.

    PI: Can we as planners be anything other than outsiders? This question relates to our efforts to translate things from theory into a practical situation. What does it mean for the process if we are constantly on the outside?

    HS: Outsiders are so taken by the situation, so immersed in it, that actions, decisions, judgments, are by necessity short-term. Bjørn Bøe, an engineer working for the Norwegian Peoples Aid (NPA), once asked me: "How can one think long-term if people are dying in the streets?" So, as humans, not just as nongovernmental organizations (NGOs), when stressed, we will think short-term. We are blinded by it.

Skotte pointed out a paradox of the humanitarian planner's position as outsider. Charged with designing and implementing the overall plan, an external consultant placed in the field can find the immediate situation of the refugees overwhelming. To frame this dilemma, Skotte cited Daniel Kahneman's discussion of two systems of thinking, one immediate or "fast" and the other more reflective or "slow."[11] The connection between psychology and planners during the on-site planning process bears more research and poses important questions about the connection between subjective responses and the "anchoring effects"—predetermined values or objectives—of basic planning principles. Iwansson added to this logic with the idea that refugee camps are lodged between circumstances of control and need. Refugees' loss of mobility and suppression of liberties often complicate the objectives of these camps to meet safety and other imperative needs. Within this framework, the planning process itself ranges between top-down mandates from agencies to more community-oriented programs that involve refugees in the design process.[12]

PI: Our theory is that we should think long-term. If you read studies written after the initial emergency has passed, they often come to the conclusion that everything is wrong because the planners and the implementers didn't consult enough with the clients. But how can you fully connect in the urgent situation? The position of designers is made worse because we are also in a position of power. We have to negotiate with governments, and ultimately what we say should be done is often done.

HS: The behavior of the external experts often aggravates their position as outsiders. It also influences the way they practice when there is not a discussion with locals. A lot of it has to do with the way they address things on the ground. My experience is that the external experts are not always certain of the context but typically feel secure about the practical tasks at hand, which tends to alienate the local planners. Given this sort of attitude, there's a lot of animosity, which is what I felt both in Bosnia and Sri Lanka. At the same time, however, these designers do have a degree of expertise when it comes to logistics and practicalities because many of them have been into emergency areas before.

Bridging between Temporary Shelter and Permanent Housing

Planners talk about "planning horizons" to indicate how long into the future a strategic plan extends. These horizons for camps are indeterminate. A 2004 UNHCR report titled *Protracted Refugee Situations* cited seventeen years as the duration of the average refugee camp, but Iwansson and Skotte contended that the figure is higher—closer to twenty-six years.[13] Statistics—longevity, population, economy—for camps are difficult to pin down because of the sheer scale, the lack of research, and the fluctuations within the protracted situations of the camps. Iwansson noted that a second generation, and now a third, has come to know the Dadaab camps as home. In the camps, infrastructure and shelter are typically makeshift, but the goals to assist and protect extend into the future. Skotte found the opposite to be true in emergency and relief operations in Bosnia, where housing was built to last, while the conflict and the dynamics of displacement—and the concomitant goals of protection and assistance—remained in flux: "The means were long-term, but the objective was short-term."[14]

My questions about design bridging spurred a thread that began to link the problematics of design and its relevance to the demands of emergency settlements. A disconnect emerges between the urgency to plan the initial response, which is prompted by crisis and characterized by a position as outsiders with a degree of power, and the necessity to plan for camps, which will inevitably last beyond the original emergency situation. What have designers learned from these disconnections?

HS: My doctoral research argued that we have to think long-term.[15] It is an obvious mistake to think short-term when designers, planners, and NGO's are making a long-term investment. I think one of the main explanations for this mistake and its shortsightedness is the fact that those of us who respond to these emergencies are totally swallowed by the misery and the urgency of the overall situation.

PI: When I was dropped into Kenya in 1992, there was a daily influx of one thousand people into the camps, and we came in out of the blue. I remember thinking how on earth would I, or indeed other people who were there at the same time, be able to resolve the issues of time and knowledge in the short term, with the need to think about the long term. Besides, most of the Somali refugees were nomads who moved around and had never lived in any kind of urban environment, much less in the kind of environment of a camp. There were some who were town people, who had been living in the European quarters of Mogadishu [in Somalia] including doctors and engineers, but they were the minority.

HS: It's very easy for designers and planners to be obsessed with the stable forms and predictable techniques of development because that's how we're trained. We have not yet overcome the incrementalism in this. We do not know how to deal with the planning of things when we don't know how long they will last.

Responding to your question about how design can bridge, I think about the provision of housing for Syrian refugees where there are spaces that can be completed with the efforts of the refugees. [There are] camps where, after some years, residents have transformed [particular areas] and made them their own—many times, quite simply, out of sticks and reclaimed materials, along with the plastic sheeting they receive. As designers, it is important for us to remember that design occurs over time, and likewise time is a fundamental feature in design. Time builds.[16] We have to imagine these projects over a long-term period. What are the developmental potentialities and possibilities of what we design? Answering such questions is a determining factor for us to address in the design process. That's one aspect. The second is that the inhabitants, the people, the refugees, are part of the design team.[17]

PI: I agree with that point of view. From my experiences in Africa, I learned that if you are in an emergency situation, it is important to understand that the situation will likely endure for a long time, and that it's possible to develop from that. We can provide fair-sized spaces where the settlements can expand. It's important to realize that camps don't grow by the effort of a designer but by the effort of the people living there, which is true for any informal housing situation, and even more formal housing schemes. So, from a design point of view, planners should provide something that will last.

Bridging between Short Term and Long Term

As our conversation continued, I picked up on the idea of bridging that Skotte had introduced when he talked about the "bridge between stable and temporary," which he termed the potential for "permanent emergency housing solutions" and for sustained financial support.[18] Word choice is critical when talking about camps, and Iwansson and Skotte prefer "housing" and "settlement" rather than "shelter," a term freighted with the disconnects between conditions on the ground and the aid organizations who provide assistance. During his work in Bosnia, Iwansson saw the misguided solutions of collective heatable tents as temporary shelters for the internally displaced during the conflict in 1992.

Skotte noted that this was Ian Davis's conclusion twenty years before Iwansson's experiences in Bosnia. Davis recommended "bypassing or circumventing the tent phase and going straight into housing." He was an important figure in the generation of planners and designers with whom Iwansson and Skotte identify. Iwansson noted: "My conclusion is the same as Davis's. I read him, even before I was directly involved in emergency response. He was one of the figures that interested me as an architecture student. He was adamant about thinking in terms of permanence from the beginning."[19] As debates about the duration of camps continue, Davis's dissertation on emergency housing (considered the first of its kind) and his subsequent writings, such as *Shelter after Disaster* (1978), in which Davis uses the term "shelter" in place of "housing," are as relevant as ever, almost five decades since his initial research and work.[20]

An extension of this model of housing is the integration of refugee accommodation within communities. During our conversations, Iwansson called the projects in Bosnia and Herzegovina "camps of permanent houses"—housing with "temporal use" that was "supposed to bridge into something more permanent." Skotte talked about the possibilities of integrating housing for refugees built into the existing urban fabric and linked with the local population, citing an example in Gračanica, in Bosnia and Herzegovina, where emergency housing was built within the city on abandoned land. Skotte himself grew up in a similar form of housing in Norway, in one of the 650 houses provided by Sweden during World War II and built into the urban fabric as housing settlements that could initially house two families and then eventually convert to single-family housing. Skotte talked about this plan as "the ideal model."

> PI: But it does go back to the starting point. You still have to design what will be the first phase of the incremental housing, so another question that comes up is about alternative ways to deliver a whole

house as a sequence: Why not make the floor slab, which may be difficult for refugees at the time, and then provide resources for construction—material on the ground for people to use? That's one of the strategies we used for reconstruction projects in Bosnia and Herzegovina. We gave people materials and technical as well as financial assistance.

HS: The Norwegian Refugee Council (NRC) practiced this kind of system for a number of years and yet they have no record of it. The process involved giving money in three installments. First, the plinth—foundations and basement—and then money was provided for the next stage, and then eventually a final phase of building. NRC pioneered this, and no one knows about it. They were providing that when I first came to Bosnia in 1995.[21]

At the heart of the original edition of *Shelter after Disaster*, Ian Davis included tables of what he called "myth" and "reality," which show evidence for how "assumed situations" after disaster or displacement are quite different from the "actual situations."[22] This latter category offers designers and planners opportunities to evaluate not only the relevance of a particular proposal but also the innovative solutions that refugees create to adapt a plan.

PI: The marketplaces of the camps in Kenya were typically built of prefabricated wall sections. Local carpenters made these panels from sticks and straw. I learned of these systems when I proposed the quite radical reorganization of part of the camp in Walda.

When I asked merchants in the market to move for a new road, they simply untied the connections between these wall sections, lifted them up, and walked away with the lightweight panels to set up the market stalls and shops nearby. Ian Davis had already talked about a local society's design and material resources. I'm very skeptical of products like the Ikea hard tents and similar design solutions that architects and schools of architecture love to propose and publish.[23]

HS: Most refugee camp designs, even if they are locally produced, are done by urban architects, and yet most of the refugees we're talking about are rural. When I was in Sri Lanka after the tsunami, I saw schemes for units and settlements, all organized into what looked like a western suburb. But the units that were provided—and I've seen thousands in Sri Lanka—did not address the social and

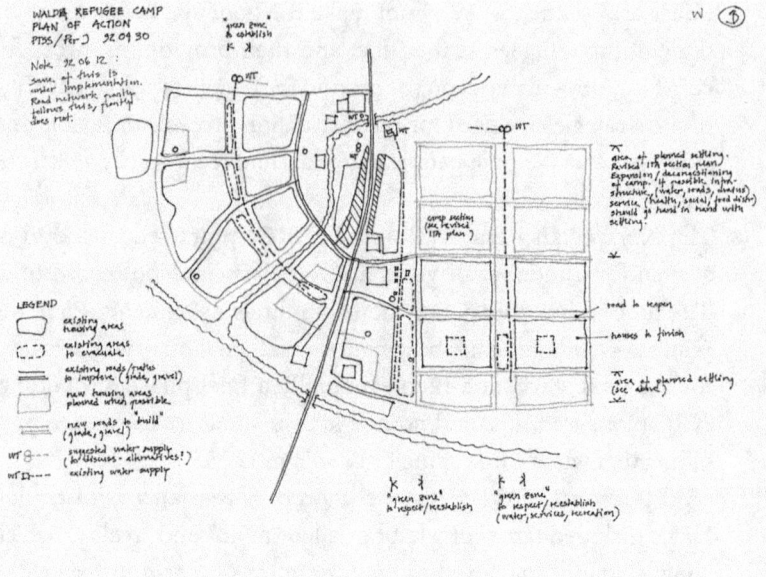

FIGURE 5.2. Per Iwansson, "Walda Refugee Camp Plan of Action," Walda, Kenya, April 30, 1992.

cultural practices of the victims, particularly in terms of the localized practices and rituals of eating and making food. All of the units that I saw had makeshift additions for kitchens built by the occupants to make room for these practices. Toilets were added as well. Food-making and sanitation are so filled with mores and cultural practices that design has the potential to impose unwanted changes in those practices.

PI: Cooking and eating habits are a very important issue in parts of Africa where there are large rural populations, and people don't always cook and eat in a house. For these refugee camps, a design consideration is not necessarily the actual construction of a kitchen but the provision of space for it. As a consultant for UNHCR in Sierra Leone, I reviewed the planning of a camp that did not account for these practices. The houses were well-built huts of mud and wattle with straw roofs, but they were placed so close to each other with only a small pathway in between that people had to cook and eat in turns in this narrow space. Each family group had their shift. I asked why this had happened, and the administrators of the camp told me: "Well, this is how the planner drew this camp." I made proposals to enlarge the camp and to move every second row of houses to make room for these practices.

"Created Spontaneity"

How do designers and planners balance the need for organization with more organically driven living patterns? Aid agencies and their workers can use the grid for orientation and navigation, but how is that concern balanced with the necessary connections between local family groups and local ways of inhabiting a place? How do planners and designers balance the needs of organization with flexibility? Between standardization and self-organization? In one respect, Iwansson and Skotte acknowledged the deployment of basic planning elements in the near term, but they also sought to avoid long-term restrictions on refugees' abilities to generate livelihoods. In this last section, a discussion of the block returned to frame a planning objective that Iwansson called "created spontaneity." Here, the simple plan of blocks accommodates change and localized transformations. Iwansson posited walking as a basic tool of the site-design process that similarly offers direct access to the essential qualities of the place—the site and contours of the camp and the local materials and resources. Earlier, Skotte had made the point that, despite advanced tools in the planning process such as satellite imaging, the core issues of design remain. Such technology can further distance designers and planners from the camp's context.[24] When Iwansson drafted plans under simple shade structures in Walda and Dadaab and when he walked to study the site, he was there in the hot air, blowing dust, and equatorial sun. He was, for a brief time, part of that climate, the environment, and the community.

PI: How do we know from the beginning which particular aspects to consider? It's easier to come in and review a camp that has been functioning for a while, see how things have evolved and how the camp is set up according to the original planning, and then figure out how to facilitate everything. During my experiences in Kenya, I thought about all these things, and there is so much to consider all at the same time. How much space does a family need? That is a unit that varies with the context.

I found out what my UNHCR predecessor in Kenya had used. Werner Schellenberg set up a basic unit of eight by sixteen meters when planning the Dagahaley camp. The size of this family unit corresponded to observations I had made on how people used plots for housing in a small new town in Mozambique, so I was fairly certain about that, and it was a useful size. I had nothing against the grid dividing a quarter into individual plots, but the important thing I found was the larger urban grid. With a structure of fairly large-size spatial units on which a number of people settle, [refugees] can say that they live in a particular unit, and [aid workers] can find their way in these camps. I was both lucky and unlucky with my experience in Kenya to enter first into Walda, a camp that had grown more or less spontaneously, so I could observe how it had been settled and draw conclusions about which elements of spatial organization were needed.

I talked to the future administrators of the camp, and I noted that they did not have to set out each individual plot. [. . .] They could decide that a certain number of people were in this area, and then let them [self-organize]. And some of that has happened—some of Hagadera's so-called blocks of about five hundred people are totally spontaneous and self-organized with winding paths between

FIGURE 5.3. Refugee settlement in Walda, Kenya, April 1992. (Photograph by Per Iwansson)

houses; some of them are rigid with paths in strict grids; some have open common spaces in the blocks, and others don't. I find that very interesting. I know that blocks closer to the center have become seriously over-crowded, probably because people have subdivided and unofficially sold part of their dwelling. They have also taken in renters, which happens in the typical informal settlements. Kibera in Kenya is 80 percent rental housing, rental shelter.

The grid needs to be adapted. I do think that, as a planning tool, a block of between four hundred and six hundred people is necessary. It can be smaller or bigger, depending on context. For example, a plan I'm working on in a municipality in the south of Sweden has twisted grids with little places in the streets, quite nice if they carry it out. It's a quite different situation, but the adaptation of the grid is similar. The blocks are of course much smaller, and they should house between one and two hundred people.

What I'm doing here in Sweden, and what I hoped to do there in Kenya, is what I have called "created spontaneity." If there is a grid, it should ideally be disturbed; it should be altered by something, so it has its own identity—now, I'm talking as an architect. It should have some way of identification and orientation [. . .].

One of my favorite architects was Bruno Taut, and I have the German edition of one of his books.[25] He designed quite a few housing schemes in Berlin in the 1920s and early 1930s, and he [wrote] about his design process at a time they were studying light and sun and different housing typologies [. . .] to base design on science. Even with all the knowledge generated, he found these studies were never enough to create good housing areas. After he was done with all this on paper—and I'm certain this is good—he then would walk and walk and walk around on site. Inevitably, before it was finished, he would realize he needed to twist the orientation of a house or move a road. He could never explain this rationally, but that's how his best design came about.

When we talk about refugee camps, it's not so much the grid that poses problems. For me, what they lack is enough public spaces for events or things that happen around the street, places where a street widens to become a public area. Hagadera had a system of housing blocks of similar size and separated by roads, and then there were wider "green" or "service" corridors, which I set up hoping that they

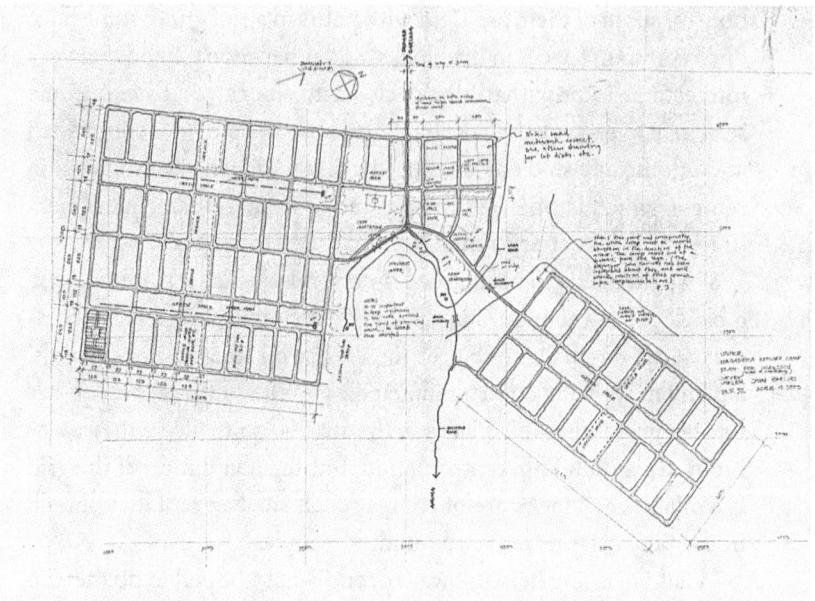

FIGURE 5.4. Per Iwansson, plan scheme for Hagadera camp, Dadaab, Kenya, 1992.

would preserve the trees there. They were also wide enough to put a school there. If I could redo it, these corridors would widen but then become narrower, and then widen again. What is right is that there is a center, there is the market, which has a bus station, and it's located [in a way that makes it accessible for] most people [. . .].

HS: The fundamentals of urbanism emerge from these places. Where there are a lot of people, activities emerge.

PI: People need space to develop, and they find it, even in the camps in Kenya. Of course, you have to know about how much space is needed for such activities. When I look at Hagadera on Google Earth, I see the market occupies the same space that I drew in 1992. If the plan is restrictive, is it too much? Or is it enough? Was I right about the size for the market at the time? It's hard to know for sure, although I can read what others have written about that market.[26]

It is also important to estimate how much space is needed for infrastructure and food distribution. I could calculate some things, like the number of Rubb Halls, the large tents for food storage, and the space they occupy, spaces for the offices for the different NGOs, spaces for people to queue for food distribution, and for the school, and for other services. But spaces for other things that belong to normal life, which are less easy to quantify, must also be provided— space for meetings, recreation, culture, for commerce to develop.

SH: This process reflects urban dynamics. For example, in a settlement for internally displaced persons in Mihatovići, near Tuzla in Bosnia, a refugee who lived in the corner flat where most people passed by had a successful shop. He diversified his inventory, made a lot of money, and eventually moved out of the settlement. This was in a way all predictable as it is aligned to basic principles of urban design. If you look at these places that start out as grids, you [can] see the activities that have emanated, particularly by certain people with initiative and drive. It's important to look into how these settlements shape up, how they develop over time. [This exercise] provides a lot of knowledge for urban planners in general.

IP: When I look back at the few resources I had, I'm quite amazed at what we managed to get on paper during the time in Kenya, and I wonder what it would be like now with computerized design and drawing tools.

When I was determining the size of a housing block for Hagadera camp, I had a few reference points: Dagahaley, which was implemented from what Schellenberg had planned, and the previous experience at Walda. While I was laying out Hagadera, I went to Dagahaley and asked whether [a particular element] was a reasonable size. And if it seemed right, I didn't try to alter it; but in other cases, I drew a road that was a kilometer in length, and then I said, "OK, what is a kilometer?" And then I walked it on the future site of Hagadera. I said, "OK, the future road starts here, and then goes for a kilometer." I actually knew my time for running one kilometer [...] and I did run it as a way of measuring.

So, I tested these things on the site. I would put something in the drawing, then went out to observe it in the field before the drawing was finalized. And that I think was good practice. Also, my experience at Walda proved to be a good learning curve.

Conclusion

At the conclusion of his work, Iwansson filed a report with UNHCR. *Mission Report 92/44* begins with an abstract that summarizes planning goals for refugee settlements in Kenya: "A Physical Planner (Consultant) undertook a two-month mission to Kenya with the main purpose of planning new refugee settlements as part of emergency operations. In Walda, the consultant made recommendations on how to restructure the camp. Refugees will be moved from the most congested areas to a new sector of the camp. Recommendations were also made on general site planning and land-use management, site-plan concepts, shelters and latrines."[27]

Iwansson's report is a significant contribution to the institutional knowledge of UNHCR's work in addition to the work of NGOs and agencies involved in planning and designing emergency settlements. However, what this report doesn't tell are the stories of the planner's deep connections to the site, to the local agencies and surveyors, to refugees themselves, and to the walks—and the runs—that Iwansson took through the landscape. On these walks, he met refugees, encountered trees, contours, and sometimes evidence of water. Iwansson recalled his first week in Walda camp:

> PI: I was supposed to solve problems, but nobody could give me instructions. So I thought: "What can I do, what am I useful for?" I reckoned: "What I can do is draw plans; I can put things in drawings." But the first thing I needed was an idea of how the camp looks. In Walda, I started walking all over the camp, and then I drove a car and kept measuring distances, making observations, driving and then walking again until I found some main paths and [...] the edge of the river [...]. I made this very simple map—it looked like a child's drawing—just one line is a road, a symbol for the river, and dense housing as dots. I spent a week walking around among the refugees trying to figure out how the spontaneous place worked.[28]

Iwansson's "simple plans" started as field notes made during his brief encounter with the place. Walking, Iwansson navigated the place as he also traversed the full range of a built environment's capacity for organization—from spontaneity to rigidity. Iwansson and Skotte similarly revisited ways that design might traverse and bridge the paradoxes and complexities of camps. The breadth and depth of their experiences point toward the value of a continued examination of the difficulties, pitfalls, and relevance of short-term responses to enduring settlements, which must balance present and future concerns for safety and livelihood.

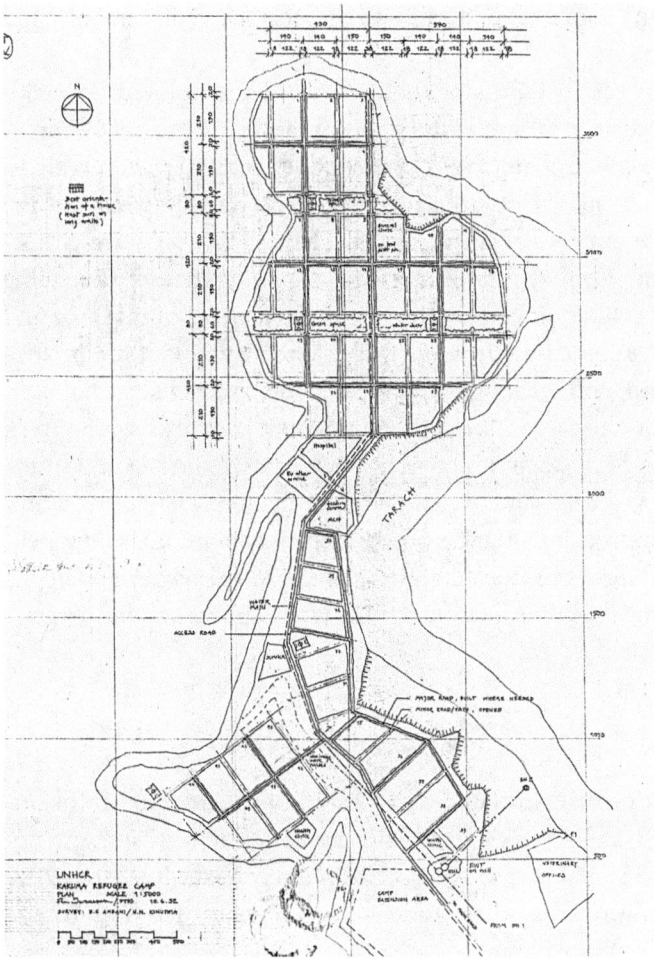

FIGURE 5.5. Per Iwansson, plan scheme for Kakuma camp, Kenya, June 10, 1992.

In Walda, Iwansson's on-the-ground experience influenced how he proposed reorganization. He concluded that the micro-management of individual lots did not work and that the infrastructure of the camp was the most significant aspect for access, location, and orientation. As he walked, took field notes, and drafted plans, Iwansson's work on site at Walda, Hagadera, and Kakuma was critical for an environmental responsiveness that, while imperfect, attempted to adapt the camp's nascent plan to topography, settlement patterns, and water sources. His work suggests that a simple plan might emerge from its local context and that, when left open in its diagrammatic form, it can be more readily adapted to site conditions than a set of normative dimensions, requirements, and universal standards.

Iwansson's notes to the plans for Kakuma demonstrated how diagrams might inform a camp's fit to its terrain and how phases of implementation—he called them "eight points of adjustment"—can address the growth of a camp.[29] Underscoring his approach to simple plans, the points follow the process of site planning. They are not only straightforward and efficient but also tuned to the incremental nature of making a camp. These points move from the technical aspects of marking and surveying to the contextual features of the land (laying out roads, subdividing clusters, and locating the camp's center), to the stages of construction for communal resources (building roads and locating services), and then to the final stage of housing. They bring a measured attitude to the necessary "haste" and urgency of the situation. They bring a unified but open approach that underpins a nascent community. Ultimately, Iwansson's work floats the idea that the "simple" might accommodate the complex, making room for internal agency while addressing the urgency of providing aid.

Postscript

This conversation was initiated as a prelude to Iwansson's return to Hagadera and Kakuma in order for him to continue to assess the implications of the initial plans. Iwansson's untimely death in March 2019 leaves those continued studies, and a legacy of work, for present and future designers and planners.

Notes

1. While working for the United Nations High Commissioner for Refugees (UNHCR), Iwansson spent two months in Kenya in the summer of 1992, starting at Walda camp, where he studied how to structure and enlarge the mostly spontaneously settled camp and how to restructure and enlarge parts that had been planned but had failed. Iwansson then worked in the Dadaab camps, where he focused on plans for a new camp in Hagadera and subsequently planned Kakuma camp in northern Kenya. As Iwansson continued to draft plans for Hagadera's extension, Kenya's refugee population exceeded three hundred thousand, an increase of more than a quarter million refugees over the previous year.

2. Iwansson had first asked this question in email correspondence in 2014. See Charlie Hailey, "Camps, Corridors, and Clouds: Inland Ways to the Ocean," in *Wet Matter*, eds. Pierre Bélanger and Jennifer Sigler, special issue of *Harvard Design* 39 (2014): 24–31.
3. Our working definition of design for this conversation included not only schematic design and its process but also the practice of planning camps, particularly through what is often called urban design.
4. An arrival rate of nearly a thousand people a day, with the majority coming to the camps at Dadaab, meant that urgency was the norm. Based on figures of 280,000 between March 1991 and March 1992. See Laura Hamilton, "Somali Refugee Displacements in the Near Region: Analysis and Recommendations," paper for the *UNHCR* Global Initiative on Somali Refugees, accessed August 10, 2018, http://www.unhcr.org/55152c699.pdf.
5. Iwansson refers to the first edition of UNHCR's *Handbook for Emergencies* (Geneva: UNHCR, 1982).
6. Compare the first edition of UNHCR's *Handbook for Emergencies* (1982) with its second (2000) and fourth (2015) editions. See James Kennedy, *Structures for the Displaced: Service and Identity in Refugee Settlements* (Delft: International Forum for Urbanism, 2008), 39–43. For a complete discussion of handbooks and guides for refugee camps, see Charlie Hailey, *Camps* (Cambridge, MA: MIT Press, 2009).
7. The pitfall of reductionism should also be noted. From the viewpoint of operations, at an early stage of emergency-response scholarship, sociologist Enrico L. Quarantelli argued that principles should not be oversimplified: "I will suggest that there are certain principles of disaster planning. These may appear simple on the surface, but which, if ignored, make for poor response by operational personnel in a disaster situation. What is clear is that . . . much can be intelligently planned ahead of time." See "Social Aspects of Disasters and Their Relevance to Pre-Disaster Planning," *Disasters* 1.2 (1977): 101. Ian Davis builds on the role of principles by positing them at the start of each chapter in his book *Shelter after Disaster* (Oxford, UK: Oxford Polytechnic Press, 1978). For more recent examples of the complexities of principles for refugee camp planning, see Tom Corsellis and Antonella Vitale, *Transitional Settlement/Displaced Populations* (Oxford, UK: Oxfam GB, 2005).
8. A growing body of literature has studied the urbanization of camps and transitions from camp to town. Specific to the camps in Kenya, see Bram J. Jansen, *Kakuma Refugee Camp: Humanitarian Urbanism in Kenya's Accidental City* (Chicago: University of Chicago Press, 2018). For the case of Dadaab's camps, see Ben Rawlence, *City of Thorns: Nine Lives in the World's Largest Refugee Camp* (New York: Picador, 2016). Marc-Antoine Perouse

de Montclos calls this process "urbanization in the making." See Perouse de Montclos, "Refugee Camps or Cities? The Socio-economic Dynamics of the Dadaab and Kakuma Camps in Northern Kenya," *Journal of Refugee Studies* 13.2 (2000): 219.

9. See Michel Agier, "Between War and City: Towards an Urban Anthropology of Refugee Camps," *Ethnography* 3.3 (2002): 317–41; and Michel Agier, *On the Margins of the World: The Refugee Experience Today*, trans. David Fernbach (Cambridge, UK: Polity, 2008).

10. Aid workers are also seen as outsiders by the communities adjacent to the refugee camps they serve. See Ekuru Aukot, "It Is Better to be a Refugee Than a Turkana in Kakuma: Revisiting the Relationship between Hosts and Refugees in Kenya," *Global Movements for Refugees and Migrant Rights* 21.3 (2003): 73–83. See also Johan Pottier, "Relief and Repatriation: Views by Rwandan Refugees—Lessons from Humanitarian Aid Workers," *African Affairs* 95.380 (1996): 408. Pottier discusses how refugee camps are "a wilderness for the outsider" who must navigate the needs of refugees as well as the complex logistics of providing aid.

11. See Daniel Kahneman, *Thinking Fast and Slow* (New York: Farrar, Straus and Giroux, 2011).

12. For a recent exploration of the relation of planning and power, see Ayham Dalal et al., "Planning the Ideal Refugee Camp," *Urban Planning* 3.4 (2018): 64–78.

13. The Executive Committee of the High Commissioner's Programme reports: "It is estimated that the average duration of major refugee situations, protracted or not, has increased: from 9 years in 1993 to 17 years in 2003." See "Protracted Refugee Situations: The Search for Practical Solutions," proceedings of June 10, 2004, 30th Meeting of the Standing Committee, 2, www.refworld.org/pdfid/4a54bc00d.pdf.

14. Skotte noted that these "permanent housing solutions were in part a consequence of the unsuccessful experience with tents" originally deployed in Bosnia. Although heated, the tents were not suited to the Bosnian climate, and this experience demonstrates one of the differences between the conditions in Kenya and Bosnia.

15. See Hans Skotte, "Tents in Concrete: What Internationally Funded Housing Does to Support Recovery I Areas Affected by War—The Case of Bosnia-Herzegovina" (PhD diss., Norwegian University of Science and Technology, 2004), https://ntnuopen.ntnu.no/ntnu-xmlui/handle/11250/230994.

16. Skotte referenced the PREVI competition and a study of its development. See Fernando Garcia-Huidobro, Diego Torres Torriti, and Nicolas Tugas, *¡El tiempo construye!/Time Builds!* (Barcelona: GG, 2008).

17. Active engagement with refugees and community participation in the design process, though challenging in emergency situations, is an effective way to connect site plans with local input. See Marianne Jahr et al., "Approaches to the Design of Refugee Camps," *Journal of Humanitarian Logistics and Supply Chain Management* 8.3 (2018): 323–45. Also see Camp Coordination and Camp Management Cluster, "Localising CCCM Responses," *Retreat Report 2015* (Oslo: NRC, 2015), http://cccmcluster.org/documents/retreat-report-2015; and CCCM, "Camp Management Toolkit," accessed April 2, 2019, https://www.globalcccmcluster.org/system/files/publications/CMT_2015_Portfolio_compressed.pdf.
18. Per Iwansson and Hans Skotte, interview by Charlie Hailey, May 13–14, 2018, Lund, Sweden.
19. Iwansson and Skotte interview, May 13–14, 2018.
20. See Davis, *Shelter after Disaster*. This original edition, which played a critical part in Iwansson's and Skotte's education as designers and planners, has been released as a second edition by IFRC and OCHA (2015). Here, Davis uses "shelter" in a form more closely allied with their use of "housing." Davis argues that shelter "must be considered as a process, not as an object" (28).
21. For discussions of similar programs, see Cash Learning Partnership, "The State of the World's Cash Report: Cash Transfer Programming in Humanitarian Aid," February 28, 2018, https://reliefweb.int/report/world/state-world-s-cash-report-cash-transfer-programming-humanitarian-aid; and Hannah Tappis and Shannon Doocy, "The Effectiveness and Value for Money of Cash-based Humanitarian Assistance: A Systematic Review," *Journal of Development Effectiveness* 10.1 (2018): 121–44.
22. Davis, *Shelter after Disaster*, 25–30.
23. Ikea has developed what it calls the "Better Shelter" for responses to refugee crises. See Camilla Tubertini, "Good Design That's Doing Good," Ikea website, accessed June 14, 2019, https://highlights.ikea.com/2017/better-shelter. The shelter's vulnerability to fire led to a redesign in 2017.
24. Aerial surveys and satellite imaging do offer insights and data that were previously difficult to gather. Skotte cited the example of Nasr Chamma's use of aerial imaging to study changes that took place in the layout of Jordanian camps over a period of twelve months. The results demonstrate how refugees transformed the grid by moving their houses into groups. See Nasr Chamma and Carmen Mendoza Arroyo, "Rethinking Refugee Camp Design: From 'Temporary' Camps to Sustainable Settlements," paper presented at the Symposium of Architecture in Emergency, Istanbul Kültür University, Faculty of Architecture, November 17, 2016.
25. Bruno Taut, *Architecturlehre* (Hamburg: VSA, 1977).

26. See, for example, Rawlence, *City of Thorns*.
27. Per Iwansson, *Kenya: Site Planning Consultancy: 12 April—15 June 1992*, Programme and Technical Support Section (PTSS), Mission Report 92/44 (Geneva: UNHCR, 1992).
28. Later, Iwansson told me the story of Ik Hajji, who grew up near Dadaab and was working for an environmentalist NGO in Hagadera camp. Ik contacted Iwansson through Facebook, and when Iwansson sent him the article he was writing about planning the camps, Ik recognized his father as one of the refugee workers hired to cut sight-lines through the bushes and trees for roads. Ik also recalled meeting Iwansson and an MSF volunteer as a child when he and his mother were collecting wood outside the camp. Iwansson was surveying the camp's context and helping orient the volunteer, but Ik's mother thought they were lost and directed them back to Hagadera.
29. Per Iwansson, "Planning Refugee Camps in Kenya," unpublished English manuscript. The article was published in Portuguese: "Planeamento de campos de refugiados no Quénia: Notas para futura pesquisa," *Espaços Vividos e Espaços Construidos* 1.6 (2017): 88–99.

6

DESIGNING EMERGENCY ARCHITECTURE

RAUL PANTALEO AND TAMASSOCIATI,
TRANSLATED BY ELISA DAINESE

Designing architecture in a refugee camp or a war zone means knowing how to combine ethics, aesthetics, and economy within the constraints of time. It also implies that architects should know how to give practical and rapid responses to emergency situations, while still questioning near-future scenarios for a better world. Our "frontier projects" in places of poverty and war start from a simple principle of justice and the assumption that living in a clean, well-designed, harmonious, and "beautiful" place helps us to imagine the future. This human right is independent from the place where it is applied; it is a matter of neither costs nor context, but of project culture. It is simply something that works better, because, I believe, there is no doubt that in a "beautiful" place one achieves a better quality of life. This is true in all parts of the world, in places of wealth and comfort and in places of the deepest despair.

The approach of TAMassociati is extremely practical and works within the broad scope of creating a "utopia"—a beautifully designed and well-kept building is a sign of hope in a place of degradation and poverty. This utopist point of view helps us consider a different future at a global scale by overcoming emergency through imagination.

It is precisely through imagination that architecture takes care of people. Indeed, recognizing symbolic elements and anchoring them to local cultures help to develop trust. For example, coral stone inserts, typical of traditional Port Sudan constructions, immediately created a sense of familiarity with the clinic we designed there.[1] However, when we discuss "beauty" as an aspect to define our humanitarian projects—such as those we carried out in areas afflicted by war and economic instability in Darfur, Sudan, Central Africa, Sierra Leone, Afghanistan, and Iraq—we always register great astonishment in our listeners, as if beauty is not a valuable quality in the context in which we operate.[2]

One should actually be surprised that it is not a consideration. Why should a war hospital not be beautiful? There is no rational reason and no practical justification. This is why for us beauty becomes an essential necessity, a question of justice, especially in places where it is totally absent.

However, "beauty" is a sneaky word. Nowadays, it is difficult to trace the initial meaning of the concept: its origin is from the Greek word *kalón*. The Greeks connected the beautiful and the good—in antiquity, beauty could not be separated from the notion of utility and service to the community. We therefore preferred to coin a new word and talk about *bellitudine*.[3]

Creating a new word allowed us to free beauty from age-old philosophical disquisitions. Our *bellitudine* is a dirty, imperfect concept that welcomes the harshness of life. It is a concept not possessing the ethereal distance of classical beauty; it simply means caring about the world, its details and proportions, loving people, and above all embracing the environment.

This is why in our frontier projects great importance is given to environmental issues—because a fairer and therefore more beautiful future starts from the possibility of intervening with cutting-edge criteria in terms of consumption and sustainability, even in the most remote places. This is a solid, practical, pragmatic and nonideological way of interpreting the theme of sustainable development, which we consider an essential right anchored to the place where it is implemented. Therefore, making ethical architecture in the most extreme conditions—war or poverty or natural disaster—means that we seek maximum energy and environmental efficiencies in a short time and with very limited resources. This results in a constant effort to simplify, which starts with the analysis of the context and its associated problems. The process reduces the superfluous elements, becoming the method and the paradigm of our design approach.

Ours is very practical work, so it is useful to present some examples of how our words and principles have become real through the buildings we design. In this chapter we will discuss four health facilities built for the Italian NGO Emergency in Darfur, Sudan, Afghanistan, and Iraq. The first two buildings we discuss are located in different areas in Sudan afflicted by very recent wars and, as in Darfur, regions that are still surrounded by strong social and political instability: the Pediatric Clinic of Nyala, capital of the state of South Darfur; and the Clinic of Port Sudan, in the northeast of the country. These small health facilities provide medical care and prevention for a population that still suffers from otherwise easily treatable diseases, but they are also, and above all, cultural experiments intended to develop a different approach to cooperation. Indeed, the ideas behind these buildings are generated from a very simple assumption: they are service structures for people who have the right, like those who live in the so-called developed countries, to be treated in welcoming, high quality, efficient, and (why not?) beautiful buildings.

The last two buildings presented in the chapter are located in areas of the world still engulfed in war: Afghanistan and Iraq. These two regions suffer from a common destiny of destruction and adversity. In Afghanistan we designed the new maternity block for the Anabah Hospital, which is a major hospital operated by the NGO Emergency in the Panjshir valley. We were called to Iraq, where Emergency has run surgical centers for the victims of wars since 1995, in 2014 to work in the refugee camps and build more "humane" clinics for them. Here too we tried to demonstrate how, even working within reduced budgets, we could repurpose the same resources already used in the prefabricated structures of the camps and create a recognizable and beautiful architecture capable of reconstructing the social fabric through its very presence. These small architectures are instrumental to what Gino Strada, physician, activist, and founder of Emergency, calls "humane reconstruction." In war not only are peoples' lives lost but also their artistic and architectural heritage, tearing apart the relationship between human beings and their dignity.

Pediatric Clinic, Nyala, Darfur, Sudan (2010)

We completed the Pediatric Clinic in 2010. The project is located in a particularly critical area of the country and of the African continent. Indeed, Nyala had been at the center of bloody clashes during a war that ended with peace agreements in 2006. The area is still today a place where instability and insecurity reign.

With our proposal we wanted to give voice to an idea of innovative and sustainable modernity for the city and the region of Darfur through the development of two key themes: the relationship between architectural continuity and comfort, and the relationship between architectural continuity and technological innovation.

Continuity and Comfort

The Pediatric Clinic in Nyala situates harmoniously within the local context and territory, thus conferring a sense of continuity to the area population, aided by a very limited environmental impact. The project developed as a very simple building around a huge *tabaldi* (the local name for the baobab tree). The clinic adopts settlement principles typical of sub-Saharan cultures, which minimize the façades exposed to the sun by opting for a hollow-space configuration in perfect harmony with traditional building systems.

The clinic proposes an architecture that seeks its contemporary appearance in the morphology of the place, in dialogue with—and integration with—the context. This is expressed through the use of "enclosed" walls that define and mark a precise and inviolable internal microcosm. The project investigates this topic, but, at the same time, its walls create passages that allow us to catch glimpses of the inside world. Indeed, the building forms a safe closure able to protect those who live there from the instability of the area. This enclosed space is also capable of opening up to the world by revealing its modernity to the city with respect and discretion, without disturbing the urban and local harmony.

The main roof employs a system commonly used in Sudan in the past, which consists of a lowered brick vault called *jagharsch* (from the Arabic word *harsch,* arch). This system is protected from direct sunlight by a higher, secondary roof in sheet metal, which, in addition to thermally insulating the *jagharsch* roof, creates a ventilated chamber between the two structures that keeps the temperature of the roof low.

The masonry of the walls is of great thickness; it is composed of two layers of locally produced bricks with an interposed ventilated chamber. This innovative choice allowed us to obtain a first level of environmental comfort, cooling down the heat flow that crosses the walls during the hottest hours of the day and allowing the building to reach the optimal environmental phase shift in around twelve to sixteen hours. Thus, the heat flow peak arises only in the coolest hours of the day (for example, if the peak is at two p.m., it enters the building between two and six a.m. the following day). Furthermore, the use of a massive envelope improves the overall comfort under the influence not only of external heat loads but also of internal ones. In fact, during the greatest indoor crowding, the massive walls contain the heat load of the clinic's internal surfaces thanks to their ability to absorb heat from within and without.

However, the simple use of this type of masonry was insufficient to guarantee complete environmental comfort. It was therefore necessary to limit the number of openings (and screen them from the outside) and seek adequate ventilation (natural and, where necessary, mechanical). The limited number of openings and their dimensions considerably reduced the direct solar gain during the day (fig. 6.1). Similarly, the application of shading systems on the façades transformed them into an integral part of thermal control. Important from the functional, cultural, and aesthetic points of view—because they were inspired by local weaving techniques—woven bamboo screens were placed to protect walkways and resting areas. This technique is inspired by the traditional system of making fences, especially in the refugee camps. An adequate ventilation allows the clinic to dissipate the heat that the massive envelope

FIGURE 6.1. Pediatric Clinic, Nyala, Darfur, Sudan, 2010. Showing the south façade with small openings and the *badger* (the chimney-like structure on the right side of the building). (TAMassociati and Raul Pantaleo)

FIGURE 6.2. Pediatric Clinic, Nyala, Darfur, Sudan, 2010. Main façade with the shading system. (TAMassociati and Raul Pantaleo)

accumulates during the day and that during the night tends to transfer to the internal environment. In this way, we obtained the double benefit of refreshing the indoors and cooling the walls (fig. 6.2).

This set of actions allowed us to reduce considerably the use of cooling systems and their cooling capacity in the clinic. These choices also supported an efficient exploitation of the resources available on site, thus limiting the costs of implementation. (We had a very limited budget.) The use of local materials and techniques also simplifies future maintenance and management.

Continuity and Technological Innovation

For long periods of the year in South Darfur, temperatures reach and often exceed 50°C (122°F), with a humidity level between 5 and 10 percent. Together with the dust generated by strong desert winds, these climatic factors made necessary a thorough study of specific cooling, insulating, and filtrating technologies. To mediate the climatic conditions, the project used technologies that reduce the energy consumption of the building to a minimum while taking into consideration the maximum living comfort of the structure.

This is why air recycling was achieved using a treatment method inspired by the *badgir*, the traditional natural ventilation system used in

Iran, which we integrated with a mechanical cooling system and the use of industrial evaporative coolers.[4] Similar to what happens in the traditional *badgir,* the eight-meter-high external chimneys capture the freshest air that the prevailing winds (from north to south) have cleaned, bringing it through a technical shaft that follows a labyrinthine path down to the basement of the building. In addition to slowing down the speed of the air, the impact against the walls of the labyrinth allows most of the sand and dust in the air to settle. This very simple system proved to be quite efficient and affordable. Furthermore, it requires almost no maintenance except for some occasional cleanings of the basement (see fig. 6.1).

In addition to this strategy, an adiabatic absorption system further intervenes on the air treatment. With the installation of two very simple air-cleaning machines similar to evaporative coolers, the project achieves a total absorption of 6KW for cooling and air exchange when operating at full capacity. This system allows a reduction of electric consumption used for air conditioning, which is estimated at about 70 percent. During various field-testing exercises, we were able to verify a temperature reduction of about 10°C even in the most critical conditions. For example, with an initial temperature at the ventilation tower of 38.7°C and a humidity rate of 21 percent, in the internal spaces destined for hospitalized patients we register a temperature of 28.4°C, a humidity of 44 percent, and a feeling of high comfort. Such a system represents an innovation for Sudan and for all sub-Saharan climate zones: the technology used is, above all, extremely simple and cheap to install.

The task of promoting health, beauty, and ecology in the same project is one of the challenges for Africa and the world of the new millennium. Growing a culture that cares about environmental rights could restore a future in countries where development has often been undermined and slowed down by the (in)discriminate exploitation of energy and natural resources. This objective is of even greater importance where the exploitation has generated excruciating and destructive civil wars with all the devastating resulting consequences.

Pediatric Clinic, Port Sudan, Sudan (2012)

The Pediatric Clinic is located in a suburban area of Port Sudan, a city of strategic importance for Sudan as its only access to the sea. In the last twenty years the area has experienced enormous demographic growth, from 30,000 inhabitants at the beginning of the millennium to almost 500,000 in 2007.[5] This exponential and dramatic growth has been caused by the development of the port, by the abandonment of the countryside triggered by increasingly frequent droughts, and, above all, by the huge numbers of refugees coming from various nearby conflict areas who have concentrated in the city. In particular, the Pediatric Clinic is located in the expansion area northwest of the port, in a large desert sector between two residential settlements of shacks and mud houses. Refugees scattered in the rest of Port Sudan have been rounded up and concentrated in this area; it is a sort of "new city" within the city. In this vast, impoverished sector, the clinic is one of the few health outposts providing basic care for local children.

In our design for the clinic, simplicity became a fundamental element to generate beauty. We focused on what could be useful and indispensable for the project without reducing our design to a set of poor or "technical" answers to practical needs. Claiming a return to a civic and uncynical design meant putting the theme of simplicity at the center of the project with the aim of achieving maximum results with minimum effort and costs. The project of the Pediatric Clinic of Port Sudan follows an approach that aims at providing essential, useful, and beautiful design to support important social aspirations. To achieve these results, we focused on three themes: the relationship between protection and sociability, the dialogue between materials and tradition, and the relation between traditional techniques and innovation.

Protection and Sociability: The Enclosure and the Garden

The single-story building developed from the idea of an enclosure with very few external openings that is structured around a succession of courtyards. In the project, the hierarchy between masses and voids was reversed in favor of the latter—to the point that the void represented by the central patio became the generating element of the project. The entrance to the clinic is dominated by a tree located at the center of the waiting area. This is a fundamental sign, an element of life in continuity with the outdoor garden. The interiors are characterized by a strong control of direct sun radiations, which was implemented by limiting the exposed openings and shielding them with natural-fiber panels. These design techniques physically isolate the spaces in the hospital from the oppressive external heat. The internal spaces become fresh and protected places illuminated by zenithal light chimneys that also evacuate the latent heat, especially in the common areas. This is also a way to rethink and repurpose the atmospheres and architectural types of the traditional Arab way of living.

The project was also envisioned to create a center of social revitalization for the nearby neighborhoods. The square/garden at the entrance side of the building hosts activities for adults, while the public park on the east side creates a garden for children to play and a small field for sports activities where the community can come together to share fun moments of various kinds. We could define this area a "pediatric garden" where the green—irrigated by wastewater and the purification system— represents the true social catalyst of the whole area but is also an element of care in itself. In the physical and human desert of the surrounding neighborhoods, the garden represents a vision of a better future that acquires a very strong, symbolic value because it is a prelude of the care that will come.

Materials and Tradition

We wanted to create a building made entirely of bricks produced in local furnaces and thereby support local economies. Thus, we used the already tested and applied construction system (ventilated, hollow walls and *jagharsch* ceilings) that had been used in the project for the Pediatric Clinic of Nyala, described above.

For the design of the main façade, we diversified the materials by inserting sections of coral stone, one of the common traditional building materials in the area. This material is deeply rooted in the local culture and can be reclaimed across the whole area of Port Sudan, where abandoned piles of rubble are left from the demolition of old buildings. The whole city was in fact built with coral stone, which is now no longer available but was once the only building material available along the entire coast.[6] By using this material, the construction site became a laboratory of restoration and memory recovery, where one could remember the roots and beauty of the place.

Further elements that characterize the main façade are the wooden sunshades, whose design was inspired by late colonial buildings and which evoke another legacy of the Ottoman Empire. The typical wooden

FIGURE 6.3. Pediatric Clinic, Port Sudan, Sudan, 2012. The clinic in its dusty context. On the right are the locally sourced natural-fiber shading panels that form part of the building envelope. (TAMassociati and Massimo Grimaldi)

shutters were in fact common at that time and were designed so that women could observe street activities without being seen. These shields, called *mashrabiya,* protect from direct sunlight and act as thermal mechanisms for shading and ventilation. They are perfect, simple, and effective architectural elements (fig. 6.3).

It was not easy to revive and bring these elements back to life, although they identified a distinctive character that could be found in the Ottoman world, from the Balkans to Africa. Our greatest difficulty was reintroducing these practices in a place where past knowledge has been lost in favor of an empty technicality and the myth of modernity.

Traditional Techniques and Innovation

From an engineering point of view, we wanted to build a clinic able to meet the needs of comfort and hygiene required by the clients while taking advantage of the experiences already gained in Nyala, where we had created simple systems representing a compromise between traditional and innovative techniques. In this case, the building was conceived as a passive envelope, using hollow ventilation systems for its walls and roofs and a protective skin that would shelter it from direct sunlight. The cooling and ventilation system of this structure was implemented by enforcing adiabatic and filtration techniques similar to those successfully developed in Darfur.

As stated in the report of the mechanical engineer who collaborated on the project: "We tried to work on the fluid dynamic efficiency of air distribution and verify the effective performance of the adiabatic cooling system in the climate of Port Sudan. There the capacity of an adiabatic system is usually strongly limited by external conditions very close to the saturation curve, which cools the air less. In order to obtain for this system a minimum, acceptable value of cooling capacity, it was necessary to correctly size the air flow in the two air-handling units. Adiabatic systems are necessarily all-air outdoor systems (given the need to guarantee a continuous supply of water to the air being treated), a condition not at all unfavorable in hospital environments."[7]

If designing also means accepting new challenges, this time the choice was even more radical. We attempted to demonstrate that quality, functionality, energy efficiency, and (why not?) beauty do not necessarily have to be economically and technologically demanding choices.

Refugee Camp, Sulaymaniyah, Iraq (2015–2017)

In 2014 Emergency was called to intervene in the refugee camps of the province of Sulaymaniyah in Iraqi Kurdistan. The goal was to bring "human reconstruction" and health centers to those areas that we could define as real emergency citadels. A few kilometers distant from the war, between Sulaymaniyah and Khanaqin, the survivors of the Syrian butchery gathered. It was the "all against all" battle that transformed Syria and Iraq into places where the only possible choice was to escape. Thus, thousands of people sought refuge in Europe, which has proved to be less and less hospitable, while the most desperate and poor have found refuge in the neighboring areas, such as the city of Sulaymaniyah in Iraq.

The clinic that we discuss below was the first of a series of five clinics.[8] It was built in the camp of Arbat, located near the city of Sulaymaniyah. The challenge of the project was to use the same standard, prefabricated modules used in the refugee camp and normally used for this kind of clinic. Our project was completed using the same number of modules in prefabricated sandwich panels, with the same finishes and at the same cost. We entered into the processes of design for refugee camps by trying to prove that with those budgets, those space-time limitations, those materials and elements, we could still generate humane places. One element we used, the color red—which is very recognizable and also delineates the NGO Emergency—created welcoming spaces, gave our buildings an identity, and transformed architecture into a recognizable landmark. On this occasion we demonstrated how it is possible in the face of an emergency to put at the center of a project not only its functionality but also the right of people to be treated in beautiful places. It was a difficult challenge, accomplished in a context in which the cold, technical accounting of the emergency had usually prevailed, as if the refugees were numbers and not people. A first demonstration of the success of our approach was the fact that our clinic became a standard reference model proposed by the Kurdish-Iraqi Ministry of Health. The project defeated the logic that usually builds the refugee camps and that often makes them resemble concentration camps rather than temporary cities. The real challenge was to start our design by thinking about people and not the emergency. For us this meant insisting on a particular principle: architecture can make a difference within war dynamics usually dominated by the immediacy of the needs arising from the emergency. Architecture is an integral part of the psychological healing process: a well-designed and beautiful place can produce a very strong feeling of relief even among suffering people.

Maternity Center, Anabah, Afghanistan (2015)

Beginning in 2003, Emergency has operated a maternity center within the Anabah War Surgery Center in Afghanistan to offer specialized assistance in obstetrics, gynecology, and neonatology. In light of the gradual increase in the gynecological and neonatal activities of the maternity center and the growing needs of the local population, in 2015 work began on the construction of a new building that would allow up to seven thousand deliveries per year and which saw us involved as designers.

In the Panjshir valley, we found small villages of mud houses. It is an architecture that merges with the colors of the landscape—mimetic, docile, and formed by buildings slowly reabsorbed by time without leaving a trace. The project of the new maternity block fell into this delicate context as a bridge between contemporary architecture and tradition, but it was also a sign of continuity and renewal. Designing its spaces required immersion in this complex and archaic culture, and it was difficult to work out a delicate balance between respect for the place and the needs of a modern maternity block (fig. 6.4).

The new maternity center represents a hope for the future, both in the services it offers and in its architecture. While searching for a dialogue with the preexisting hospital, the new intervention marks a break by forwarding a message of modernity and beauty. Our compositional choices were characterized by a certain lightness, a joyful and playful language. The front is marked by windows of different sizes and varied positions, as if they could evoke a group of children playing. In continuity with other projects that we carried out, the building is also characterized by a strong anthropomorphism. Indeed, we wanted its form and shape to evoke a face. This was extremely important in the maternity center, where friendly architecture can challenge the inability of a region marked by poverty to welcome the joy of an extraordinary moment like birth.

FIGURE 6.4. Maternity Center, Anabah, Afghanistan, 2015. The building meshes with the mountains in the background. (TAMassociati)

The result of this experiment is a project capable of reconciling the need to achieve high technological standards with the principles of simplicity, beauty, and eco-sustainability.

Conclusion

We are convinced—and we trust that we have shown it with these few examples—that even in an emergency situation it is possible to have the courage to talk about beauty. It is this quality that makes the difference in a humanitarian project and triggers the imagination of a better tomorrow.

Our projects are very concrete utopias. They provide new trees in a desert refugee camp, a colored wall in the abandonment of Port Sudan, a clean building in the degradation of Darfur—places of peace amid the din of war. Their presence translates into strategic actions able to help populations that suffer or have suffered injustice to get beyond the brief vision of the emergency. The beauty we have sought in our work is solid and does not follow the latest fashion. It speaks of permanence, it is made to last, and it abhors the ephemeral. Our architecture is well rooted— with its feet on the ground and with an eye to tradition—but it is, and always will be, facing the future. Our response to emergency has become an opportunity to rethink architecture in an unconventional way through the design of places where the right to beauty is exercised by combining functionality, design, utility, and grace.

Notes

1. For more on this topic see the section entitled "Pediatric Clinic, Port Sudan, Sudan (2012)."
2. For the work of the NGO Emergency, see "Who We Are," accessed June 15, 2021, https://en.emergency.it/who-we-are/organization/.
3. From the Italian words *bellezza* (beauty) and *attitudine* (inclination).
4. The *badgir*, or wind tower, captures the air, channels it to the inhabited areas, and cools rooms through evaporation and convection.
5. The data has been confirmed by local experts.
6. A similar situation can be found in the archaeological site of Suakin, a few kilometers away from the area. Historically, Port Sudan played a crucial role in the trade and cultural developments of the region. Even from an architectural perspective, its golden age began in the early sixteenth century when

its port was conquered by Sultan Selim I. The city remained under Ottoman domination until the mid-nineteenth century.
7. Marco Paissan, technical report, Pediatric Clinic, Port Sudan, Sudan (internal report, 2012).
8. TAMassociati also designed clinics in the refugee camps of Arbat and Quoratu in Iraq.

7

TEACHING CULTURALLY SENSITIVE DESIGN

ALEKSANDAR STANIČIĆ, INTERVIEW WITH AZRA AKŠAMIJA

This chapter reflects on the pedagogical and research methods developed by Assoc. Prof. Azra Akšamija from the MIT Department of Architecture in her trailblazing course Culturally Sensitive Design, taught in the spring semester of 2017–18 academic year. The course was one in a series of five courses that Akšamija conducted that were focused on the context of refugee camps in Jordan. Culturally Sensitive Design concerned the Al Azraq Refugee Camp, built in 2014 for refugees of the Syrian Civil War. The camp was developed by the United Nations High Commissioner for Refugees (UNHCR) in conjunction with the government of Jordan, and it currently hosts around fifty thousand refugees from Syria. Unable to return to their home country under the rule of Bashar al-Assad, and not being allowed to take roots on Jordanian soil—or to integrate into Jordanian society—refugees at the camps resort to artistic production as a way to preserve their culture and make political statements denouncing their unenviable position.

The introduction to the course begins with the following lines: "Culturally Sensitive Design introduces a cross-disciplinary and inclusive model for education and civic innovation through the lens of art and design, with a focus on creative responses to conflict and crisis."[1] From this starting point, the students develop their own design models for (artistic and architectural) interventions that aim at enhancing intercultural collaborations and the quality of life in the camp. The course echoes noble efforts of the Future Heritage Lab, also led by Professor Akšamija, to "develop and implement projects and alternative educational formats at the intersection of art, culture, and technology to address the emotional, cultural, and practical needs of communities in threat."[2] Professor Akšamija kindly invited me to participate in the course as a guest critic, so I had the pleasure of witnessing in person some of her students' work and spirited discussions that inspired the projects. This chapter highlights pedagogical methodologies and comments on the projected impact of these experimental approaches, while also touching on some larger issues in the field of postwar art and architectural production. The applied form of an interview-article gives an adequate format for an expanded discussion in which the actual transcript of the interview is supplemented with additional comments, references, and explanations.[3] The chapter can be also read as continuation of many dialogues Azra Akšamija and I had during the course, which have continued ever since.

Art as a Bridge between Cultures

The course on Culturally Sensitive Design recognizes and tackles an alarming phenomenon emerging in the most recent world conflicts: the purposeful and calculated destruction of art and architecture of "others," as András Riedlmayer defines it.[4] From former Yugoslavia to Iraq and Syria, this destruction has served as an efficient weapon of alienation. Its main purpose has been the revision of cultural memory and the ultimate fragmentation of social connections among people of different ethnic and cultural backgrounds who share a specific territory. The result is the "homogenization" of both the societal fabric and related spatial features. Targeting places that constitute cultural identity and a sense of collective belonging—such as religious buildings, national museums, and libraries—has caused irreparable trauma and outrage among citizens who are the direct victims of such violence. The erasure of shared pasts that do not fit within new nationalist narratives has become the crucial factor in the creation of homogeneous nation-states. The ultimate confirmation that art serves as a bridge between cultures—if we ever needed one—therefore came from an unlikely source: the "barbaric minds of city-haters."[5]

Beginning with this realization, the key premise of the Culturally Sensitive Design course led by Akšamija was that art can be used as a counter-weapon of war in the complex processes of postwar reconciliation. The hypothesis that served as a starting point for the course was that rebuilding transcultural relations would ultimately lead to the incremental expansion of social tolerance thresholds. Compelling examples from the Al Azraq Refugee Camp in Jordan show that culture is an essential human need and that the fight for preservation of traditions and culture equals the fight for physical survival. Cultural production has not only a therapeutic effect in dealing with destruction and trauma, but the aesthetics of it also engenders a sense of pride and high morale in difficult times. The question with which we ought to start, then, is,

ALEKSANDAR STANIČIĆ: What exactly is the agency of cultural heritage in war and postwar contexts?

AZRA AKŠAMIJA: The motivation for a lot of my work, in which—in the broadest sense—this course is also part of, is the meaning of cultural heritage that I came to understand through the wars in Yugoslavia, but it can also be seen on a larger scale in the iconoclasm and cultural destructions that are happening right now in the Middle East. As you know, during the war that accompanied the breakup of Yugoslavia, particularly in Bosnia between 1992 and 1995, cultural heritage was systematically targeted.[6] Building on the work of András Riedlmayer, I have done extensive research on this subject, looking on the one hand at the quantity [of destruction], but also qualifying the way culture was destroyed.[7] To give you a broader picture: in Bosnia, for example, over two thousand religious monuments, mosques, synagogues, and churches (both Catholic and Orthodox) were demolished. However, the numbers [of targeted sites] are very different, so you have approximately fourteen hundred mosques and approximately two hundred churches—mostly Catholic churches—destroyed. Depending on the area and what kind of battles were fought there, cultural heritage and signifiers of ethnic and religious identity were specifically targeted.

This destruction went beyond mere identifiers of one ethnic group's presence; it was also about destroying history and any evidence that one particular group was living in a certain area. Therefore libraries, archives, and even cemeteries were destroyed—the graveyards were dug out and moved to other locations. In my qualitative analysis of the destruction, I realized that there was something that went beyond the mere removal of traces of cohabitation: the genocidal nature of this destruction had a certain sadistic component, and I asked myself why. The way, for example, architecture was destroyed invoked certain cultural taboos: houses of worship were destroyed on religious holidays to intensify the destruction and the experience of destruction in the eyes of the affected community. Those who were destroying were celebrating the destruction. On the other hand, the experience of suffering for those who were affected was intensified through public executions of their religious leaders, such as imams, which sometimes happened on top of religious buildings. I argue that this type of violence was meant to antagonize people to the extent that they would never want to live together in the future. These strategies not only aimed to erase history; they were also planned to prevent the possibility of future coexistence.

When we zoom out and look at this broader picture, we realize that those who destroyed cultural heritage [sites] were not simply following orders—they really understood cultural symbols as an embodiment of those who were targeted for erasure, almost as if architecture is not just a symbol but really the personification of the enemy. Both perpetrators and survivors share the same understanding—many people tend to take on this discourse and identify themselves with those buildings that represent them. Similarly, in the process of reconstruction, the first thing that people restore is not a house but a mosque or a church as a statement: "We have survived as a collective; we are coming back; you didn't manage to destroy us." That process, of course, points at a number of different issues: questions of identity, coming to terms with trauma, and the memory of a violent past. Also, nationalisms are resurgent, while certain political agendas are also playing a role in the way these buildings and reconstruction processes are shaped.

For me, the answer to the question "Why was this heritage destroyed?" was among the biggest lessons I learned from the Balkans. From here comes the idea of architecture as a bridge between cultures. When you look at these destructions of architecture in Bosnia, it was an attempt to erase the fact that in every little Bosnian town and village you have a church and a mosque standing next to each other. What was targeted were mainly those sites that provide a testimony of how people managed to live together, as neighbors, for centuries. Maybe this coexistence was not always peaceful, but the extent of destruction was unprecedented. Culture has tremendous power both as (in this case) evidence of coexistence, but also as a medium to shape this coexistence. In the whole region of the Balkans the different ethnic groups have learned from each other for centuries. You have mosques whose minarets look like church towers (especially in Herzegovina); there are carpets in Orthodox churches similar to those in mosques; you have Islamic geometry in synagogues—which points at the rich history of transcultural cross-fertilization. The craftsmen who were traveling around and executing these different buildings were also exchanging knowledge from one cultural context to another. At least in the place I come from, that is, Sarajevo, we have celebrated all religious and cultural holidays and cultivated respect for difference. While everyone lived their lives according to their own tradition, people were intermingling, intermarrying, and respecting everyone else's customs. That I think is really something beautiful and I hope not fully destroyed in Bosnia.

I think it is important to state that "culture," in the way I use the term, is inherently hybrid and [a fusion of traditions and customs]. There is no such thing as one "pure" culture; I think that every civilization learns, evolves, and builds on top of the knowledge of preexisting people. We see that all across the world. Culture is inherently hybrid and our identities are multilayered, complex, multidimensional. This opinion stands in contrast to those claims that nationalists make, seeking to portray cultures as homogenous and a response to certain parameters that they set, which are usually defined by a certain historical moment, often identified as the birth of a nation and/or its golden age.

Production of Future Heritage

Postwar shutdown of (trans)cultural institutions and the suppression of free and critical artistic production contributes to singular nationalistic narratives and the building of nation-states. Instead of reconciliation through culture, what usually happens after the war is the creation of new cultural memories at the perimeters of political processes. Independent, free-thinking artists and architects are, however, excluded from these developments. The best examples are ideological and openly biased museums (often privately funded or dark-funded), which are, essentially, state-making projects. By telling the one-sided and often fabricated (hi)stories of only a small part of the population, such projects purposefully deny the possibility for transcultural collaborations, hence serving as a powerful weapon in the frozen conflict that stretches long into seemingly peaceful times.[8]

The goal of the course Culturally Sensitive Design reflects the mission of the Future Heritage Lab, which is to give power back to cultural and artistic productions by using the arts as a tool of postconflict cultural dialogue. During the course students were encouraged to (re)interpret the refugee-led design found at the Al Azraq Refugee Camp through the lens of their own cultural background (figs. 7.1 and 7.2). By learning from the Syrian refugees, students got the chance to participate in a creative process that literally and symbolically transcends (cultural) borders to critique the architectural limitations of the refugee camp, such as the inadequacy of offered housing solutions and necessary infrastructure, made worse by a construction/adaptation ban.

The success of such approach is already validated in Azra's past art projects, such as the "Museum Solidarity Lobby," the "Future Heritage Collection," and the "Cultureshutdown" initiative, which are all powerful statements against the oppression and weaponization of culture, and hence share a borderline with social activism.[9] However, the goal of the course, producing future heritage artifacts, can also lead to a treacherous path, since, as mentioned previously, every production of cultural memory or heritage can be ultimately considered a political project.

AS: How can we ensure that the intended message is transmitted and prevent the hijacking of art for the wrong purposes? To what extent can we actually design the experience of heritage and control the political messages it sends?

AA: To link back to the previous examples from Bosnia, we have seen that what came after the war was a kind of competition for the space of identity and how that has been framed and produced architecturally and culturally. We see this battle and conflict continuing through instrumentalization of language, music, clothing, architecture—everything basically. One danger—and this is again something I learned from Bosnia—is that in that process of restoring, especially if we are not critically reflecting but just trying to

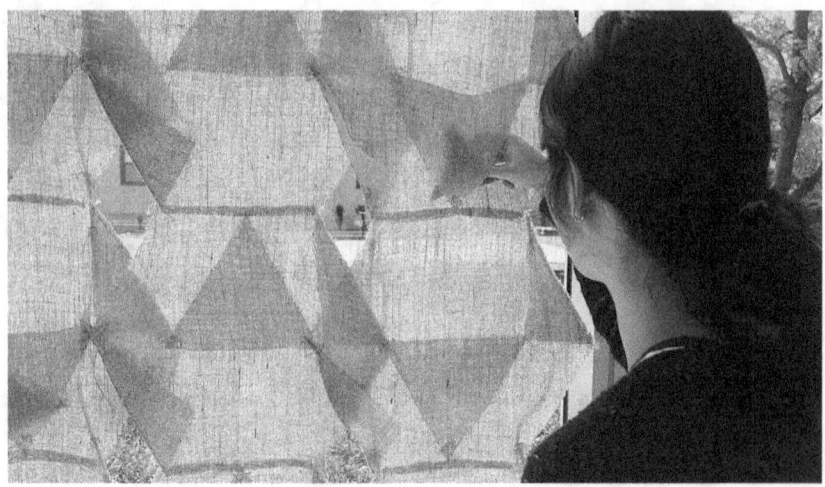

FIGURES 7.1 AND 7.2. A prototype for multiuse food packaging for humanitarian aid by Catherine Lie and Marcas Smith. Individual rice bags, made of burlap, can be disassembled and reassembled to create modular shading and privacy fabrics. (Images courtesy of Catherine Lie)

"replace" or "reinvent" ourselves, the danger is to homogenize or flatten those multilayered complexities of history mentioned before. You see that in the very vulgar and aggressive type of postwar architecture built all around the Balkans and specifically in Bosnia. In these places, and especially where the most destruction happened, people rushed to reconstruct—just look at Mostar and the competition of church towers and minarets happening there. This competition for visual dominance over a territory is signifying of that flat and narrow idea of history, producing along the way finite erasure of the multicultural nature of the city.

In my pedagogy I start by first explaining the importance of cultural memory in the context of conflict and crisis, and then I move to the critical role the preservation of cultural heritage can have (figs. 7.3 and 7.4). Students look at different examples and different approaches to preservation, from those practices that are maybe considered traditional and fixed through international codes to transcultural approaches, meaning strategies to preservation that may vary in different contexts. Look, for example, at the Japanese Shinto temples that are being "reconstructed" by being taken apart and reassembled, and it is that process of restoring that constitutes the memory of that place. Compare that to the places where material preservation itself matters immensely, and we see the heavyweight debate around them, specifically in the context of Palmyra, where people are now fetishizing the ruins themselves, even though that very place has been the palimpsest of different building and rebuilding iterations throughout history. For me the prevalent questions are, What segment of history do we choose to restore and reconstruct? What are the parameters on which we base those decisions? These are really the fundamental questions. And then: Who is involved? Who makes these decisions? Who is the expert? Who is included and excluded? For instance, in class we discussed the example of Cecilia Giménez—the painter from Spain who restored a fresco in the Sanctuary of Mercy church in Borja near Zaragoza.[10] She found herself to be an expert, even if she is a painter. The Sanctuary is her church, and she wanted to restore something that is very dear to her and her community. While her preservationist effort was mocked and laughed at by the international media, her restored fresco became a globally known internet meme. I see the value of it as a critical act of preservation.

I am taking an investigative and maybe deconstructivist approach to these questions to understand how to transmit critical thinking about cultural heritage to the students: not simply to give my opinion but to have the students think about these processes. In the production of "Future Heritage," we came to ask these questions: "As a student you have to think about what is being restored. To what

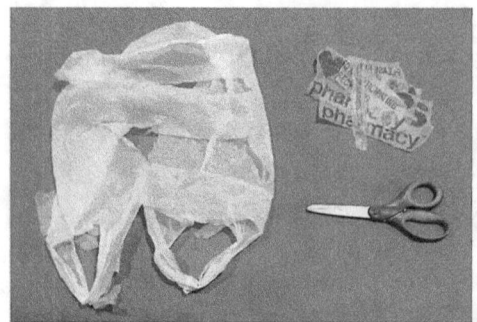
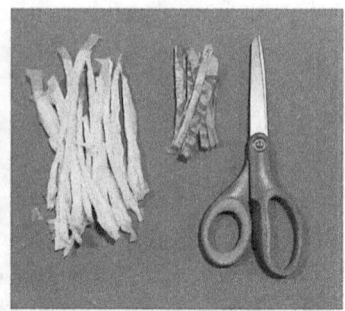

FIGURES 7.3 AND 7.4. Inspired by decorative geometric tiles from the Azm Palace, an eighteenth-century palace that is now a museum in Damascus, Syria, Ellen O'Connell created a prototype for a "displaced Azm Museum" in Al Azraq Camp. The individual marble tiles of the palace are recreated in collaborative workshops by melting colored plastic bags. (Images courtesy of Ellen O'Connell)

end? Who benefits from it?" Then the process is also about reinterpretation: interpretation is a creative, critical act. A new story is being created. How far we take this innovation depends on the creativity of the student and what message is intended. For example, right now [2019] we are working with displaced Syrians in refugee camps in Jordan on a project that creates a cultural space by combining references from nomadic tents with the history of palatial architecture. Those range from the Azm Palace in Damascus to the Doge's Palace in Venice, because I would like them to investigate not only Islamic historical influences but also Byzantine cultures, while also pointing at the need for civic spaces. The assignment is not about creating a copy of a historical precedent but about the cultural needs of refugees and a possibility of creating civic spaces within the context of containment. We test this possibility by creating mobile architectural forms out of recycled clothing, so there are different materials that embody the memories of the many people who wore them, and their formal reference is to these historical buildings. At the same time, the materials point at the environmental and social costs of our consumer lifestyle, costs that are carried by those who are excluded from that way of living. The students and other project participants are telling their own story through the selection and creative translation of their references. The whole course is about the narration of that shared knowledge and the transmission of knowledge from one region to another.

AS: In pedagogies that revolve around design and creativity, sometimes it is more about the process of design, how you unpack and repack things, than the final product (fig. 7.5). This has everything to do with the deficiencies of design evaluation—the success of intermediate mini-tasks can be quantified and objectively measured, but the aesthetic assessment of the design itself cannot be done without a dose of subjectivity. Also, a shared concern among students and professors alike is that the approach to these topics inside the protected environment of a students' design studio is not realistic, is somehow less rigorous than it would have been in an actual (artistic or architectural) production in the so-called real world. This is practically inevitable because students' final products are deprived of the limiting factors typically associated with actual realization and implementation of design projects. Do you see those two processes

FIGURE 7.5. Beside individual projects, the students collaborated on a project called "Digital Muqarnas." Learning about Islamic geometry involved an academic exchange with Prof. Mohammad Yaghan from German-Jordanian University in Amman, Jordan. (Image courtesy of Azra Akšamija)

[i.e., pedagogical versus professional] differently, or do you think that they are essentially part of the same method?

AA: I think that both methods are important—both the processes of creating and the outcome itself. Sometimes I have to adjust the course to the type of participants and the duration of the class, especially because we are working remotely and hence are unable to implement things immediately, so a lot of these works develop in phases. For example, the research about the refugee camp was carried out by one class, another one continued it, the third developed the idea for the "Code of Ethics," the forth one developed the idea for the mobile cultural space, et cetera. Thus, things are being prototyped and discussed; each class builds on each other in the hope that someday these ideas will be implemented by (or in collaboration with) refugees "on the ground." It is important that, at the end, you get good results, which, of course, also depend on the parameters that are set at the beginning. On the one hand, I use art and design as a vehicle to investigate and discuss certain problems; on the other hand, I consider design itself and the act of creation and craftsmanship to be a form of thinking and a statement. Sometimes, of course, design projects could be better developed, but we have only three months to really articulate a certain idea, so it is not that much time for introducing students who, oftentimes, have never done any kind of design work. Therefore, the results are very different based on the entry level of students. At MIT students from different disciplinary backgrounds are allowed to choose courses they like. Usually my students are artists, architects, mechanical engineers, some urban planners, even mathematicians, and now and then business school students. Some are highly skilled in craftsmanship, others not at all, and usually this is an issue (fig. 7.6). Similarly, in the refugee camps we prototype certain ideas with both camp residents and students and test what works and what doesn't. We use this mode in both thinking and in the act of creation. On the other hand, in the refugee camp there is a different kind of dynamic—I don't want to come to this context as a "white savior" trying to teach the residents something at any cost. There, this pedagogy works more as a form of knowledge exchange. Creative work becomes a way of generating meaning and dignity in the context of an absolute battle

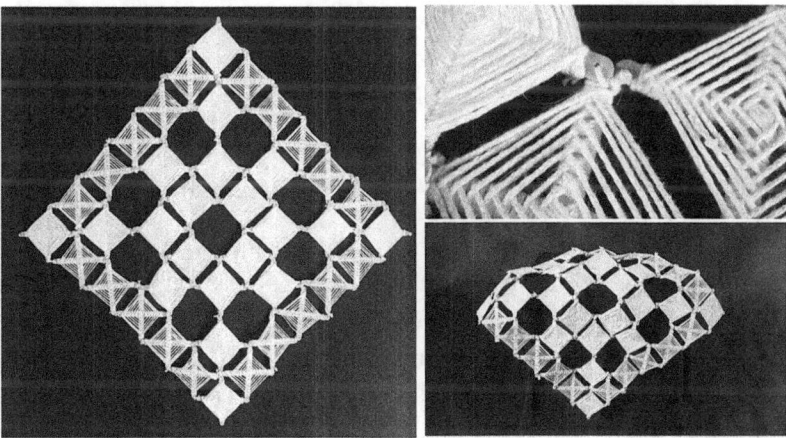

FIGURE 7.6. Erika Anderson created a modular system of "woven tiles" made of recycled plastic bottles and yarn scraps. Small pieces created by individuals can be connected into a collective fabric. The collaborative process is meant to foster social cohesion and relationships. (Image courtesy of Erika Anderson)

for survival and overcoming the dehumanizing aspects of humanitarian design. I try to organize the classes in the camp differently so that we always have a group of host community students, different people from the camp, different age groups, and also international people—sometimes those are my students, sometimes people who are simply there in Jordan, but always from different backgrounds. In this very diverse context, everyone has something to contribute and people are learning from each other even if it doesn't mean that there is necessarily an expertise in certain technical skills, or it could be just that you are an expert in your own life. For example, you may be an expert in living and surviving in the camp, and we can learn from that. These different audiences within the same course supposedly function in both contexts; their work just has different application.

In 2018 the main assignment of the Culturally Sensitive Design course at MIT included the design of a carpet (ground), ceiling, and seating. Students could choose between these areas and ask themselves: How do we sit? On the one hand, they learned that you can maybe sit differently; however, they also learned as students in the US about the context of absolute scarcity. If they want to design something here, at MIT, it is easy to laser-cut it at school. However, you don't have laser-cutters in the camp. You don't even have any material, so you have to create it out of trash. The attempt to make something and to fail doing so teaches students a lot: How is it possible to actually do anything in the context of the refugee camp?

Code of Ethics/Ethics of Intervention

One issue that came up a lot in the course was the question of interpretation: What does "heritage" actually mean? It was very interesting to observe how students from different cultural backgrounds reacted to the specific setting of the refugee camp and how they all tried to incorporate parts of their own culture into design solutions, constantly translating and rethinking this mixture of different influences. Something else that was often brought up in our discussions was the question of cultural appropriation: Who owns the art? Who benefits from it? We also examined the engagement of the international community, large companies, and nongovernmental organizations as well as MIT's interest in the topic and its ethical role in these processes.

This inevitably leads us to the question of ethics, which is one of the most complex and multilayered questions in postwar architectural and artistic production. Even the abstract and free interpretation of art forms can trigger the question of cultural appropriation. Defining the elusive essence of what constitutes one's culture is a difficult task, best seen in the constantly contested work of architectural preservationists. It is practically impossible to make an intervention in space or create an art project without asking: What is (un)ethical about it? How does it engage with the community? Who benefits from the intervention and at whose expense?

Students in Akšamija's course tried to answer these questions by responding to the "Code of Ethics" questionnaire. Through the analysis of given or selected works of art, they had to extrapolate what is, in their own view, (un)ethical about those projects. The key points, as stated in questionnaire, were as follows:

a. *Example of a cultural intervention.* Provide an example giving insights into ethical concern.
b. *Ethical considerations.* Extract 3 questions from your example (Is it ethical to . . . ? Who benefits from . . . ? How might we . . . ?)
c. *Lesson learned.* What have I learned for my practice?[11]

Curiously taking part in this exercise, I chose one example I know really well, the *Memorial in Exile,* in Stratford, London.[12] However, I found it very difficult to give straightforward answers. The discussion that followed within the class revealed some (to me, at least) unknown concepts, such as *"zekat"* (in the Muslim world, giving alms without acknowledgement), and led to some deep philosophical questions: "Am I doing good only if my work is being recognized?" Or "Is there a selfless good deed?" To complicate things even further, we rightfully asked ourselves about the ethics of the code of ethics: Who are we to impose our code of ethics upon others' system of values?

On its website the Future Heritage Lab offers some short universal guidelines about personal behavior, communication inside the community, issues of education and economy, and finally art and design in culturally sensitive environments.[13] However, the dilemma remains.

AS: Will the "Code of Ethics" ever be able to give definite answers to these complex questions on ethics and its relation to design?

AA: The "Code of Ethics" project evolved out of our frustration with the ongoing situation, but also from learning different lessons and realizing our own biases in the process of entering these spaces such as refugee camps. I felt there was a need to self-reflect and share some of those dilemmas and experiences with others who also would like to work and contribute to alleviate some of people's needs in the context of conflict and crisis. Initially we thought that it would have been beneficial to come up with a set of guidelines that we could share in order to inform design policy. Soon I learned that this, of course, is not possible because ethics vary in different cultural contexts—what is customary in one place cannot with certainty be accepted in another. Instead, the first step should be to create awareness around ethics. So far, the code functions really well as a critical and pedagogical tool. I use it effectively in classes—students fill out a form, and in doing so ask critical questions and evaluate or reflect upon ethics versus esthetics in socially engaged art and design projects. On the other hand, we are trying to establish a broader ethical platform that would function online. We use the "Code of Ethics" in a series of events in different places. For example, at the Amman Design Week there was a curated dinner table where the code was written and rewritten on the tablecloth.[14] In this way, we created a temporary moment of reflection.

The project acknowledges that there is no singular ethical perspective—hence, its title [originally had] a question mark at the end ("Code of Ethics?"). The proposal seeks to raise awareness of and broaden the scope of questions that need to be asked and that people need to be aware of. It also aims to share the "Code of Ethics" across different disciplines. In my career, I've seen a lot of situations in the refugee camps where artists are the ones who need to demonstrate sensibility. For example, when someone is taking a picture of the refugees, the question we should ask is, What is the endgame here? That's maybe not problematic to some people who seek to raise awareness about the needs of children, but in my eyes, as an artist, it is like: "Oh my God, am I potentially using this child to promote my cause?" Similar thinking applies the other way around: artists often use these contexts to promote and gain social capital around their own projects, and that would be unethical in the context of humanitarian aid and of the community itself. It is a very difficult sphere to navigate; my goal here is not to come up with one ethical guideline that fits everything, but to use my skill as an artist to inspire people to have these difficult conversations, create this bridge between disciplines, so we can learn from each other and reflect, raise awareness that these questions exist, know what should be asked, and also question our own actions. One acknowledgement here is what I learned through the iteration of this process: when you work in the humanitarian context, you always have one foot in the dirt, so to say, because we all bring our own biases; by not being refugees, we come from a privileged position. (We can leave the camp anytime and people in the camp cannot.) But then I ask myself: "Shall I do nothing? Shall I just sit in my own bubble and not use my resources to help?"

When it comes to production of artifacts, I try to find a multidimensional format that works for me as an artist. For example, with my current class, I am working on the prototypes for the T-Serai project, a portable palace inspired by tent traditions of the MENA region made out of recycled textiles. My artwork gives the overall framing and the concept of this project—the idea of the portable palace called the T-Serai—through modular tapestries as one type of generative design. However, it is a participatory project, which has different dimensions. One dimension is educational: vocational training in the camp where people can learn sewing, for example. Then there is creative expression, creating tapestries just to create something and feel like a human being, or simply to spend time productively. Then there is a component of preserving living cultural practices with this process: where a grandmother can teach a kid to embroider certain cultural patterns and also teach me about it along the way. The same project, which is also the art project that I have created and exhibited in the Sharjah Museum of Islamic Civilization, thus has different meanings and is made fully different in the context of the camp. I don't claim the one that is made in the camp as my own artwork, but I use the one that I created for the museum in Sharjah to commission refugee designers in the camp to create their own work. In addition, if local people create their own tapestries, those will belong to them, as they are their own artifacts.

Who Owns the Art?

AS: A question related to the one on ethics is, Who owns the art? Or better yet, Who has the right to make financial profit out of it? Is it ethical to monetize cultural practices to ensure survival of people/culture/art? If we put aside for a moment the academic and educational aspect of small-scale initiatives that do not have immediate or long-term impact on the ground, the interest of big players becomes painfully obvious. International institutions such as UNESCO and the World Bank have more global agendas, which make them not shy about self-promotion, while local stakeholders often seek short-term (and short-sighted) financial gains at the expense of underprivileged and/or oppressed refugee communities.

How the projects are financed reveals all the complexity of the power-plays between international and local actors, each of them claiming the right to financially exploit local cultural production. Who, then, has the agency to decide who owns the culture?

AA: Coming from a privileged position can be really problematic; one needs to be really sensitive on how to approach this context. I think we should first acknowledge and then use our privilege, of course, as we cannot change the world fully from scratch, but we need to be fully aware of our own biases and the problems that come with our own fundraising campaigns. We need to understand what it means to be involved and who actually benefits at the end from what we do. This is also a very difficult question in the art context, as artists do not usually constitute NGOs or humanitarian organizations, me included. Art should not be measured by the parameters of impact of the humanitarian work. Indeed, it is impossible to qualify and quantify the impact that making something can have on a person, or how it can put a smile on his/her face for one day, or in some ways validate that same person as a human being in this context of imprisonment in which people are completely dehumanized and patronized. Cultural interventions are hard things to measure, so to say, using the same criteria as the impact of other disciplines, but they are, nevertheless, very important. At the same time, there is a danger in putting art in the sphere of humanitarian work and just instrumentalizing it for the sake of trauma therapy or PR-ing something. And again, there is this artists' responsibility to reflect on themselves and on what exactly is their contribution. This makes me think of Ai Weiwei's work (and his photograph mimicking the drowned Syrian child, Alan Kurdi, on the beach) and the awareness he is trying to raise. About what exactly are we not aware? That refugees exist? That we don't care about drowning refugees? How great exactly is the benefit for the artist versus the benefit of actual refugees, and what are the kinds of costs involved in the production of these works? This is a big dilemma for me, and that is why I decided not to go with [the whole class] to the refugee camps anymore, as the question became: "Do I pay $15,000 for the students' flight tickets, or can I save that money and put it into use in the refugee camp in other ways?" Also, "Should I make money by selling my work?" I don't do that because generally I don't want to sell this type of art; luckily, I am privileged, and I don't have to. Another reason is that I don't believe in that art-market system, especially having in mind the kind of work I'm doing. Remember, for example, my "Monument in Waiting" project? This carpet depicts the stories of genocide survivors, and for this project to be sold and end up hanging in someone's garage or a private living room would defeat the whole purpose of the proposal itself—I don't even want to think about selling this piece. It is the kind of story that should belong to everyone. I think it is important that certain things, the kind of works that we make—especially when unprivileged people are involved in creating the work—do not belong to me or to the UNHCR. It is fundamental that they belong to the people who made them.

AS: What struck me the most in our class discussions was the realization of how much money is lost in the process and never reaches the people who need it the most. For example, money from international funds, such as UNESCO, predominantly goes to local governments and contractors, so one has to be really careful about the redistribution of funds and their misuse.

AA: Yes, that is absolutely true. It is very difficult because the corruption in the humanitarian system is a well-known problem. At the same time, we need humanitarian agencies, and we do need some humanitarian aid to be organized at the international level, but the problem of forced displacement is so huge that I don't know how it can be managed by a single organization. It requires heavy work. I've seen also the work that humanitarian workers do—it is hard work. They get moved from one country to another every five years . . . Who wants to live that kind of lifestyle? You live in a high-risk location, under stress and in extreme heat. However, compared to local salaries, their paydays are huge! There are a lot of misuses, of course, but we have to be cautious not to put everyone in the same pot. Working with these organizations I've seen both really amazing people driven by empathy and good intentions, and I have also seen people—like in any organization—who are not doing such a great job. How the corruption can be controlled is certainly beyond the scope of this conversation, but within the field of architecture and design there is corruption as well. For example, we can ask ourselves if our work is using the suffering of these people to boost our own careers. That is a kind of corruption we could critique within our own field. In my work, I express this critique by focusing on the potential of art and design as a contribution to alleviating human suffering but also to preserving heritage and promoting some kind of dialogue. I think there is a lot that art can do. As I mentioned earlier, it is amazing when you do creative work with the people in the camp—it doesn't even need to lead to anything; it can be just about creating something constructive in a moment when you have nothing. This type of work creates a sense of dignity and purpose, and if that process can also be educational, that is even better! Art can have the power to inspire young people and create excitement about learning, and this is especially important when you are in the camp, where many kids are dropping out of school because they don't see the point of going to school. They think they will be imprisoned in the camp forever. Here, creating a sense of hope is important. And then, on a broader scale, I seek to raise critical awareness in both ourselves and others about the cultural and emotional needs of displaced people, from multiple perspectives; this is something art can open up.

(The Road to Hell Is Paved with) Best Intentions

We learn from history—especially in the sphere of urban and architectural development, which innately deals with predicting and designing the future—that well-meant initiatives often produce devastating long-term results. This happens mainly because not all people have the same vision of the future—one person's benefit is another person's misery. However, in artistic and heritage productions (especially ones that deal with transcultural overlaps), bad results happen because people tend to get lost in translation—not only linguistic but also the translation of symbolic meanings as well. In the safety of a design studio, every theme—no matter how controversial—is thoroughly discussed; every design decision is contextualized, tested, and explained among peers. But when those designs are presented to the untrained eye of a nonprofessional, in an unfamiliar setting, instant judgements often distort desired interpretations. The most important question then becomes, How do we mediate our projects?

Assumptions that the language of architecture is universal may come up as erroneous because images, and especially symbols, do not function on the same level cross-culturally. Then there is the question of framing the narratives around heritage production and using appropriate terminologies. One example that came up during class was that insisting on cultural empowerment entails admitting that some groups of people are powerless.

Culturally sensitive design argues that the refugees should have a voice in choosing their own artistic expression and heritage preservation strategies. In the end, "Refugee inventions demonstrate how art, architecture, and design inspire hope and underpin innovation in a humanitarian context."[15] The book *1002 Inventions: Art and Design in Al Azraq Refugee Camp* reveals the hidden but rich cultural life present in the camp and shows us how local artistic responses to conflict can be creative. The work of humanitarian agencies, then, should focus more on informing humanitarian aid: providing guidance, advice, and knowledge exchange.

AS: How can we make sure that the best intentions we have do not get misunderstood, abused, or misused when making the transition from a thought exercise to actual implementation?

AA: That's the dilemma, right? I think it is important to know your audience, basically, to whom one is speaking, and to be very explicit in communication. For example, when the students are designing projects as if they are taking place in the refugee camp, it is important for me to teach them that they are not designing for refugees. They need to unlearn that agenda, which is often promoted in the problem-solving impetus of institutes such as MIT, which in this context might be patronizing. However, through thinking about the context and how one would design if he or she was living in the refugee camp, students also learn empathy and the constraints of humanitarian design. They also serve as a prototype format for a lesson that could be tested as a design challenge in the camp. A lot of these projects that we've done with students serve as thought exercises. We also discussed them in the camp, where I said, "Here is the problem: How do we create a seating or a floor without access to tools or materials?" This is how a conversation can also be created through design prompts and tests without students necessarily doing this and taking the agency away from the refugees. For this type of knowledge exchange, I do not need to take MIT students to the camp. It is more about co-creation, so we have different groups with different skills, and everyone pitches an idea. I bring in the voices of MIT students to prototype new designs with camp residents.

I've faced this issue before, in my earlier work, such as the "Wearable Mosques," for example.[16] The question of audience is very important; when I present my wearable mosque project in an artistic context, it is understood clearly as an artwork that has a purpose of posing critical questions about identity and mosque architecture and about the fight over certain symbols and the minority groups' right to visibility, et cetera. When I present the same project in political settings, the context frames the meaning of the piece; the project may not be understood as a critical artwork but as a design solution to the problem of visibility of Muslims in the West. As such, the mediation of the work becomes really problematic because you can have people claiming that we don't need to build mosques—we can wear them. I think knowing the audience and the context in which the work is presented is really important in regard to the publications, to the design work, to the tools of mediation. What that means in educational context, for me, is that it is often about unlearning certain assumptions—for example, the notion of "designing for refugees." This is something we are unlearning in our course; instead, we explore designing with or within the context of certain constraints.

Epilogue/Lessons Learned

AS: We agreed earlier on the idea that the agency of this course and artistic production in a postwar context in general are meant to remediate the consequences of targeted destruction of art and architecture. This is especially true when the whole purpose of the destruction is not only the erasure of common heritage and history but also breaking up ties among people. The agency of the Culturally Sensitive Design course—the one that, at least in theory, should be the goal of every architectural reconstruction—is to learn how to remediate those consequences to establish some kind of dialogue between cultures. The one-year time distance between the course and the interview gives us the opportunity to evaluate some initial results and findings. Since this is a boundary-breaking work, the question that imposes itself is, Have your predictions, but also expectations of your students, been realized, and to what extent? How did the refugees in Al Azraq Camp respond to students' projects, and how did the international/professional community? Will there be any kind of further collaboration as the outcome of this project? Most importantly, have the envisioned goals on pedagogies development, design policies creation, and reconciliation through art been met?

AA: I mentioned at the beginning that the Culturally Sensitive Design course is only one in a five-partite miniseries that has refugee camps in Jordan as their main focus (fig. 7.7). As such, it is part of the process of building a certain perspective and method on preservation and a pedagogy around the context of conflict and scarcity. This course has created an important milestone in our thinking and in design pedagogy that now is part of a larger framework that I call "performative preservation." This approach questions how we think about creating heritage and approaching preservation in the context of war, destruction, and displacement. I think this context of conflict is very particular, especially when you are facing displaced populations on a huge scale and a huge scale of destruction. We have to rethink the way we are approaching preservation; we cannot come with standard approaches that focus on specific monuments or humanitarian aid that takes the culture fully out of account. Therefore, Culturally Sensitive Design is part of a

FIGURE 7.7. The students' final projects were presented in the main lobby of the MIT MediaLab, within the Future Heritage Lab's installation called "Digital Majlis." Light effects based on embroidery patterns, developed by FHL with Syrian refugees in Al Azraq Camp in 2017, transmitted the culturally sensitive ethos of the class to the corporate spaces of MIT. (Image courtesy of Azra Akšamija)

bigger picture that I am creating that argues for the cultural lens to be more central in the context of humanitarian assistance. On the other hand, in the context of humanitarian preservation, Culturally Sensitive Design is about focusing on aspects of the living culture through the act of interpretation and the dynamics of creation. It aims at revitalizing and restoring the links between people as the conflict is still taking place and exposing young people to different worldviews and transcultural perspectives, and to the transcultural nature of heritage. Should the war stop? Or should these people be resettled in another place? This will inform their way into integrating into another context. In any case, the culture is happening now, it continually reconstitutes itself, and heritage is what we create today. This is the process that we are shaping through critical reflections and imaginative creations.

Notes

1. A brief course outline for Culturally Sensitive Design can be found on MIT's Art Culture Technology website, accessed June 13, 2021, https://act.mit.edu/academics/courses/advanced-projects-in-art-culture-and-technology-culturally-sensitive-design/.
2. Future Heritage Lab is a transdisciplinary initiative started by Azra Akšamija and hosted at MIT. It combines diverse practices in art, design, and cultural preservation with MIT expertise in new technologies to produce creative responses to crisis and conflict. For more, visit the FHL website, accessed June 13, 2021, https://www.futureheritagelab.com/about.
3. On this type of writing, see Graham Cairns, *Reflections on Architecture, Society and Politics* (London: Routledge, 2018). The formal interview with Azra Akšamija was conducted via Skype on April 1, 2019, almost one year after the end of the course.
4. András Riedlmayer, "The War on People and the War on Culture," *New Combat* (Autumn 1994): 16–19.
5. Bogdan Bogdanović, "Assassino della città," *Spazio e Società* 64 (1994): 72–75.
6. There are many (official and unofficial) surveys of destroyed cultural heritage sites in former Yugoslavia during the 1990s. Perhaps the most thorough ones come from András Riedlmayer, such as "Killing Memory: The Targeting of Bosnia's Cultural Heritage," testimony presented at a hearing of the Commission on Security and Cooperation in Europe, US Congress, April 4, 1995, Community of Bosnia Foundation, accessed June 13, 2021, https://www.ischool.utexas.edu/~archweek/2002/killingmemory.doc.
7. Azra Akšamija, "Our Mosques Are Us: Rewriting National History of Bosnia-Herzegovina through Religious Architecture" (PhD diss., Massachusetts Institute of Technology, Dept. of Architecture, 2011).
8. One example that immediately comes to mind is from Belgrade's Museum of Genocide Victims, where the exhibition "NATO War Crimes in 1999" was framed in the same context as World War I, World War II, and the Bosnian War, and then exhibited in Republika Srpska, accessed June 13, 2021, https://www.muzejgenocida.rs/images/izlozbe/1999_opt.pdf.
9. Azra Akšamija, "Museum Solidarity Lobby," Ljubljana, Slovenia: Museum of Modern Art, 2019.
10. See, for example, "Spanish Fresco Restoration Botched by Amateur," BBC News online, August 23, 2012, https://www.bbc.com/news/world-europe-19349921.

11. Students' video responses (and some additional feedback from earlier surveys) can be found at the Code of Ethics website, accessed June 13, 2021, https://www.codeofethics.online.
12. Better known as the ArcelorMittal Orbit in the Queen Elizabeth Olympic Park in Stratford, London, the project was designed by Turner Prize–winning artist Sir Anish Kapoor and Cecil Balmond of engineering Group Arup. For more on the controversy surrounding this work, see the Forensic Architecture project "Four Faces of Omarska," accessed June 13, 2021, https://cetirilicaomarske.wordpress.com.
13. On these topics, see the Code of Ethics website, https://www.codeofethics.online/new-page/.
14. See the Amman Design Week website, accessed June 13, 2021, https://ammandesignweek.com.
15. The works of art produced by refugees in Al Azraq Refugee Camp are summarized in Akšamija, Azra, *1002 Inventions: Art and Design in Al Azraq Refugee Camp* (Cambridge, MA: MIT SA+P Press, 2019). This short excerpt from the book summary is from the Graham Foundation website, accessed June 13, 2020, http://www.grahamfoundation.org/grantees/5850-1002-inventions-art-and-design-in-al-azraq-refugee-camp.
16. More details can be found on MIT's Art Culture Technology website, accessed June 13, 2021, http://act.mit.edu/event/azra-aksamija-wearable-mosques.

CONCLUSION

RECONCEPTUALIZING DESIGN AFTER DESTRUCTION

ELISA DAINESE AND ALEKSANDAR STANIČIĆ

The destruction of art and architecture through violence and war shapes not only the built environment but also the societies and cultures that encompass destroyed sites. The (fear of) devastation affects every aspect of life, from social to economic to political; so much so that—if not properly addressed—desolation becomes an integral part of a culture itself. When war affects urban settings, it produces evident, immediate, and overwhelming effects, which over time can turn into less recognizable, long-term ramifications. Normalizing the threat of violence through defensive architecture or the prolonged use of urban planning as a weapon of war are only some of the phenomena elaborated in detail in this book.[1] Others include the permanent breakup of social bonds, violent erasure of cultures and histories, and environmental impacts through increased extraction of natural resources. Millions of refugees and families fleeing war in both Africa and the Middle East have lived in exile for generations, trying to make a home in unfamiliar land while awaiting reconstruction of their own destroyed houses.[2] Developed for the short term, emergency camps designed to provide shelter are demonstratively unable to transform according to refugees' evolving needs.[3] Having all this in mind, what can be said about the role of design and designers in building a more inclusive postwar environment?

As the examples discussed in *War Diaries* explain, rebuilding—as a new construction operation and/or as a preservationist effort—confirms its potential to work toward peace-building and trigger new social contracts. Rebuilding can also perpetuate conflict. Called to participate in recovery projects, architects, artists, and other design experts struggle to find their role within redevelopment processes, often swamped by the need to generate practical, sustainable, and effective solutions and puzzled by the awareness that design could perpetuate dividing ideologies. Especially in postconflict settings, a reconceptualization of design after destruction is therefore necessary to prepare the way for critical interpretations of complex urban dynamics, and so is the need to highlight creativity, imagination, and design as a primary rather than peripheral topic in these contexts.[4]

Even if reconstruction processes begin immediately following destruction, urgent postconflict design has been undervalued in research on urban resilience and recovery. Instead, we would like to propose that only the promotion of design as a foregrounding discipline in postwar urban conversations can illuminate and add to the overt exploration of how cities and societies recover from military devastation. If the realities of working in contested territories and communities are, by their very nature, comprised by politics and geography, design expertise can not only share knowledge on the transformation of the physical environment but also map it across media, scales (the artistic, architectural, and urban ones), and disciplines (practical, academic, and nonprofit sectors). The goal is to build bridges between local actors affected by war and those institutions involved in humanitarian aid and reconstruction—which could include educational, international, local, governmental organizations, NGOs, and the private sector—as well as the other experts working in emergency contexts. The resulting concentrated and original efforts presented in this book can initiate a dialogue on the role of design in postwar reconstruction and emergency, whose bases lay on theoretical, contextual, and practical investigations of design responses to urban warfare and violence against art and architecture.

Some topics can be singled out as they emerge with great urgency when we bring design and aesthetic questions to the fore. By examining design successes and shortcomings, strategies and approaches during the first phases of design after destruction, these themes question the role of the artist/designer in the complex political conversations that dominate postconflict work. Featured discussions in the volume reassess designers' involvement in the process and reevaluate the interpretative tools to be used during postwar rebuilding. These discussions also bring forward some conclusions whose summary is offered in these final remarks. First, the interconnection of media and conflict transcends the global media coverage of violence and destruction, as explained in Gabriel Schwake's contribution (chapter 3) on the weaponization of design and aesthetics. New technologies for site survey, visualization, and analytics—such as satellite and drone imaging, remote sensing, and automated cross-referencing of large datasets, for example—bring awareness to the unexpected consequences of spatial conflicts. Some investigations even expose hidden territorial tensions. The visual representations based on new information extracted from these technologies are pertinent for the work of policy makers, activists, and even tribunals, and they raise multiple points for discussion on media tools, techniques, and underlying theories of (architectural and artistic) design.[5] Expertise in design has become an invaluable competence in the reinterpretation of visual and territorial data, bringing innovation into traditionally inert disciplines such as human rights violations and prosecutions—and creating the profession of designer-investigator in the process.

The chapters in *War Diaries* also highlight this less overt role played by designers and the tensions emerging from it that may affect the process of design in postwar situations. Indeed, as several authors in this book point out, design remains a core discipline in the mediation of the complex postwar relations between stakeholders, especially, but not only, in the urban and public realm. While planners, architects, and artists are often participants in the public discourse on risks and objectives of postwar urban recovery, they also play the role of translators of the sociopolitical forces articulated into built form.

Results also affirm the need for a more critical reading of the role of architects, planners, and artists who operate in postwar settings, as both Kai Vöckler and Azra Akšamija maintain in chapters 1 and 7, respectively. Architecture and planning are only two disciplines among many others applied in the postwar field—designers working together with local communities, doctors, nurses, logisticians, officers, and administrators. Examples such as that of Sri Lanka, affected by a twenty-year civil war and a tsunami in 2004, show the incongruities of the promises to quickly "build back better" while bound by the inconsistencies of the international aid system and its multiple actors.[6] As Deen Sharp explains in chapter 4, the question of who is making decisions regarding the design and reconstruction of damaged architecture and art in Beirut reveals power plays between all kinds of actors, especially when it comes to contested territories in a state of permanent or "frozen" conflict. It is not difficult, then, to recognize in those instances various militaristic strategies of oppression, segregation, and social inequality embedded into legal and urban parameters, codes, and policies.

Furthermore, the inflow of capital, both domestic and international, is conditioned by all kinds of agendas, ideologies, and political and economic demands that often have little regard for the actual needs of local communities. International organizations and institutions, even when well-intentioned, bring their own interests, aesthetics, and related symbolisms into reconstruction proposals, often completely misreading sensitive situations on the ground, an oversight that can lead to increased tensions rather than a deescalation of conflict.[7] From such circumstances arises the recognition of the need for designers to play the role of interpreters mediating conflicting interests among different stakeholders, and the idea of design as a moment of knowledge exchange. That, of course, cannot be done if designers do not recognize and acknowledge their own cultural backgrounds, positions of power and privilege, and potential biases. If we take as an axiom the fact that each of us comes with a preinstalled set of cultural values, opinions, and beliefs, then designing in and for a context that is different from our own represents by default an act of cultural merger, interpretation, and even appropriation. This is recognized in the work of the Future Heritage Lab at MIT, led by Azra Akšamija, who has tried to formalize a set of ethical guidelines for designers in the proposed "Ethics of Intervention" rule book. Educators and educational institutions play exceptionally responsible roles here, not only in educating future experts and practitioners but also in holding themselves to a higher standard and leading by example.

The intention of this varied collection—and our decision to favor a multiple narrative instead of single one—comes from this awareness. At first glance, such a panoply of places and actors might appear to substantiate the received image of postwar design as a practice with no cohesive trends beyond a strong desire to (re)build. But if these individual voices and practices are examined in the context of a participatory discourse, a more coherent picture emerges. Even more compelling outcomes appear when we consider all the nuances arising from the understanding of local cultures, in contrast to the decontextualized, conceptual, and even dogmatic approaches to design promoted by some planners and architects. This point is emphasized in chapter 2 (Armina Pilav) and chapter 6 (Raul Pantaleo and TAMassociati). In opposition to ideas that consolidate the concept of the "genius-designer," *War Diaries* highlights approaches that encourage the emergence of significant diverging opinions and ethical perspectives—reinforcing the belief that only from understanding and acknowledgment can emerge reconciliation and integration. However diverse are the practitioners, theorists, and artists we invited to participate in this project, however varied are their visions of art and architecture, they are united in their conviction that neither the notion of "shelter" nor the concept of "top-down design" are idioms that sufficiently respond to the character and circumstances of postwar society and culture.

Our intent is to articulate a renewed design practice that critically diverges from contemporary design discourse and systems that still support a hierarchical or even condescending articulation of design. Global initiatives that come from international platforms, even when well-intended, are at risk of sounding tone-deaf. Awarded competition entries judged solely by the "attractiveness" of their proposed designs or the ingenuity of their technical solutions may lack physical feasibility or take no consideration of local cultural contexts.[8] Today this regularly happens in the competitions for designs for emergency humanitarian architecture, although, as shown in the interview by Charlie Hailey and in the interview-article with Azra Akšamija, the best results are achieved when locally available resources and the refugees' origins are taken into account. As many observers recognize, the architecture and spatiality of modern-day refugee centers often "limit the capacity of refugees to build their own spaces and their own lives."[9] According to Andrew Herscher, "The tension between development and humanitarian relief [...] in architectural terms, has pitted 'dwelling' against 'shelter.' [...] Each raises the stakes for expertise differently: the former by ennobling the shared mission of architecture and humanitarianism, and the latter by reducing it to functionalist, instrumentalized science."[10] If we consider as a reference these examples of state-of-the-art humanitarian emergency architecture in a postwar context, then we can argue that architectural design still needs to find its way between patrons and benefactors of functional, scientific impetuses in order to bridge these two seemingly different worlds and philosophies.

As a contrast and an alternative to these practices, the authors featured in this volume propose the development of a practice that seeks the inclusion of marginalized perspectives and condemns the idea of relying on a delivery of expertise supported by the backing of ideologies and political power, and the top-down deployment of nationalist policies. While architects can serve as mediators working across the aisle, by insisting upon participatory design and planning, they can give voice to local and even marginalized communities. Especially in societies divided by warfare, only co-creation under the assumption of equality for all, just leadership, shared goals, and the vision of a prosperous future can help (re)build social tolerance.[11] Design approaches, practices, and tools become fundamental as they promote the meaningful involvement of multiple and diverse participants while activating and promoting memory resilience, transitional justice, and reconciliation.

Considering the issue from multiple and diverse perspectives also offers us reflections on the modalities in which architectural design can be employed to address the violent past and make ethical statements after trauma. At the center of the discussion are voluntary and involuntary resettlements after devastation and the development of urban and social recompositions, reinterpretations, and reinventions of memory and tradition after violent eradication. Fundamental is the recognition of the need for a code of shared ethics of involvement among participants and stakeholders. The designer has here the difficult role of developing personal as well as sharable ethics of interpretation to mediate among actors and build an enlarged design team.

More than fixed guidelines, what emerges are shared principles that sustain exchange and openness—some authors, such as Charlie Hailey in chapter 5, even call it "creative spontaneity"—at multiple levels. New strategies imply a constant participatory effort and attentive studies of the context (both geographic and interventional) and its characteristics. When working on culturally sensitive design, architects, planners, and artists are called upon to be open to the idea that transformations can occur through time or can affect sensitive social balances on the ground. Transformative ideas can change not only the practice of design but also its theories and methods. This fluidity could make final interpretations seem impossible, so to overcome difficulties, designers need to reconceptualize design itself and relearn the practice of knowledge exchange. We believe this awareness would help designers and planners take a stronger position when faced with postwar challenges in the future, or at least would encourage them to understand the effects and significant consequences of their actions.

Notes

1. War normalization in architectural design was addressed in chapter 3 by Gabriel Schwake, while in chapter 4 Deen Sharp writes on the relation

between planning, urban design, and war. See also Nan Elin, ed., *Architecture of Fear* (Princeton, NJ: Princeton Architectural Press, 1997).
2. On the generational issue and so-called protracted refugee situations, see, for example, Anooradha Iyer Siddiqi, "Seventeen Years a Refugee," *Harvard Design magazine* 44 (2017): 153.
3. On the design of refugee camps, see Ayham Dalal et al., "Planning the Ideal Refugee Camp," *Urban Planning* 3.4 (2018): 64–78; Andrew Herscher, *Displacements: Architecture and Refugee* (Cambridge, MA: MIT Press, 2017); Franziska Laue, "Shelter Architecture—Emergency Versus Innovation, Contextualisation and Flexibility," *Trialog* 112/113, special issue, Camp Cities (2013): 18–29. As a result of poorly conceived planning, camp inhabitants often end up deprived of freedom of movement, public spaces, access to land, and legal employment. On humanitarianism and its discontent, see, for example, Michael Barnett, *Empire of Humanity: A History of Humanitarianism* (Ithaca, NY: Cornell University Press, 2011). See also Michel Agier, "Afterword: What Contemporary Camps Tell Us about the World to Come," *Humanity: An International Journal of Human Rights, Humanitarianism, and Development* 7.3 (Winter 2016): 459–68.
4. The most important books already published on this subject still focus on destruction more than the role of design in postconflict reconstruction.
5. Goldsmiths-based *Forensic Architecture* studio is a global leader in this field. They undertake advanced spatial and visual media investigations into cases of human rights violations using tools that traditionally belong to the field of architecture, such as digital and physical models, 3-D animations, virtual reality environments, and cartographic platforms. See the Forensic Architecture website, accessed June 13, 2021, https://forensic-architecture.org.
6. On the "Build Back Better" initiative in Sri Lanka, see, for example, Sandeeka Mannakkara and Suzanne Wilkinson, "Build Back Better: Lessons from Sri Lanka's Recovery from the 2004 Indian Ocean Tsunami," *International Journal of Architectural Research* 7 (2013): 108–21. See also the example of Haiti: Jean-Marc Biquet, "Haiti: Between Emergency and Reconstruction," *International Development Policy* 4.3 (2013): n.p., http://journals.openedition.org/poldev/1600.
7. An example that immediately comes to mind is the reconstruction of the Old Bridge (Stari Most) in Mostar, Bosnia and Herzegovina. See Emily Gunzburger Makaš, "Rebuilding Mostar: International and Local Visions of a Contested City and Its Heritage," in *On Location: Heritage Cities and Sites*, ed. D. Fairchild Ruggles, n.p. (New York: Springer Verlag, 2012).
8. One such example is the "MatterBetter" competition for postwar housing in Syria from 2016. The fact that the location was never precisely defined is an indication of the survey character of the competition. Unbound by the spec-

ificities of a local context, with the main requirement being creating "living conditions that will be attractive for once-displaced Syrians to return to," submitted designs all had a conceptual and even abstract character. Results of the competition can be viewed here: "Syria: Post-War Housing Competition," e-Architect website, https://www.e-architect.com/syria/syria-post-war-housing-competition.
9. For more on this, see Andrew Herscher, "Designs on Disaster: Humanitarianism and Contemporary Architecture," in *Routledge Companion to Critical Approaches to Contemporary Architecture,* eds. Swatti Chattopadhyay and Jeremy White, n.p. (London: Routledge, 2019).
10. Herscher, "Designs on Disaster."
11. This point is also discussed in Aleksandar Staničić and Šijaković Milan, "(Re)building Spaces of Tolerance—A 'Symbiotic Model' for the Post-War City Regeneration," *Architecture and Culture,* 7.1 (2019): 113–28.

BIBLIOGRAPHY

Agier, Michel. "Afterword: What Contemporary Camps Tell Us about the World to Come." *Humanity: An International Journal of Human Rights, Humanitarianism, and Development* 7.3 (Winter 2016): 459–68.
———. "Between War and City: Towards an Urban Anthropology of Refugee Camps." *Ethnography* 3.3 (2002): 317–41.
———. *On the Margins of the World: The Refugee Experience Today*. Translated by David Fernbach. Cambridge, UK: Polity, 2008.
Akar, Hiba Bou. *For the War Yet to Come: Planning Beirut's Frontiers*. Stanford, CA: Stanford University Press, 2018.
Akšamija, Azra. "Museum Solidarity Lobby." Ljubljana, Slovenia: Museum of Modern Art, 2019.
———. *1002 Inventions: Art and Design in Al Azraq Refugee Camp*. Cambridge, MA: MIT SA+P Press, 2019.
———. "Our Mosques Are Us: Rewriting National History of Bosnia-Herzegovina through Religious Architecture." PhD diss., Massachusetts Institute of Technology, 2011.
Alexander, David. "From Civil Defence to Civil Protection—and Back Again." *Disaster Prevention and Management* 11.3 (2002): 209–13.
Allais, Lucia. *Designs of Destruction: The Making of Monuments in the Twentieth Century*. Chicago: University of Chicago Press, 2018.
Amaratunga, Dilanthi, and Richard Haigh. *Post-Disaster Reconstruction of the Built Environment: Rebuilding for Resilience*. Chichester, UK: Wiley-Blackwell, 2011.
Anderson, Sean, and Stephen Sloan. *Historical Dictionary of Terrorism*. Metuchen, NJ: Scarecrow Press, 1995.
"Anti-cementism in Lebanon: Beirut Is Still Arguing over its Post-war Reconstruction." *The Economist*, July 11, 2019.
Apter, Emily, Thomas Keenan, et al. "Humanism without Borders: A Dossier on the Human, Humanitarianism, and Human Rights." *Alphabet City: Social Insecurity* 7 (2000): 40–67.
Archis Interventions. *Manual on the Legalization of Structures Built without a Construction Permit*. Archis Interventions in cooperation with the Municipality of Prishtina with the support of the Association of Kosovo Munici-

palities and Co-PLAN, Tirana, 2009. Accessed June 10, 2021. http://www.seenetwork.org/files/2010/11/16/3/Archis%20Interventions_Prishtina_Manual_2009.pdf.

Architecture for Humanity. *Design Like You Give a Damn: Architectural Responses to Humanitarian Crises*. New York: Metropolis Books, 2006.

Arendt, Hannah. *Lectures on Kant's Political Philosophy*. Chicago: University of Chicago Press, 1982.

Aukot, Ekuru. "It Is Better to be a Refugee Than a Turkana in Kakuma: Revisiting the Relationship between Hosts and Refugees in Kenya." *Global Movements for Refugees and Migrant Rights* 21.3 (2003): 73–83.

Barakat, Sultan, ed. *After the Conflict: Reconstruction and Development in the Aftermath of War*. London: Tauris, 2005.

Barenstein, Duyne E. Jennifer, and Esther Leemann. *Post-Disaster Reconstruction and Change: Communities' Perspectives*. Boca Raton, FL: CRC Press, 2012.

Barnett, Michael. *Empire of Humanity: A History of Humanitarianism*. Ithaca, NY: Cornell University Press, 2011.

Baumann, Hannes. *Citizen Hariri: Lebanon's Neo-liberal Reconstruction*. London: Hirst, 2017.

Ben-Aharon, Rachel. "National Centre of Israeli Robustness." *AIQ* 106 (2016): 89–95.

Bevan, Robert. *The Destruction of Memory: Architecture at War*. London: Reaktion Books, 2007.

Beyhum, Nabil, Assem Salaam, and Jad Tabet, eds. *Beyrouth: Construire l'Avenir, Reconstruire le Passe?* Beirut: L'Urban Research Institute, 1995.

Biquet, Jean-Marc. "Haiti: Between Emergency and Reconstruction." *International Development Policy* 4.3 (2013): n.p. http://journals.openedition.org/poldev/1600.

Bittner, Regina, Wilfried Hackenbroich, and Kai Vöckler, eds. *UN Urbanism: Mostar Kabul*. Berlin: Jovis, 2010.

Björkdahl, Annika, and Stefanie Kappler. *Peacebuilding and Spatial Transformation: Peace, Space and Place*. London: Routledge, 2017.

Boano, Camillo. "Disruptive Design: On Design Gestures, Breathing and Non-Doing." Guest editor Isabelle Doucet in conversation with Camillo Boano. *Candide* magazine 10+11 (December 2016): 114–15.

Bogdanović, Bogdan. "Assassino della città." *Spazio e Società* 64 (1994): 72–75.

Borasi, Giovanna, ed. *The Other Architect: Another Way of Building Architecture*. Leipzig: CCA, Spektor Books, 2015.

Brand, Ulrich, Alex Demirovic, Christoph Görg, et al., eds. *Nichtregierungsorganisationen in der Transformation des Staates*. Muenster: Westfälisches Dampfboot, 2001.

Büschel, Hubertus. "*Geschichte der Entwicklungspolitik.*" In *Docupedia-Zeitgeschichte*, November 2, 2010. http://dx.doi.org/10.14765/zzf.dok.2.591.v1.

Cairns, Graham. *Reflections on Architecture, Society and Politics*. London: Routledge, 2018.

Calame, Jon, and Esther Charlesworth. *Divided Cities: Belfast, Beirut, Jerusalem, Mostar, and Nicosia*. Philadelphia: University of Pennsylvania Press, 2009.

Camp Coordination and Camp Management Cluster. "Localising CCCM Responses." *Retreat Report 2015*. Oslo: NRC, 2015.

Carabelli, Giulia. *The Divided City and the Grassroots: The (Un)making of Ethnic Divisions in Mostar*. Singapore: Palgrave Macmillan, 2018.

Cash Learning Partnership. "The State of the World's Cash Report: Cash Transfer Programming in Humanitarian Aid." February 28, 2018. https://reliefweb.int/report/world/state-world-s-cash-report-cash-transfer-programming-humanitarian-aid.

Chamma, Nasr, and Carmen Mendoza Arroyo. "Rethinking Refugee Camp Design: From 'Temporary' Camps to Sustainable Settlements." Paper presented at the Symposium of Architecture in Emergency, Istanbul Kültür University, Faculty of Architecture, November 17, 2016.

Charles, Kelly. "Limitations to the Use of Military Resources for Foreign Disaster Assistance." *Disaster Prevention and Management: An International Journal* 5.1 (1996): 22–29.

Charlesworth, Esther Ruth. *Architects without Frontiers: War, Reconstruction and Design Responsibility*. Amsterdam: Architectural Press, 2006.

———. *Humanitarian Architecture: Fifteen Stories of Architects Working after Disaster*. London: Routledge, 2014.

Chytry, Josef. *The Aesthetic State*. Berkeley: University of California Press, 1989.

Coaffee, Jon, et al. *The Everyday Resilience of the City*. Basingstoke, UK: Palgrave Macmillan, 2009.

Cohen, Sheli, and Tal Amit. "Public Shelters to Protective Space: The Privatisation of Civil Defence." In *Living Forms: Architecture and Society in Israel*, edited by Sheli Cohen and Tal Amit, 124–43. Tel Aviv: Am Oved, 2007.

Corsellis, Tom, and Antonella Vitale. *Transitional Settlement/Displaced Populations*. Oxford, UK: Oxfam GB, 2005.

Coward, Martin. *Urbicide—The Politics of Urban Destruction*. New York: Routledge, 2009.

Dalal, Ayham, et al. "Planning the Ideal Refugee Camp." *Urban Planning* 3.4 (2018): 64–78.

Davie, Michael. "La gestion des espaces urbains en temps de guerre: Circuits paralleles a Beyrouth." In *Reconstruire Beyrouth: L es paris sur le possible,* edited by Nabil Beyhum, 157–93. Lyon: Maison de l'Orient Méditerranéen, 1991.

Davis, Ian. *Shelter after Disaster.* Oxford, UK: Oxford Polytechnic Press, 1978.

Debrix, François. "The Sublime Spectatorship of War." *Journal of International Studies* 34.3 (2006): 767–91.

De Man, Paul. *The Resistance to Theory.* Minneapolis: University of Minnesota Press, 1986.

Department of Construction and Engineering of Israel. *Open Architectural Competition.* Tel Aviv: Ministry of Defense, 2016.

Douer, Yair. *Our Sickle Is Our Sword.* Tel Aviv: Yad Tevenkin, 1992.

Eddé, Henri. *Le Liban d'ou je viens.* Paris: Buchet-Chastel, 1997.

Efrat, Elisha. "Changes in Israel's Urban System after Forty Years of Statehood (1948–1988)." *Eretz-Israel: Archaeological, Historical, and Geographic Studies* (1991): 19–26.

Efrat, Zvi. *The Israeli Project.* Tel Aviv: Tel Aviv Museum of Art, 2004.

Elin, Nan, ed. *Architecture of Fear.* Princeton, NJ: Princeton Architectural Press, 1997.

Everill, Bronwen, and Josiah, Kaplan. *The History and Practice of Humanitarian Intervention and Aid in Africa.* Houndsmill, UK: Palgrave Macmillan, 2013.

Executive Committee of the High Commissioner's Programme. "Protracted Refugee Situations: The Search for Practical Solutions." Proceedings of June 10, 2004, 30th Meeting of the Standing Committee. www.refworld.org/pdfid/4a54bc00d.pdf.

Featherstone, Mike. *Consumer Culture and Postmodernism.* London: Sage, 1996.

Fisk, Robert. *Pity the Nation: Lebanon at War.* Oxford, UK: Oxford University Press, 1990.

Fontenot, Anthony, and Ajmal Maiwandi. "Reconstructing Kabul: Past, Present and Future." *Volume* 40, Architecture of Peace Reloaded (2014): 30–39.

Forde, Susan. *Movement as Conflict Transformation: Rescripting Mostar, Bosnia-Herzegovina.* Singapore: Palgrave Macmillan, 2019.

Foucault, Michel. *Discipline and Punish: The Birth of the Prison.* Translated by Alan Sheridan. New York: Vintage Books, 1995.

———. "Space, Knowledge, Power." In *Rethinking Architecture—A Reader in Cultural Theory,* edited by Neil Leach, 367–80. London: Routledge, 1997.

Gaffikin, Frank, and Mike Morrissey. *Planning in Divided Cities.* Chichester, UK: Wiley-Blackwell, 2011.

Garcia-Huidobro, Fernando, Diego Torres Torriti, and Nicolas Tugas. *¡El tiempo construye!/Time Builds!* Barcelona: GG, 2008.

Gavin, Angus, and Rami Maluf. *Beirut Reborn: The Restoration and Development of the Central District.* London: Academy Press, 1996.

Gonçalves, Miranda Rui, and Federica Zullo, eds. *Post-Conflict Reconstructions: Re-Mappings and Reconciliations*. Nottingham, UK: Critical, Cultural and Communications Press, 2013.

Government of Israel. *National Outline Plan 38*. Jerusalem: State of Israel, 2012.

———. *1951 Civil Defense Act*. https://www.nevo.co.il/law_html/law01/125_001.htm.

Graham, Stephen. *Cities, War, and Terrorism: Towards an Urban Geopolitics*. Oxford, UK: Blackwell, 2004.

———. *Cities under Siege: The New Military Urbanism*. London: Verso, 2011.

Gunzburger Makaš, Emily. "Rebuilding Mostar: International and Local Visions of a Contested City and Its Heritage." In *On Location: Heritage Cities and Sites*, edited by D. Fairchild Ruggles, n.p. New York: Springer Verlag, 2012. https://uncc.academia.edu/EmilyMakas.

———. "Representing Competing Identities: Building and Rebuilding in Postwar Mostar, Bosnia-Herzegovina." PhD diss., Cornell University, 2007.

Gutwein, Daniel. "The Class Logic of the 'Long Revolution.'" *Iyunim Bitkumat Israel* 11 (2017): 21–57.

Hackenbroich, Wilfried, and Kai Vöckler. "The Re-Urbanisation of Kabul by the International Community or: What can we learn from Kabul?" In *UN Urbanism: Mostar Kabul*, edited by Regina Bittner, Wilfried Hackenbroich, and Kai Vöckler, 79–99. Berlin: Jovis, 2010.

Hailey, Charlie. *Camps*. Cambridge, MA: MIT Press, 2009.

———. "Camps, Corridors, and Clouds: Inland Ways to the Ocean." In *Wet Matter*, edited by Pierre Bélanger and Jennifer Sigler, special issue of *Harvard Design* 39 (2014): 24–31.

Hamilton, Laura. "Somali Refugee Displacements in the Near Region: Analysis and Recommendations." Paper for the UNHCR Global Initiative on Somali Refugees. Accessed August 10, 2018. http://www.unhcr.org/55152c699.pdf.

Harris, William. *The New Face of Lebanon: History's Revenge*. Princeton, NJ: Markus Wilener Publishers, 2006.

Hason, Yael. *Three Decades of Privatization*. Tel Aviv: Adva Center, 2006.

Healey, Patsy. *Collaborative Planning: Shaping Places in Fragmented Societies*. New York: Palgrave, 1997.

Herscher, Andrew. "Designs on Disaster: Humanitarianism and Contemporary Architecture." In *Routledge Companion to Critical Approaches to Contemporary Architecture*, edited by Swatti Chattopadhyay and Jeremy White. London: Routledge, 2019. https://www.routledgehandbooks.com/doi/10.4324/9781315688947-3.

———. "Wararchitectural Theory." *Journal of Architectural Education* 61.3 (January 2008): 35–43.

Herscher, Andrew, Nikolaus Hirsch, and Markus Miessen, eds. *Displacements: Architecture and Refugee.* Berlin: Sternberg Press, 2017.

Herzfeld, Michael. "Developmentalism." In *Anthropology: Theoretical Practice in Culture and Society,* edited by Michael Herzfeld, 152–70. Oxford, UK: Blackwell, 2001.

Hourani, Najib. "Transnational Pathways and Politico-Economic Power: Globalisation and the Lebanese Civil War." *Geopolitics* 15.2 (2010): 290–311.

"Insecurities: Tracing Displacement and Shelter." MoMA exhibition, October 1, 2016–January 22, 2017.

"Iqtisad Solidere fi azma maaliyya khatria" [Solidere's economics in dangerous financial crisis]. *MTV,* July 12, 2019. https://www.mtv.com.lb/News /إقتصاد/886161/سوليدير_في_أزمة_مالية_خطرة.

Israeli Civil Defence, Home Front Command (IDF, HFC). *Shelter Maintenance Instructions.* Ramleh: IDF, 2006.

Iwansson, Per. *Kenya: Site Planning Consultancy: 12 April—15 June 1992.* Programme and Technical Support Section (PTSS), Mission Report 92/44. Geneva: UNHCR, 1992.

———. "Planeamento de campos de refugiados no Quénia: Notas para futura pesquisa." *Espaços Vividos e Espaços Construidos* 1.6 (2017): 88–99.

Jabareen, Yosef, and Hakam Dbiat. *Architecture and Orientalism in the Country.* Haifa: Technical Institute of Israel, 2014.

Jahr, Marianne, et al. "Approaches to the Design of Refugee Camps." *Journal of Humanitarian Logistics and Supply Chain Management* 8.3 (2018): 323–45.

Jakupi, Arta. "The Effect of the International Community Presence in the Urban Development of Post Conflict City. Case Study: Kosova." PhD diss., Bauhaus University Weimar, 2012. https://e-pub.uni-weimar.de/opus4/frontdoor/deliver/index/docId/1831/file/Arta+JAKUPI-+The+Effect+of+the+International+Community+Presence+on+Urban+Development+of+Post+Conflict+City_pdfa.pdf.

Jamaković, Said. "Sarajevo Is Growing in the Sky." *Slobodna Bosna/Free Bosnia* magazine, August 31, 2008.

Jansen, Bram J. *Kakuma Refugee Camp: Humanitarian Urbanism in Kenya's Accidental City.* Chicago: University of Chicago Press, 2018.

Jerliu, Florina, Wilfried Hackenbroich, and Kai Vöckler (in collaboration with Visar Geci, Vloar Navakazi, Thilo Fuchs). "Post-Conflict Planning: Archis Interventions in Prishtina, Kosovo." In *SEE! Urban Transformation in Southeastern Europe,* edited by Kai Vöckler, 52–71. Vienna: Lit Verlag, 2012.

Kabbani, Omar. *The Reconstruction of Beirut.* Oxford, UK: Centre for Lebanese Studies, 1992.

Kahneman, Daniel. *Thinking Fast and Slow.* New York: Farrar, Straus and Giroux, 2011.

Kaldor, Mary. "Cosmopolitanism Versus Nationalism: The New Divide?" In *Europe's New Nationalism: States and Minorities in Conflict*, edited by Richard Caplan and Jon Feffer, 42–58. New York: Oxford University Press, 1996.

Kant, Immanuel. *Critique of the Powers of Judgment*. Edited by Paul Guyer. Translated by Eric Matthews. Cambridge, UK: Cambridge University Press, 2001.

Kellner, Douglas. "9/11, Spectacles of Terror, and Media Manipulation." *Critical Discourse Studies* 1.1 (2004): 41–64. https://doi.org.10.1080/17405900410001674515.

Kennedy, James. *Structures for the Displaced: Service and Identity in Refugee Settlements*. Delft: International Forum for Urbanism, 2008.

Khalaf, Samir, and Philip Khoury, eds. *Recovering Beirut: Urban Design and Post-War Reconstruction*. London: Brill, 1993.

Khalidi, Walid. *All That Remains*. Washington, DC: Institute for Palestine Studies, 1992.

Kimmerling, Baruch. *The End of Ashkenazi Hegemony*. Tel Aviv: Keter, 2001.

———. "Militarism in Israeli Society." *Teoria U'Bikoret* 4 (1993): 123–40.

———. *Zionism and Territory: The Socio-Territorial Dimensions of Zionist Politics*. Berkeley: Institute of International Studies, University of California, 1983.

Knapp, Eberhard. "The Need for One 'Urban Vision' and Many 'Masterplans.'" In *Development of Kabul. Reconstruction and Planning Issues*, edited by Babar Mumtaz and Kaj Noschis, 101–9. Lausanne: Comportment, 2004.

Kruger, Thomas. "Alles Governance? Anregungen aus der Management-Forschung für die Planungstheorie." *RaumPlanung* 132/133 (2007): 125–30.

Landis, James M. "Morale and Civilian Defense." *American Journal of Sociology* 47.3 (1941): 331–39.

Laue, Franziska. "Shelter Architecture—Emergency Versus Innovation, Contextualisation and Flexibility." *Trialog* 112/113. Special issue, Camp Cities (2013): 18–29.

Law, Johnathan. *The Reconstruction of Lebanon*. Washington DC: US Businessmen's Commission on the Reconstruction of Lebanon, 1984.

Lefebvre, Henri. *The Production of Space*. Translated by Donald Nicholson-Smith. New York: John Wiley and Sons, 1991.

Leslie, Jolyon. "City of Contest." In *UN Urbanism. Mostar Kabul*, edited by Regina Bittner, Wilfried Hackenbroich, and Kai Vöckler, 94–99. Berlin: Jovis, 2010.

Machlis, Gary E., Thor Hanson, Zdravko Špirić, and Jean E. McKendry, eds. *Warfare Ecology: A New Synthesis for Peace and Security*. Dordrecht: Springer Netherlands, 2011.

MacIver, Robert M. *The Modern State*. Oxford, UK: Oxford University Press, 1926.

Makarem, Hadi. "Actually Existing Neoliberalism: The Reconstruction of Downtown Beirut in Post-Civil War Lebanon." PhD diss., London School of Economics, University of London, 2014.

Makdisi, Saree. "The Architecture of Erasure." *Critical Inquiry* 36 (2010): 519–59.

———. "Laying Claim to Beirut: Urban Narrative and Spatial Identity in the Age of Solidere." *Critical Inquiry* 23.3 (1997): 661–705.

Mann, Michael. "The Autonomous Power of the State: Its Origins, Mechanisms and Results." *European Journal of Sociology* 25.2 (1984): 185–213.

Mannakkara, Sandeeka, and Suzanne Wilkinson, "Build Back Better: Lessons from Sri Lanka's Recovery from the 2004 Indian Ocean Tsunami." *International Journal of Architectural Research* 7 (2013): 108–21.

Marx, Sven-Patrick. "Stadtplanung zwischen Umbruch und Kontinuität." In *Strategieorientierte Planung im kooperativen Staat*, edited by Alexander Hamedinger, Oliver Frey, Jens S. Dangschat, et al., 87–101. Wiesbaden: VS Verlag für Sozialwissenschaften, 2007.

Melčák, Miroslav, and Ondřej Beránek. "ISIS's Destruction of Mosul's Historical Monuments: Between Media Spectacle and Religious Doctrine." *International Journal of Islamic Architecture* 6.2 (2017): 389–415. https://doi.org/10.1386/ijia.6.2.389_1.

Missiroli, Antonio. "Disasters Past and Present." *Journal of European Integration* 28.5 (2006): 423–36.

Mitchell, David F. "NGO Presence and Activity in Afghanistan, 2000–2014: A Provincial-Level Dataset." *Stability: International Journal of Security and Development* 6(1).5 (2017): n.p. http://doi.org/10.5334/sta.497.

Mumtaz, Babar, and Kaj Noschis, eds. *Development of Kabul: Reconstruction and Planning Issues*. Lausanne, Switzerland: Comportment, 2004.

Naor, Moshe. *Social Mobilization in the Arab/Israeli War of 1948*. New York: Routledge, 2013.

Nucho, Joanne Randa. *Everyday Sectarianism in Urban Lebanon: Infrastructures, Public Services, and Power*. Princeton, NJ: Princeton University Press, 2017.

Paissan, Marco. Technical report for TAMassociati. Pediatric Clinic, Port Sudan, Sudan, 2012.

Perouse de Montclos, Marc-Antoine. "Refugee Camps or Cities? The Socioeconomic Dynamics of the Dadaab and Kakuma Camps in Northern Kenya." *Journal of Refugee Studies* 13.2 (2000): 205–22.

Pilav, Armina. "Before the War, War, After the War." *International Journal of Disaster Risk Science* 3.1 (2012): 23–37.

Pilav, Armina, Marc Schoonderbeek, Heidi Sohn, and Aleksandar Staničić, eds. *Mediating the Spatiality of Conflicts*. International Conference Proceedings,

TU Delft Faculty of Architecture and the Built Environment. Delft: BK Books, 2020.
Polman, Linda. *War Games: The Story of Aid and War in Modern Times.* London: Penguin, 2010.
Pottier, Johan. "Relief and Repatriation: Views by Rwandan Refugees—Lessons from Humanitarian Aid Workers." *African Affairs* 95.380 (1996): 408.
Quarantelli, Enrico L. "Social Aspects of Disasters and Their Relevance to Pre-Disaster Planning." *Disasters* 1.2 (1977): 101.
"Rad sharika solidere ala' takrir al-MTV bitarikh 12 haziran 2019" [Response by Solidere to the MTVJuly 12, 2019]. *Solidere,* July 12, 2019. http://www.solidere.com/sites/default/files/attached/pr_sol_13_06_2019.pdf.
Rawlence, Ben. *City of Thorns: Nine Lives in the World's Largest Refugee Camp.* New York: Picador, 2016.
Riba, Naama. "The Next Objective of the IDF: An Architectural Revolution." *Haaretz,* October 10, 2016. https://www.haaretz.co.il/gallery/architecture/.premium-1.3092731.
Riedlmayer, András. "Killing Memory: The Targeting of Bosnia's Cultural Heritage." Testimony presented at a hearing of the Commission on Security and Cooperation in Europe, US Congress, April 4, 1995. Community of Bosnia Foundation. Accessed June 13, 2021. https://www.ischool.utexas.edu/~archweek/2002/killingmemory.doc.
———. "The War on People and the War on Culture." *New Combat* (Autumn 1994): 16–19.
Ristić, Mirjana. *Architecture, Urban Space and War: The Destruction and Reconstruction of Sarajevo.* London: Palgrave Macmillan, 2018.
Rizzo, Anthony, dir. *Duck and Cover.* 1952. New York: Archer Productions.
Rokem, Jonathan, and Camillo Boano, eds. *Urban Geopolitics: Rethinking Planning in Contested Cities.* London: Routledge, 2017.
Rose Viejo, Dacia, and M. L. S. Sørensen, eds. *War and Cultural Heritage: Biographies of Place.* Cambridge, UK: Cambridge University Press, 2015.
Salam, Assem. "The Reconstruction of Beirut: A Lost Opportunity." *AA files* 27 (1994): 11–13.
Salem, Paul. "Framing Post-war Lebanon: Perspectives on the Constitution and the Structure of Power." *Mediterranean Politics* 3.1 (1998): 13–26.
Sasson-Levy, Orna. "Where Will the Women Be? Gendered Implications of the Decline of Israel's Citizen Army." In *The New Citizen Armies: Israel's Armed Forces in Comparative Perspective,* edited by Stuart A. Cohen, 173–95. New York: Routledge, 2010.
Schneider, Jane, and Ida Susser, eds. *Wounded Cities: Destruction and Reconstruction in a Globalized World.* London: Berg, 2004.

Schwake, Gabriel. "Post-Traumatic Urbanism." *Cities* 75 (2018): 50–58.
Scott, James C. *Seeing Like a State: How Certain Schemes to Improve the Human Condition Have Failed.* New Haven, CT: Yale University Press, 1998.
Segal, Rafi, David Tartakover, and Eyal Weizman. *A Civilian Occupation: The Politics of Israeli Architecture.* London: Verso, 2002.
Siddiqi, Anooradha Iyer. "In Favor of Seeing Specific Histories." *Grey Room* 61 (2015): 86–91.
———. "On Humanitarian Architecture: A Story of a Border." *Humanity: An International Journal of Human Rights, Humanitarianism, and Development* 8.3 (2017): 519–21.
———. "Seventeen Years a Refugee." *Harvard Design* 44 (2017): 153.
Skotte, Hans. "Tents in Concrete: What Internationally Funded Housing Does to Support Recovery I Areas Affected by War—The Case of Bosnia-Herzegovina." PhD diss., Norwegian University of Science and Technology, 2004. https://ntnuopen.ntnu.no/ntnu-xmlui/handle/11250/230994.
Sontag, Susan. *Fascinating Fascism.* New York: Vintage Books, 1974.
Staničić, Aleksandar, and Milan Šijaković. "(Re)building Spaces of Tolerance—A 'Symbiotic Model' for the Post-War City Regeneration." *Architecture and Culture* 7.1 (2019): 113–28.
State Comptroller of Israel. *Resistance of Buildings and Infrastructure in Earthquakes.* Jerusalem: Office of the State Comptroller, 2011.
Stoppani, Teresa. "Architecture of the Disaster." *Space and Culture* 15.2 (2012): 135–50.
Stratis, Socrates, ed. *Guide to Common Urban Imaginaries in Contested Spaces: The "Hands-on Famagusta" Project.* Berlin: Jovis, 2016.
Štraus, Ivan. *Arhitekti i Barbari/Architects and Barbarians.* Sarajevo: Međunarodni centar za mir/International Center for Peace, 1995.
———. *Arhitektura Jugoslavije 1945–1990/Architecture of Yugoslavia 1945–1990.* Sarajevo: Svjetlost, 1991.
———. "Poziv stručnjacima Europe/Invitation to European Experts." *Business* (April 1996): 74.
Stular, Aleksandr. "'Mostar was a very specific case . . .'" In *UN Urbanism: Mostar Kabul,* edited by Regina, Bittner, Wilfried Hackenbroich, and Kai Vöckler, 157–64. Berlin: Jovis, 2010.
Tannous, Nicole. "Re-envisioning Beirut: A Critique of Populism and Neoliberalism in Modern City Planning." Master's thesis, California State University, 2015.
Tappis, Hannah, and Shannon Doocy. "The Effectiveness and Value for Money of Cash-based Humanitarian Assistance: A Systematic Review." *Journal of Development Effectiveness* 10.1 (2018): 121–44.

Tarabulsi, Fawwaz. *A History of Modern Lebanon*. London: Pluto, 2007.
Tarraf, Giorgio. *Beirut: The Story of a City Destroyed by Peace*. Master's thesis, Lebanese American University, 2014.
Taut, Bruno. *Architecturlehre*. Hamburg: VSA, 1977.
Trent, John E. *Modernizing the United Nations System: Civil Society's Role in Moving from International Relations to Global Governance*. Farmington Hills, MI: Barbara Budrich Publishers, 2007.
Tubertini, Camilla. "Good Design That's Doing Good." Ikea website. Accessed June 14, 2019. https://highlights.ikea.com/2017/better-shelter.
Tzfadia, Erez. "Militarism and Space in Israel." *Israeli Sociology* 11.2 (2010): 337–61.
Union of International Associations. *Yearbook of International Organizations*. Accessed June 14, 2021. https://uia.org/yearbook.
United Nations. *Handbook for Emergencies*. Geneva: UNHCR, 1982.
United Nations International Strategy for Disaster Reduction. *2009 UNISDR Terminology on Disaster Risk Reduction* Accessed June 8, 2021. https://www.unisdr.org/files/7817_UNISDRTerminologyEnglish.pdf.
Vale, Lawrence. *Architecture, Power and National Identity*. London: Routledge, 2008.
Vale, Lawrence, and Thomas J. Campanella, eds. *The Resilient City: How Modern Cities Recover from Disaster*. Oxford, UK: Oxford University Press, 2005.
van der Tas, Jurjen. "Social Services, Access to Land and Transportation as Core Sectors for the Future Growth of Kabul." In *Development of Kabul: Reconstruction and Planning Issues*, edited by Babar Mumtaz and Kaj Noschis, 67–72. Lausanne, Switzerland: Comportment, 2004.
Vathi, Zana, and Richard Black. *Migration and Poverty Reduction in Kosovo*. Development Research Centre on Migration, Globalisation and Poverty, February 2007. Accessed June 4, 2021. https://pdfs.semanticscholar.org/3eb1/23d94df5f49864b316cf254c5cfc52f9cea0.pdf.
Verdeil, Éric. "Reconstructions manquées à Beyrouth : La poursuite de la guerre par le projet urbain." *Les Annales de la recherche urbaine* 91.1 (2001): 65–73.
Vöckler, Kai. "Four Strategies to Counter the Division of Cities." *Volume* 40, Architecture of Peace Reloaded, special insert "The Good Cause: Architecture of Peace—Divided Cities," exhibition catalog, Munich Architecture Museum (2014): 28–31.
———. "Politics of Architecture." In *SEE! Urban Transformation in Southeastern Europe*, edited by Kai Vöckler, 14–18. Vienna: Lit Verlag, 2012.
———. "Politics of Architecture." *Volume* 26, Architecture of Peace, special insert "SEE: Archis Interventions in Southeastern Europe" (2010): 1–7.

———. "Politics of Identity—The Example of Mostar, Bosnia-Herzegovina." NECE conference paper, 2010. Accessed June 14, 2021. https://www.bpb.de/veranstaltungen/netzwerke/nece/66608/conference-pre-workshop-city-and-diversity-challenges-for-citizenship-education.

———. *Prishtina Is Everywhere: Turbo Urbanism: The Aftermath of a Crisis*. Amsterdam: Archis, 2008.

———. "Stateless Urbanism." *Volume* 11, Cities Unbuilt (2007): 146–47.

Wakim, Najah. *The Black Hands* [al-ayādī as-sawwad]. Beirut: Sharikat al-matbuʿat lil-tawzi, 1998.

Walzer, Michael. *Thick and Thin: Moral Argument at Home and Abroad*. Notre Dame, IN: University of Notre Dame Press, 1994.

Warchitecture. ARH magazine, special edition. Sarajevo: Association of Architects Sarajevo, October 1993.

Weizman, Eyal. *Hollow Land: Israel's Architecture of Occupation*. London: Verso, 2007.

———. *The Least of All Possible Evils: Humanitarian Violence from Arendt to Gaza*. London: Verso, 2011.

Weiss, Srdjan Jovanović. "NATO as Architectural Critic." *Cabinet* 1 (2000): 84–89.

Woods, Lebbeus. *Radical Reconstruction*. New York: Princeton Architectural Press, 1997.

———. *War and Architecture*. New York: Princeton Architecture Press, 1993.

World Bank. "Assessment Study Entitled the Council for Development and Reconstruction." World Bank Group Archives, Washington DC, 1990.

———. "Lebanon Stabilization and Reconstruction: Vol. 2." Report no. 11406-LE. World Bank Group Archives, Washington DC, 1993. https://documents.worldbank.org/en/publication/documents-reports/documentdetail/213051468055439952/sectoral-annexes.

———. "Project Completion Note, Lebanese Republic, Reconstruction Project, Loan 1476-LE." World Bank Group Archives, Washington DC, 1995.

———. "Republic of Lebanon Recent Economic Developments and Emergency Rehabilitation and Technical Assistance Needs in Selected Priority Sectors." World Bank Group Archives, Washington DC, 1991.

Yahya, Maha. "Forbidden Spaces, Invisible Barriers: Housing in Beirut." PhD diss., Massachusetts Institute of Technology, 1995.

Yassin, Nasser. "Violent Urbanization and Homogenization of Space and Place: Reconstructing the Story of Sectarian Violence in Beirut." *World Institute for Development Economics Research* 2010/18 Working Paper, 2010.

Yiftachel, Oren, and Sandy Kedar. "Landed Power: The Making of the Israeli Land Regime." *Teoria U'Bikoret* 16 (2000): 67–100.

CONTRIBUTORS

DR. ELISA DAINESE is a theorist and historian with architectural background, and she is currently Assistant Professor of History and Theory of Architecture at the Georgia Institute of Technology. She works on issues of decolonization and postcolonial theory; global history and globalization; modernism, architectural design, and urbanization with a focus on the transoceanic exchange between African, European, and American architecture. She holds a PhD from the IUAV in Italy. She has published widely in architectural books and magazines (*Journal of the Society of Architectural Historians, Journal of Architecture, e-flux, Thresholds,* and *Bauhaus*), and her research has received grants and awards from Columbia University, the Bruno Zevi Foundation, the CCA, GAHTC, the Graham Foundation and the University of Pisa (Italy). Her book projects include this work and *African Dimensions of Postwar Architecture: A Global History of the Sub-Saharan "Habitat"* (sole author, forthcoming).

PROF. CHARLIE HAILEY is a Distinguished Teaching Scholar and professor in the School of Architecture at the University of Florida, where he received his doctorate. A licensed architect, he also studied at Princeton University and the University of Texas and has worked with the designer/builders Jersey Devil. He has lectured nationally and internationally, most recently at the University of Ljubljana, the Venice Biennale, MIT, Harvard University, UCLA, NYU, and SUT in Macedonia, where he was a Fulbright Scholar. His research focuses on how emergent built environments are constructed and experienced, and he contributes to scholarship investigating material culture and cultural landscapes to discover links between phenomenology, human agency, settlement patterns, and ecology. He is the author of numerous articles and six books on camping as place-making (*Campsite*, 2008), camps as contemporary spaces (*Camps*, 2009), islands as manufactured cultural landscapes (*Spoil Island*, 2013), and the pedagogy of thinking and making (*Design/Build with Jersey Devil*, 2016). In spring 2016 he received a grant from the Graham Foundation for Advanced Studies in the Fine Arts to study Slab City, a settlement in southern California, with photographer Donovan Wylie. This project was published in 2018 (*Slab City: Dispatches from the Last Free Place*). His latest book is *The Porch: Meditations on the Edge of Nature* (2021).

RAUL PANTALEO in an architect and one of the cofounders of Studio TAMassociati, a practice that specializes in socially oriented projects in critical areas. Some of the current and completed projects include the Salam Centre for Cardiac Surgery for the Emergency NGO in Sudan; Banca Etica (Ethic Bank) headquarters in Padua, Italy; and healthcare buildings for the Emergency NGO in Darfur, Sudan. The studio also has projects in the Central African Republic, Sierra Leon, Rwanda, Afghanistan, Iraq, and Uganda. As coprincipal of Studio TAMassociati, Pantaleo has been awarded a number of prestigious prizes (2017 Lafarge Holcim Awards Acknowledgement Prize, Aga Khan Award for Architecture, Curry Stone Design, Architetti dell'anno 2014, Zumtobel Group Award). In 2016 he was a member of the curatorial team in charge of the Italian Pavilion at the 15th International Architecture Exhibition of the Venice Biennale. He graduated from the IUAV of Venice, and he holds an international certificate in Human Ecology that he obtained thanks to his postgraduate studies at the University of Padua. Since 2019 he has been an Adjunct Professor of Architectural Design at the University of Trieste in Italy.

DR. ARMINA PILAV is a feminist, architect, researcher, and lecturer at the Department of Landscape Architecture at the University of Sheffield. She received the Marie Curie Individual Fellowship for her Un-war Space research (2016–18), developed at the Faculty of Architecture and Built Environment—TU Delft. Armina's research, practice, and teaching intersect and focus on the politics of re-presentation and re-production of physical, mediated space as well as bodily experiences in extreme conditions of war destruction or other disaster conditions. Dr. Pilav uses cross-media tools, psychospatiality, and radical observations to explore ecologies of transformations of rivers and land and related natural forms, architectures, and societies during and after wartime. Her work explores and creates different processes and spaces at the same time as it archives practices, transitional architectures, and impermanent organizations of humans/nonhumans within post-traumatic landscape systems. She publishes in magazines and academic journals and exhibits regularly. Her recent research on the destruction of Sarajevo and Mostar and the inhabitants' transformation of violence has been exhibited at the Venice Biennale of Architecture (2018) and as part of the Architecture of Shame project in Matera in July 2019. Dr. Pilav is a member of the Association for Culture and Art Crvena in Sarajevo.

DR. GABRIEL SCHWAKE is an architect, planner, and researcher. He studied architecture at Tel Aviv University and completed his PhD at the TU Delft. In his work Gabriel examines the issues of identities, conflicts, and neoliberalism in the process of spatial production. Focusing on the process of spatial production, Gabriel is interested in the transforming role of the built environment in times of increasing globalization and nationalism. His areas of expertise include nation-building, geopolitics, and geoeconomics, with an emphasis on the Middle East and other contested regions.

DR. DEEN SHARP is an LSE fellow in Human Geography in the Department of Geography and Environment at the London School of Economics and Political Science. He was previously the codirector of Terreform, Center for Advanced Urban Research, and a postdoctoral fellow at the Aga Khan Program for Islamic Architecture at the Massachusetts Institute of Technology. He is coeditor of *Beyond the Square: Urbanism and the Arab Uprisings* (2016) and *Open Gaza: Architectures of Hope* (2021). Sharp has published in the academic journals *Progress in Human Geography* and the *Arab Studies Journal*. Previously, he was a freelance journalist and consultant based in Lebanon. He has written for a range of media outlets, including the *Guardian, Executive* magazine, *Jadaliyya,* and *MERIP,* and has worked for several governments, UN agencies, and international NGOs.

DR. ALEKSANDAR STANIČIĆ is an architect, theorist, and Assistant Professor at TU Delft Faculty of Architecture and the Built Environment, Chair of Methods of Analysis and Imagination. Previously he was a Marie Curie Postdoctoral Fellow at TU Delft, a research scholar at the Italian Academy for Advanced Studies, Columbia University, and postdoctoral fellow at the Aga Khan Program for Islamic Architecture at MIT. Aleksandar is on the editorial board of the *Footprint: Architecture Theory Journal* (2020–present), and author of numerous articles and special issues in the *Journal of Architecture, Footprint, Architecture and Culture,* and others. He is recipient of multiple grants and fellowships from the Graham Foundation, the European Commission, Government of Lombardy Region (Italy), and the Ministry of Education, Republic of Serbia.

PROF. KAI VÖCKLER is a founding member of Archis Interventions and program director of the South Eastern Europe (SEE) Network. He has taken part in urban development projects in southeastern Europe and urban research projects in Europe and Asia. Professor Vöckler is an urbanist, publicist, author, editor, curator of exhibitions, and lecturer on art and urban themes. He gained a PhD in Art History on urban spatial images and has professional expertise in landscape, architectural, and artistic competitions and design projects, both solo and in teams with architects. He has curated various exhibitions at European cultural institutions and museums. He is currently Professor for Urban Design at the Offenbach University of Art and Design, Germany.

INDEX

Italicized page numbers refer to illustrations.

accountability, 21, 26, 39
Addis Ababa, General Post Office and Ministry of Transport and Telecommunications, 50, *51*
aestheticization of war and violence in civilian life, 11, 70–71, 79, 84
Afghanistan, Anabah Hospital Maternity Center, 12, 141, 150–52, *151*. *See also* Kabul (Afghanistan)
Aga Khan Foundation (AKF), 23, 42–43n19
aid programs. *See* humanitarian aid; NGOs (nongovernmental organizations); *and specific NGOs and global organizations by name*
Ai Weiwei, 171
Akar, Hiba Bou, 97
Akšamija, Azra, 12, 181, 182; interview with, 154–78; "Monument in Waiting" project, 171; "Wearable Mosques" project, 174. *See also* Culturally Sensitive Design course (MIT)
Albania, 29
Algeria, 3
Amman Design Week, 168
Anabah Hospital Maternity Center (Afghanistan), 12, 141, 150–52, *151*
anthropomorphism, 151
Arab Center for Architecture, 91
ArcelorMittal Orbit (Stratford, London), 167, 178n12
Archis Interventions (Archis network), 19, 24, 25–26, 29, 37, 41n7, 43n19,
43n22, 44n35; public awareness campaign, 30, *31*, *32*
architects. *See* role of architects and designers in postwar environments
Architects Association of Sarajevo, 47
architecture: bridging through design, 7, 119–27, 157, 183; defensive, 3; of peace, 19; as personification of culture targeted for destruction, 157; prewar architecture no longer possible in postwar environment, 65; redefined in war and postwar periods, 49. *See also* competitions; destruction of art and architecture; postwar reconstruction; urban postwar reconstruction; wartime design and architecture; *and specific locations and types of architecture by name*
Architecture of Israel Quarterly, 84
ARH (magazine), 53, 54
Arhitekt (design bureau), 66n8
Arnautović, Selma, 54, 67n23
art: activism and, 10, 155; hijacking for wrong purposes, 159–63; impact even in times of emergency, 5, 170; in postwar reconciliation, 155–56; as tool of postconflict cultural dialogue, 159–61, 172, 175; as tool to alleviate human suffering, 172. *See also* Culturally Sensitive Design course (MIT); destruction of art and architecture
Assad, Bashar al-, 154

Association of Owners Rights in the Beirut Central District, 108; poster by, *109*
Atelier Parisien d'Urbanisme, l' (APUR), first attempt for Lebanese reconstruction (1977 plan), 99–101, 104
Auerbach Halevy Architects, 82
Azraq Refugee Camp, Al (Jordan), 12, 154; cultural production in, 156; inadequacy of housing and infrastructure in, 159; *1002 Inventions: Art and Design in Al Azraq Refugee Camp*, 173, 178n15; previous art projects of, 159; process of design in, 165–66; refugee-led design, Culturally Sensitive Design course applying, 159, *160*, *162*, 163

Barenstein, Duyne E. Jennifer, 4–5
Bauhaus Dessau Foundation, 19
BCD. *See* Beirut/Beirut Central District (BCD; Lebanon)
beautiful places: *bellitudine,* use of, 140; emergency health architecture as, 139–41, 145–47, 149–52; meaning of "beauty," 140; refugee camps, beautifying design of, 150
Bechtel (US engineering firm), 103
Beirut/Beirut Central District (BCD; Lebanon), 91–114, *93*, *110*, 181; APUR-led plan of 1977–86, 99–100, 104; Association of Owners Rights in, 108; Beirut Festival (1994) in, 106; change in mindset of populace about returning to (1983–84), 102–3; collapse of Wadi Abu Jamil (plot 999 Mina el Hosn), killing squatters in, 108; commodification of space in, 106; demolition of downtown and significant buildings, 102, 104, 108; difference between inside and outside of Solidere's area, *93*; Eddé Plan, 103–6; explosion damage (2020), 111; Law 117 (1991) to allow real estate company to engage in rebuilding, 104, 114n46; during Lebanese Civil War, 96–97; Lebanese Lira national reconstruction project (1978) in, 100; multiple master plans for during Civil War, 98–99, 113n24; Oger-Gemayel Plan (1983), 101–3; opposition to Eddé Plan and Solidere, 104–6, *105;* postwar reconstruction, 11, 97–106; privatization of reconstruction, 100, 103; rival militias considering as crucial site of conflict, 98; small-scale real estate corporations financing reconstruction in, 100; Solidere's role in rebuilding, 91–93, 103–5; tour "'Beauty under Stress': Practicing Public Space in Beirut Central District," 91–92, *93. See also* Port of Beirut; Solidere (Lebanese Company for the Development and Reconstruction of the Beirut Central District SAL)
Belgrade: Museum of Aviation, 50; Museum of Genocide Victims, 177n8; recognition of specific architects' works in, 58; RTS (Radio-Television of Serbia) memorial in, *6;* Serbian government building in, 2
bellitudine, 140
Ben-Gurion, David, 87
bias: inherent bias of each person's own cultural background, 168–70, 182; in postwar construction and art, 33, 46, 158–61
Bičakčić, Edhem, 60
Bjelašnica: Olympic Press Center, 52
Boano, Camillo, 49, 64
Bøe, Bjørn, 120–21
Bogdanović, Bogdan, 47
"Borba" award for best architectural achievements in Yugoslavian territory, 67n27
Borja, Zaragoza (Spain), Sanctuary of Mercy church in, 161
Bosnia-Herzegovina: antifascist memorial complexes, failure to maintain, 47; Archis Interventions in, 19; architects' ambiguous position in postwar

environment in, 59; biased postwar architecture in, 33, 46, 160–61; cultural competition for space of identity in architecture in, 159–60; ethnic coexistence in, 66n15, 158; integrating emergency housing into existing urban fabric in, 124; Iwansson's work on emergency settlements in, 124, 125; Skotte's work on emergency settlements in, 115, 119, 121, 122, 136n14. *See also* Mostar (Bosnia-Herzegovina)

Bosnian War (1992–96): Boano's work experience in, 49; cross-media analyses of architects' practices during, 49; design during and immediately after, 11, 46; multicultural coexistence prior to, 66n15, 157–58; surveys of destroyed cultural heritage sites in, 177n6; targeting of cultural heritage and religious sites in, 156, 157

BOT (build, operate, transfer) project, 79

Bouman, Ole, 41n7

building codes, 75

Bulić, Jagoda, 53

Campanella, Thomas, 4

case studies, 6. *See also specific locations and types of projects by name*

casualties in wars: civilian, 71–72, 78; Lebanese Civil War, 95, 112n7

Chamma, Nasr, 137n24

civil defense and protection: emergency drills to prepare for enemy attacks and natural disaster, 72, 73; erasing boundaries between home front and war front in, 3, 71–77; infrastructure of, 69. *See also* National Center of Israeli Resilience (*HaMirkaz LeEitanut Yisraelit*)

civil society organizations. *See* NGOs (nongovernmental organizations)

climate change, 3, 14

collaborative planning. *See* participatory planning

communication with public, 37–38

communities: destruction of neighborhood fabric by conflict and reconstruction, 35–36; fostering sense of community, 36; role in postdisaster reconstruction, 5, 9. *See also* participatory planning

competitions, 183; "MatterBetter" competition in Syria, 185–86n8; military colleges in Jerusalem, design competitions for, 86; National Center of Israeli Resilience design competition, 78–84, 82, 83, 87

conflict. *See* violence *and specific wars and locations by name*

conscious contextualization, 19, 25

Co-PLAN (Tirana-based association), 29

coral stone, use of, 139, 147, 152n6

corruption, 18, 27, 38, 64, 114n46, 171–72

cost concerns: consumer lifestyle and social exclusion, 163; emergency health facility architecture, 144; military-funded projects focusing on, 80. *See also* funding; NGOs (nongovernmental organizations)

Council for Development and Reconstruction (CDR; Lebanon), 99, 103–4, 113n26, 114n43

"created spontaneity," 127–31, 184

Croatia, 55, 67n27

cultural appropriation, 167

cultural harmony in architectural design: Anabah Hospital Maternity Center (Afghanistan), 150; Pediatric Clinic of Nyala (Darfur), 142; Pediatric Clinic of Port Sudan, 147. *See also* multiculturalism

cultural heritage: agency of, in war and postwar contexts, 156–58; calculated destruction of, 1–3, 155, 157, 158–59; critical thinking about, 161; hybrid nature of "culture," 158; importance of cultural memory, 161; international aid community focusing on landmarks of,

cultural heritage (*continued*)
  33; "new cultural memories," creation of, 158–59; preservation, teaching in Culturally Sensitive Design course, 159–66, *160, 162*; rebuilt sites as, 7, 10, 147, 148. *See also* religion and religious structures
Culturally Sensitive Design course (MIT), *9*, 9–10, 12–13, 154–76; agency of cultural heritage and, 155–58; best intentions and the potential for bad results in, 172–74; creating dialogue between cultures, 159–61, 172, 175; as cross-disciplinary and inclusive model for education and civic innovation, 154–55; cultural needs of refugees within context of containment, 163; determining who owns the art, 170–72; ethics and cultural interventions in, 166–69, 182; in five-part miniseries dealing with refugee camps in Jordan, 175, *176*; lessons learned in, 175–76; patronizing agenda of institutions, efforts to avoid, 174; performative preservation framework of, 175; process of design in, 163–66, *164, 165*; production of future heritage and, 158–66; purpose of, 154, 159
Ćurić, Borislav, 56
Cyprus, 19, 31

Dadaab Refugee Camps (Kenya), *4*, 12, 116–17, *119*, 122, 127, 134n1, 135n4. *See also* Dagahaley Refugee Camp (Kenya); Hagadera Refugee Camp (Kenya)
Dagahaley Refugee Camp (Kenya), 128, 131
Dainese, Elisa, volume chapters by, 1–15, 179–86; volume chapter translation by, 139–53
Damascus, Azm Palace in, 163; design inspired by, *162*
Dar al-Handassah (DAR; Lebanese engineering firm), 102, 103, 114n43
Darfur, Pediatric Clinic of Nyala, 12, 141–45, *143, 144*
Davie, Michael, 96–97
Davis, Ian, 124; *Shelter after Disaster,* 124, 125, 137n20
De Boeck, Lieven, *Fireworks II, Le Bleu du Ciel,* 7
de Man, Paul, 70
design. *See* architecture; postwar reconstruction; urban postwar reconstruction; *and specific locations and types of structures by name*
designers. *See* role of architects and designers in postwar environments
destruction of art and architecture: Beirut, demolition of downtown and significant buildings in, 102, 104, 108; religious structures destroyed on religious holidays, 157; social consequences of, 1–3, 155, 157, 179. *See also* Štraus, Ivan
displaced population: from Africa and Middle East, 179; art raising critical awareness about, 172; effects on infrastructure, 18; failure to return to home, 17–18, 102–3; during Lebanese Civil War, 95–96, 97, 102–3, 108; resettlement solutions for, 3; rural population relocating to city, 18, 33–36, 40n3. *See also* refugee camps
Dobrinja (Sarajevo), 54
Doucet, Isabelle, 49
Dubrovnik (Croatia), 55

earthquakes, 75
Eastern Bloc, collapse of, 72
Eastern Europe, 43n19
East Germany, Project and Access Plan (PAP) in, 35
Economist, The, on Solidere and Beirut's reconstruction, 94
Eddé, Henri, 102–4, 106
Eddé Plan (Beirut), 103–6

Elektroprivreda Building (Sarajevo): destruction of, 56, *57*; façade, 52, *53*, *57*; first Štraus design proposal for (1972), 50; purpose of building, 65n6; reconstruction of, 11, 47, *51*, *52*, 59–64, *61*, 65n2, 66n10; sculptural elements added as part of rebuilding, 61

Eliav Architects, 82; Center for Israeli Resilience design by, *82*

Emergency (Italian NGO), 141, 149, 150. *See also* emergency health facility architecture

emergency health facility architecture, 139–53; Anabah Hospital Maternity Center (Afghanistan), 12, 141, 150–52, *151*; beautiful places, right of people to receive health care in, 139–41, 145–47, 149–52; color used to give building an identity, 150; comfort combined with sense of continuity in, 142–44, 147–48, 151; cost concerns, 144; Pediatric Clinic of Nyala (Darfur), 141–45, *143*, *144*; Pediatric Clinic of Port Sudan, 141, 145–49, *148*; protection and sociability in, 146–47; simplicity as fundamental element of, 146; Sulaymaniyah Refugee Camp clinic (Iraq), 12, 149–50; technological innovation to reduce energy consumption in, 144–45, 148–49

emergency preparation for defense. *See* civil defense and protection

emergency shelters. *See* refugee camps

empowerment, 39, 86, 173

energy consumption, technological innovation to reduce, 144–45, 148–49

environmental issues, 140, 142–44; climate change, 3, 14; earthquakes, 75

ERSTE Foundation, 43n19, 43n23

ERSTE Group, 43n19

ethics: cultural interventions and, 166–69, 182; militarization of post-war architecture as violation of, 5; ownership of the art and, 170–72; reconstruction phases and, 8, 141; shared ethics among participants and stakeholders, 184

ethnic identity, destruction of, 66n15, 156–58. *See also* multiculturalism

Fawaz, Mona, 94
First Gulf War (1991–92), 74–75
Fisk, Robert, 95
flexible planning, 36–38
Foster, Norman, 93
Fouad Chehab Ring Road (Beirut), 91
frontier projects, 139, 140
funding: of Beirut reconstruction, 100; of humanitarian aid projects, 170, 171; National Center of Israeli Resilience, lack of funding for construction of, 84; of NGOs, 23
Future Heritage Lab, 154, 159, 161, 167, *176*, 177n2, 182

Gavin, Angus, 106
Gaza, missiles and rockets aimed at Israel from, 75–76
Geci, Visar, public awareness series produced by, *31*
Gemayel, Amin, 101, 102
genocide, 3, 156–57, 177n8
George Haddad Highway (Beirut), 91
Germany, Nazi aestheticizing of violence in, 70
Ghalgoul (part of Beirut), 100
Giménez, Cecilia, 161
globalization, 1, 22–23, 28, 183
Goshen Architects, 82
governance and urban postconflict development, 20–25
Gračanica (Bosnia-Herzegovina), 124
Grbavica (Sarajevo), 54

Hadid, Zaha, 93
Hagadera Refugee Camp (Kenya), 12, 115–18, *119*, 120, 128–31, *130*, 133, 134, 134n1

Hailey, Charlie, 12, 184; volume chapter by, 115–38
Hajji, Ik, 138n28
Hariri, Rafik, 98, 99, 101–4, 106–7
Hariri Foundation, 103
healing process: social relationships and, 10, 12; wartime architecture enabling, 150, 152. *See also* psychological relief
health care facilities. *See* emergency health facility architecture
Hecker, Zvi, 78
Herscher, Andrew, 183; *Wararchitectural Theory*, 53–54
Herzog & de Meuron, 93
historical landmarks. *See* cultural heritage
Holl, Steven, 93
Home Front Command. *See* Israel Defense Force (IDF)
home front versus battlefront, 3, 71–77, 87. *See also* normalization of war in civilian life
homogenization of nation-states. *See* territorial homogenization as result of destruction of art and architecture
Hoss, Salim-al, 99
Hourani, Najib, 106, 108–9
housing shortage, 33
humanitarian aid: art's impact measured differently than, 170; code of ethics and, 168–69; donor countries' sociopolitical aims applied to locality of reconstruction, 21; inconsistencies of system, 181; planner as outsider to refugees and local authorities, 120–21, 136n10; provision of facilities for, 49
human rights, 21, 181, 185n5

IAUA. *See* Israeli Association of United Architects (IAUA)
Ikea, 125, 137n23
imagination: collective, 12, 58; in emergency construction, 139; in urban war conditions, 56, 176; utopist point of view and, 139, 152
informal sector construction, 34, 44n39
interdisciplinary approach, 4, 12, 19, 25, 154–55, 168–69, 177n2. *See also* Culturally Sensitive Design course (MIT)
International Monetary Fund (IMF), 22
Iran: missile program and nuclear project, 76; traditional natural ventilation system in, 144–45
Iraq: assaults on cultural heritage in, 3; Scud missile attacks on Israel from, 74; Sulaymaniyah Refugee Camp, 12, 149–50; surgical facility in, 141
Israel: Arab Palestinian houses and ruins in, 71, 78; building codes for earthquake protection in, 75; civil defense infrastructure in, 69; Civil Defense Law (1951), 72; Civil Defense Service (*Hagana Ezrahit*, or *Haga*), 72; erasing boundaries between the home and the front in, 72–77; frontier settlements in, 71; invasion of southern Lebanon (1978), 100; Merhav Mugan (protective space) in, 75, 76; military colleges in Jerusalem, design competitions for, 86; military construction inspired by civilian architecture in, 79; Ministry of Defense's Department of Construction and Engineering, 78; missile and rocket attacks on, 74, 75–76; National Emergency Management Authority (NEMA, or *RACHEL*), 76–77, 78; normalization of war in civilian life in, 70–71, 79, 84, 86–87; private shelters in, 74; privatization of civil defense infrastructure in, 69, 77, 84; retrofitting existing buildings in, 77; role of architecture and urban development in, 69; TMA 38 plan in, 77; underground shelters in, 74, 74. *See also* National Center of Israeli Resilience (*HaMirkaz LeEitanut Yisraelit*)
Israel Defense Force (IDF), 71; Home Front Command, 11, 75, 78, 80–81, 86

Israeli Air Force Museum, design competition for, 86
Israeli Association of United Architects (IAUA), 78, 80–82
Italy, fascists aestheticizing violence in, 70
Iwansson, Per, 12, 134n1; death of, 134; interview with, 115–38; *Mission Report 92/44*, 131–32; open-ended urban design and, 118. *See also* "simple plans" approach

Jamaković, Said, 58
Jerliu, Florina, public awareness series produced in cooperation with, 31
Jerusalem military colleges, design competitions for, 86
Jordanian refugee camps, 137n24. *See also* Azraq Refugee Camp, Al (Jordan)
Jounieh (Lebanon), 98, 101
justice and transitional justice, 7, 139, 140, 152, 184

Kabul (Afghanistan), 18, 19, 31, 33, 35, 37, 40n4
Kahneman, Daniel, 121
Kakuma Refugee Camp (Kenya), 115–17, 119–20, 133, *133*, 134, 134n1
Kaldor, Mary, 23
Kant, Immanuel, 70
Karim Aga Khan IV, 42–43n19
Kenya: ethnic and territorial homogenization in, 3; growth in refugee population in, 134n1; simplicity of camps in, 115–16; Somali refugees in, 3, 122–23. *See also* Dadaab Refugee Camps (Kenya); Hagadera Refugee Camp (Kenya); Kakuma Refugee Camp (Kenya); Walda Refugee Camp (Kenya)
Khoury, Bernard, 96–97
Kibera (Kenya), 129
Knapp, Eberhard, 35
Kosovo, 19, 22, 40n3
Kosovo-Albanians, 18, 34, 40n2

Kosovo-Serbs, 18, 34, 40n2, 44n35
Kovačević, Zdravko, 50
Kurdish-Iraqi Ministry of Health, 150
Kurto, Nedžad, 50–51, 67n17

Law, John, 101
Lebanese Civil War, 94–103; assassination of American University of Beirut president (1983), 102; Battle of the Hotels, 113n23; cease-fire (1977), 99–100; Christian militias versus Syrian forces, 101; construction sector's growth in, 97; damages estimated from, 95; displacement of population during, 95–96, 102–3; militia territories' proliferation in, 96; Mountain War (1984), 102; public services controlled by militias in, 96–97; religious homogenization as goal of militias in, 96; as series of incidents, 95, 97, 102; urbanization as part of, 97; US Embassy and Marine headquarters bombing (1983), 102; War of Liberation as last stage of, 98, 103
Lebanese Company for the Development and Reconstruction of the Beirut Central District SAL. *See* Solidere (Lebanese Company for the Development and Reconstruction of the Beirut Central District SAL)
Lebanon: economic collapse of (2020), 111; financial assistance to, 98, 101; formation of Second Lebanese Republic, 107; General Labor Confederation strikes, 108; *Horizon 2000 for the Reconstruction and Development of Lebanon*, 103–4; Israeli invasion of southern Lebanon (1978), 100; missiles and rockets aimed at Israel from, 74, 75–76; national debt and default of, 106, 111; postwar reconstruction in, 91–114; repressive governance after Hariri's 1992 election, 107–8; social power in postwar era, 107–10. *See also* Beirut/Beirut Central District

Lebanon (*continued*)
(BCD; Lebanon); Solidere (Lebanese Company for the Development and Reconstruction of the Beirut Central District SAL)
Lebas, Jean-Paul, 106
Leemann, Esther, 5
Linor Project (Lebanon), 101
Ljubljana, 58
local and international organizations/interests during reconstruction, 8–9, 10, 21–27, 29–31, 30, 39, 43n22, 43n28, 44–45n40
local conditions, need to account for, 1, 6, 19–21, 34, 116, 133–34, 182
London Docklands Development Corporation (LDDC), 106
long-term versus short-term thinking when designing emergency structures, 122–23, 152
Lynch, Kevin, *The Image of the City*, 106

Makdisi, Saree, 104, 107–8
mashrabiya (shutters), 148, *148*
master plan, need for, 33–37
media's role, 1, 8, 37–38, 180–81; cross-media analyses of architects' practices during wartime, 49–50, 180
Memorial in Exile (Stratford, London), 167, 178n12
memory, cultural. *See* cultural heritage
memory studies, 10
militarization of art and architecture, 3, 5, 8, 14n13, 110, 179, 181
MIT (Massachusetts Institute of Technology). *See* Culturally Sensitive Design course (MIT); Future Heritage Lab
mosques. *See* religion and religious structures
Mostar (Bosnia-Herzegovina), 19, 31, 37, 42n13, 160, 185n7; Boano's work experience in, 49; Partisan Cemetery, 47
Mount Trebević (Sarajevo), 54, 59

Muhasilović, Halid, 50
Mujezinović, Ismet, 53
multiculturalism: in Bosnia-Herzegovina, 66n15, 157–58; erasure of, 3, 156–59, 161; Sarajevo's Unis Towers and, 50. *See also* cultural heritage

Nahas, Charbel, 102–3
National Center of Israeli Resilience (*HaMirkaz LeEitanut Yisraelit*), 11, 70, 77–86; civilian-like approach to the design of, 78–79, 86; collaborations with civilian institutions to enlarge competition outreach, 80–81; composition of competition jury for, 81; concept for, 78; criteria in design competition, 80; design competition for construction of, 78, 79–84, 87; finalist entries in competition for, 82, *82, 83*; Home Front Command role in design of, 80–81, 86; Israeli-Arab architects entering competition for, 81; lack of funding for construction of, 84; name of, 77–78; Rehavam Base as location for, 80; winning entry from Ran Blander Architects, 82–84, *84, 85*; WIZO and IAUA role in design process, 78, 80–82
National Emergency Management Authority (NEMA, or *RACHEL*, Israel), 76–77, 78
nationalist resurgence, 157, 158
NATO, 22
natural resources. *See* environmental issues
Neidhart, Juraj, 58
new technologies, 127, 137n24, 181
New Urbanism, 106
NGOs (nongovernmental organizations): architects' and designers' role in postwar environments within, 25–27; cooperation of international with local NGOs, 8–9, 21–27, 29–31, 30, 39, 43n22, 43n28, 44–45n40; criticisms

of, 23–24, 44–45n40; definition, 22; funding of, 23; internationally networked NGOs, growth of, 22, 42n16; as mediators between local and international communities, 25–26; new divide between the impoverished/displaced and global citizens of, 22–23; pooling of resources to build resilient networks, 24–25; role of, 10, 19, 20–25, 37; specialty areas of, 24
9/11 attacks, 72
normalization of war in civilian life, 70–71, 79, 84, 86–87, 179, 184n1
Norway, housing built by Sweden in, 124
Norwegian Refugee Council (NRC), 125
Nouvel, Jean, 92, 93
Nucho, Joanne, 96

OECD (Organisation for Economic Co-operation and Development), 22
Oger-Gemayel Plan (Beirut 1983), 101–3
Oger Liban (corporation), 99, 102
Open Society Foundations (OSF), 43n19
ownership: APUR in Beirut and role of property owners, 100; of art, 170–72; BCD opposition from property owners, 104; planning urban postwar reconstruction without, 36; private, 170–72; process of legalization in Prishtina, 43–44n30; reclaiming Beirut property from squatters, 105; Solidere forcing land owners into real estate corporation, 108

Palestinians living in Israel. *See* Israel
Palmyra (Syria), 3, 161
Pantaleo, Raul, 12, 182; volume chapter by, 139–53
participatory planning, 36, 37, 39, 40, 121, 123, 137n17, 173, 183–84. *See also* NGOs (nongovernmental organizations)
Pašović, Haris, 47
patronage, 26, 170, 183

Pediatric Clinic of Nyala (Darfur), 141–45, *143, 144*
Pediatric Clinic of Port Sudan, 141, 145–49, *148*
Peri Davidovich Architects, 82; Center for Israeli Resilience design by, *83*
Pilav, Armina, 10–11, 182; volume chapter by, 46–68
Planning Institute for Development of the Canton of Sarajevo, 58
Podgorica (Yugoslav city), 58
political nature of postwar building, 13, 17, 19, 37, 157, 159, 180
politicization of violence, 1–3, 70
Port of Beirut: explosion and destruction (2020), 111; rebuilding, 99, 100
Port Sudan: archaeological site of Suakin and use of coral stone, 147, 152n6; Pediatric Clinic, 12, 139, 141, 145–49, *148*; population growth in, 145–46; refugees in, 146
postwar reconstruction, 4–10; bias in, 33, 46, 158–61; criticism of, 5–6; education of new generation of designers in, 9–10; innovative design in, 5–6, *6*, 159, 183; local and international organizations/interests in, 8–9, 10, 21–27, 29–31, *30*, 39, 43n22, 43n28, 44–45n40; meaning of, 94, 179; misconceptions about later possibility of modification of, 5; religious buildings given priority in, 157; salvageable buildings, reuse of, 63; Woods and Štraus's principles of, 60, 62–63. *See also* participatory planning; urban postwar reconstruction; *and specific locations and wars by name*
preservation. *See* cultural heritage
Prishtina (Kosovo), 18, 26, 29, 31, *31,* 34–35, 37, 38, 40n2, 43n30, 44n35
Project and Access Plan (PAP, East Germany), 35
protective spaces approach, 11, 70, 75–77, 83–84, 86, 147

psychological relief: art as tool for trauma therapy, 170; cultural production's aesthetic and morale effects, 156, 172; wartime architecture enabling, 150, 152

Quarantelli, Enrico L., 135n7

Rabbat, Nasser, volume foreword by, vii–ix
Ran Blander Architects, 82–83; winning design for Center for Israeli Resilience, 84, 85
Reagan administration's support for Lebanon, 101
reconciliation: art's role in, 155–56; loss of potential for, 158–59; "simple plans" approach and, 152; understanding and acknowledgment leading to, 66, 183; urban role in, 17, 21. See also specific conflicts by name
reconstruction. See postwar reconstruction; urban postwar reconstruction; and specific countries and cities by name
reductionism, 135n7
refugee camps, 12, 14n11; "anchoring effects" and, 121; basic urban structure applicable to, 118–19, 130, 135n3; beautifying to break out of concentration camp design of, 150; choice of terminology for, 124, 137n20; community involvement in planning process for, 121, 123, 137n17, 173, 183–84; cooking and eating habits as design considerations for, 126–27; "created spontaneity" and, 127–31, 184; designing as bridging, 119–27, 183; health services, planning for access to, 118; housing versus tent phase for, 124, 136n14; humanitarian aid workers and offices, positioning of, 120; local society's design and material resources, use of, 125, 137n24; long-term versus short-term thinking when designing, 122–23, 179; negative effects of poorly conceived planning for, 185n3; planning horizons for duration of, 122–23, 136n13; power of designers in construction of, 121, 122; prefabricated panels and woven screens in, 125, 143; public space, need for, 129–31; redesign later by refugees, 137n24; rental shelter in, 129; self-organizing by inhabitants, 128–29; simple plans for, 115–38; transition from camp to town, 122–23, 135n8; urgency and challenges of implementation, 117–19, 134, 135n4; voice of refugees in artistic expression, 173. See also "simple plans" approach and specific camps and locations by name
regulation of urban development, 26–27, 35; enforceability in postwar period, 38–39; illegal development in immediate postwar period and, 34, 38, 44n39; planning used for, 37; prewar regulations still in effect, 38
religion and religious structures: coexistence in Bosnian cities and villages, 66n15, 158; Giménez's preservationist effort in Sanctuary of Mercy church, 161; in Lebanese Civil War, 95–97, 101; in Sarajevo and Bosnian War, 156–57; wearable mosque project of Akšamija, 174
resettlement solutions. See displaced population
resilience, 77, 86
restitution claims for property, 36
Riedlmayer, András, 155, 156, 177n6
role of architects and designers in postwar environments: as agents of change, 10, 26; avoidance of political ideologies, 180; "bird's-eye view," shortcomings of, 26; bridging between planner as outsider with local authorities and refugees, 120–21, 180; as mediators for participatory design and planning, 7, 183–84; within NGOs, 25–27; in pilot projects, 21; principles for, 27–28,

179–80; response to incorporate humanity and professional integrity, 64, 183; transformative ideas and, 184; in urban postconflict development, 19–20; in urban war conditions, 56
Rui Gonçalves, Miranda, 4
Rwanda, 3

safety precautions, 5, 38, 75. *See also* National Center of Israeli Resilience (*HaMirkaz LeEitanut Yisraelit*)
Saida (Lebanon), 98
Saifi (part of Beirut), 100, 102
Salam, Assem, 102
Salem, Paul, 101
salvageable buildings, reuse of, 63
Sarajevo (Bosnia-Herzegovina): Ali Pašino school and neighborhood, 59, 68n33; Boano's work experience in, 49; earthworks remaining in, 59; ethnic groups in, 66n15, 158; half-destroyed buildings remaining in, 58–59; Hotel Holiday, 50, 52; Maršal Tito barracks, 59; military siege and destruction of, 50, 53–56; Olympic Museum, 47, 48, 58, 59; postwar construction in, 57–59; private construction boom in (2008–9), 58–59; public buildings, advocating reconstruction priority for, 64; recognition of specific architects' works in, 58; Štraus's architecture in, 50, 58; Štraus's diary observing destruction of, 11, 47–48, 54–57, 66n8; Štraus's views on possible postwar reconstruction in, 63–64; Unis Towers, 50, 55, 60. *See also* Štraus, Ivan; Woods, Lebbeus
Sarkis, Élias, 99
Sassine, Rania, 91–93, 93, 111n1
satellite imaging, 127, 137n24, 181
Saudi interests in Lebanese peace negotiations, 101
scarcity: Culturally Sensitive Design course students learning about, 166, 175; in reconstruction era, 18; "simple plans" approach and architecture of scarcity, 117, 131
Schellenberg, Werner, 128, 131
Schwake, Gabriel, 11, 180–81, 184n1; volume chapter by, 69–90
Second Lebanese Republic, 107
Serbian Academy of Sciences and Art, 47
Serbs. *See* Kosovo-Serbs
Shammaa, Nassar, 114n44
Sharjah Museum of Islamic Civilization (UAE) exhibition, 169
Sharp, Deen, 11, 181, 184n1; volume chapter by, 91–114
Sierra Leone, Iwansson's work on emergency settlements in, 115, 126
"simple plans" approach, 12, 115–38; architecture of scarcity and, 117, 131; basic tools and makeshift offices, 117; "created spontaneity" and, 127–31; designing as bridging, 119–27; grid design, 117–18, 128–29; improvisation's role in, 116; local conditions, need to account for, 116, 133–34; meaning of term "simple," 115; open-ended urban design and, 118; planner as outsider, bridging with local authorities and refugees, 120–21; self-organizing by camp inhabitants and, 128–29; short-term bridging to long-term structures, 123–27; technology use versus first-hand experience in designing, 127, 131; urgency and challenges of implementation, 117–19, 134; walking as basic tool of site-design process, 127, 129, 132–33
Skopje (Yugoslav city), 58
Skotte, Hans, 12, 136n14, 137n24; interview with, 115–38. *See also* "simple plans" approach
Slobodna Bosna/Free Bosna (magazine), 58, 67n33
Socialist Federative Republic of Yugoslavia. *See* Yugoslavia, Socialist Federative Republic of

social tolerance, 7, 10, 156, 184
Solidere (Lebanese Company for the Development and Reconstruction of the Beirut Central District SAL), 11, 91–94, 103–5, *107, 110*; criticism of, 93–94, 104–5, *105*, 107–9; formation of, 99, 103, 106; legacy of, 106; new economic order created by, 106, 108–9; precursor initiatives, 97–98; share price since Lebanon's economic collapse (2020), 111; violence in approach of, 108, 110
Somali civil war, 3. *See also specific refugee camps in Kenya by name*
Sørensen, M. L. S., 5
Soros, George, 23, 43n19
Souk al-Nouriye (Beirut), 102
Souk Sursok (Beirut), 102
Soviet Union, 70
Špilja, Sabahudin, 56
Sri Lanka, 181; Skotte's work on emergency settlements in, 115, 116, 121, 125–26
Staničić, Aleksandar, volume chapters by, 1–15, 154–78, 179–86
Strada, Gino, 141
strategic planning: need for, 33–34; planning horizons and, 122–23
Štraus, Ivan, 11, 46–68, *48, 53*; *Architect and Barbarians* (published version of diary), 47–48, 54–55, 67n23; architectural works by, 50–52, 58; *Architecture of Yugoslavia from 1945 until 1990*, 54; awards and recognition of, 55, 67n27; color, use of, 52; correspondence and relationship with Woods, 11, 47, 60, 62, 64; death of, 66n14; interviews with, 47, 54, 65n2, 66n10, 67n23, 68n37; on postwar architecture and future of Sarajevo, 54; on "the present of the city," 58; on prewar architecture no longer possible in postwar environment, 65; recommendations for reconstruction process, 64; reconstruction in Sarajevo and, 59–64; on "systematic destruction of the city," 56; on territorial separation in reconstruction process, 63–64; training of, 66n14; war diary of, 11, 47–48, 54–57, 66n8; writings by, 53. *See also Elektroprivreda* Building (Sarajevo)
Sudan, emergency health facilities in, 12, 141–42. *See also* Port Sudan
Sulaymaniyah Refugee Camp clinic (Iraq), 12, 149–50
Šutej, Miroslav, 53
Sweden: grid design in, 129; Norwegian housing built by, 124
Syrian Civil War: assaults on cultural heritage in, 1, 3; refugees from, 123, 171. *See also* Azraq Refugee Camp, Al (Jordan)
Syrian role in Lebanese Civil War, 98

Tabbara, Bahij, 108
Ta'if Peace Accord (1989), 98, 103
TAMassociati, 12, 182; volume chapter by, 139–53
Taut, Bruno, 129
Tel al-Za'atar, 95
territorial homogenization as result of destruction of art and architecture, 3, 96, 155, 158, 160
Tito, Maršal, 59
tolerance. *See* social tolerance
Trablousi, Fawwaz, 96
transcultural cross-fertilization. *See* multiculturalism
transparency, 24, 26, 27, 37, 39, 42, 82
T-Serai project, 169

Ukraine, assaults on cultural heritage in, 1
UNESCO, 170, 171
UN-Habitat, 33, 36, 37
UNIS (Yugoslavian state military company), 52
United Nations, 22; on Lebanese Civil War damages, 95

United Nations High Commissioner for Refugees (UNHCR), 116, 118, 120, 126, 128, 134n1, 154, 171; *Mission Report 92/44* (Iwansson), 131–32; *Protracted Refugee Situations*, 122

United Nations Interim Administration Mission in Kosovo (UNMIK), 22, 29, 34, 35

University of Prishtina, 31

urban conflicts research, 4, 180

urban postwar reconstruction, 17–45; altered demographics and, 17–18; architects' and designers' role within NGOs and, 25–27; city as agent of political and social change, 17, 19; destruction of neighborhood fabric by conflict and reconstruction, 35–36; dissemination of lessons learned, 40; divided cities, 17; enforceability, 38–39; flexible planning, 36–38; future research on, 28–40; illegal development in immediate postwar period, 34, 38, 44n39; informal sector construction boom, 34, 44n39; master plan, need for, 33–37; NGOs, role of, 19, 20–25; planning without a future, 34–35; planning without a neighborhood, 35–36; planning without ownership, 36; recommendations, 39–40; symbolic actions in, 4; urban vision, 33–34. *See also* regulation of urban development *and specific cities by name*

urban resilience, 4, 7, 10, 77

urban warfare, 1, 179. *See also* violence *and specific locations of wars by name*

urgency in refugee camp design, 117–19, 134, 135n4

US Agency for International Development, 101

US Businessmen's Commission on the Reconstruction of Lebanon, *The Reconstruction of Lebanon*, 101

utopist point of view, 139, 152

Vale, Lawrence, 4

Venice, Doge's Palace, 163

Viejo, Dacia Rose, 5

violence: aestheticizing of, 11, 70–71, 79, 84; against architecture, as "warchitecture," 53–54; continuous conflict, even into peaceful times, 94, 110, 159; reconstruction perpetuating, 94, 110, 159, 179; Solidere's approach and, 108, 110

Vöckler, Kai, 10, 17, 41n7, 181; public awareness series produced in cooperation with, 31; volume chapter by, 17–45

Volume (architectural magazine), 25–26, 41n9

Vukovar (Croatia), 55

Wakim, Najah, 114n46

Walda Refugee Camp (Kenya), 116–18, 120, 125, *126*, 127, 128, *128*, 131–33, 134n1

Warchitecture (magazine), 49, 53, 56, 66n11

"warchitecture," development of term, 53–54

war diaries, 11. *See also under* Štraus, Ivan; Woods, Lebbeus

War on Terror, 72

wartime design and architecture: considered same as in peacetime, 5; psychological healing process enabled by, 150, 152; resulting from forced and unpredictable spatial transformations, 49. *See also* refugee camps *and specific locations and wars by name*

weaponization of built environment. *See* militarization of art and architecture

Western aid organizations, 21, 42n14. *See also* NGOs (nongovernmental organizations)

WIZO Academy of Design and Education (Haifa), 80–81

Woods, Lebbeus: blog photograph, 48; correspondence and relationship with Štraus, 11, 46, 60, 62, 64; *Elektroprivreda* reconstruction and, 52, 60–62; illustration of damaged and reconstructed residential block, 8; on prewar architecture no longer possible in postwar environment, 65; *Radical Reconstructions*, 60; Sarajevo destruction observed by, 48; Sarajevo postwar reconstruction and principles for public building reconstruction, 60; Štraus's influence on, 50; *War and Architecture*, 47, 60; war diary of, 11; "Zagreb-Free-Zone" exhibition (1991), 47, 65n4

World Bank: on construction sector's growth during Lebanese Civil War, 97, 113n26; financial assistance to Lebanon, 98, 101; global agenda of, 170; on Lebanese Civil War's displacement of population, 95–96; on Lebanon's economic collapse (2020), 111

Yugoslavia, Socialist Federative Republic of: ethnic groups in, 66n15; migration from, 50; prewar architects in, 57–58. *See also* Bosnian War (1992–96)

Yugoslavian modernism, 46, 54, 65n1

Zagreb (Croatia), 58

zekat (Muslim alms giving), 167

Zullo, Federica, 4

www.ingramcontent.com/pod-product-compliance
Lightning Source LLC
Chambersburg PA
CBHW070315240426
43661CB00057B/2654